AF512314

Revisiting Nehru in Contemporary India

Revisiting Nehru in Contemporary India

Edited by
Baljit Singh

KNOWLEDGE WORLD
KW Publishers Pvt Ltd
New Delhi

in association with

Nehru Studies Centre
University of Jammu
Jammu

Copyright © 2015
Baljit Singh

All rights reserved. No part of this publication may be reproduced, stored in a retrieval system, or transmitted in any form or by any means, electronic, mechanical, photocopying, recording or otherwise, without the prior written permission of the copyright owner.

ISBN 978-93-83649-33-4

Published in India by Kalpana Shukla

KNOWLEDGE WORLD
KW Publishers Pvt Ltd
4676/21, First Floor, Ansari Road, Daryaganj, New Delhi 110002
Phone: +91 11 23263498/43528107
Email: knowledgeworld@vsnl.net • www.kwpub.com

2011 FPBA BEST PUBLISHERS AWARD (ENGLISH)

Printed and Bound in India

Contents

Preface vii

Contributors xi

1. Locating Nehru in Contemporary India 1
Baljit Singh

2. Jawaharlal Nehru's Conception of History 27
Sukhdev Singh Sohal

3. Nehru's Idea of Federalism and Nation-Building in India 41
Ranjit Singh

4. Kashmir and Nehru: Contours of a Troubled Legacy 63
Simrit Kahlon

5. Communalism, Nehru and National Unity 79
Suneel Kumar

6. Nehru's Paradigm of Panchayati Raj and Its Contemporary Relevance 91
Ranbir Singh and Saroj Malik

7. Jawaharlal Nehru, Neo-Liberalism and Social Democracy: Mapping the Shifting Trajectories of Developmental State in India 105
Ronki Ram

8. Nation-Building, Natural Resources and Regional Development in India: Revisiting the Nehruvian Vision 133
Ambrish Dhaka

9. Foreign Policy in India's Development Since Nehru Era 145
Baljit Singh

10. Asian Security Structure and Challenges for India: Efficacy of the Nehruvian Approach 163
Rajpal Budania

11. Nehru and India's China Policy 179
Baljit Singh

12. Nuclear Technology and Nehru's Outlook 207
Suneel Kumar

13 India's Policy Towards Nepal and Bhutan: Nehru to Present 235
Debamitra Mitra

Index 257

Preface

The strength of the book lies in revisiting Nehru and finding out the relevance of his ideas in the contemporary Indian context. For instance how he helped India to consolidate as a political nation and also played a critical role in constructing India's identity in the comity of nations through his policy posture of non-alignment. The main thrust of non-aligned policy was to retain the freedom of action in foreign affairs when the world was bipolar. Freedom of action which Nehru nurtured while formulating India's foreign policy is very much relevant in the contemporary scenario. The process of federal infrastructuring that Nehru did while reorganising the states on the basis of language/ethnicity/region, has become a continuous process that has helped India in building a more inclusive political nation. However, the process is still going on to make India a more inclusive nation in political, economic and social sense. Likewise, Nehru conceived panchayati raj system as an instrument of community development programme in India, which has also become a third tier of Indian federal system besides helping India in the process of deepening of democracy.

When Nehru is judged as a leader, he is either appreciated for what he has done or blamed for what he could not do or handle properly when he was at the helm of affairs. Most of the time Nehru's performance has been assessed without placing him in the context in which he performed with all the limitations of a newly liberated state. In this volume an attempt has been made to have a fair understanding about Nehru by placing him in the time and space in which he worked and by also taking into account the challenges Post-Colonial India was facing during his time. The contributors to this volume have analysed diverse aspects of Nehru's thinking and policies to understand him keeping in view the time and space, and constraints thereof in which he worked but also to explore the relevance of his ideas in contemporary Indian, Asian and global context.

Nehru's model of economic development has become more relevant as globalisation has been making a retreat the world over. One of the major drawbacks of globalisation was that it created a dichotomy between the logics of democracy and neo-liberal market economy. Democracy believes in equality and inclusion, whereas globalisation believes in the principle of the survival of the fittest and hence promotes exclusion of vulnerable sections of society. Nehru's idea of mixed economy is not only the site where the logic of democratic politics and economic development meet with each other but it is also a device which provides substance to social democracy in India. This book further explores how the logic of neo-liberalism mismatches with social democracy.

Nehru's idea of social democracy and its contradictory relations with neo-liberalism and market economy in India are topics of great interest. Nehru's decision to reorganise states on the basis of language and thereby give practical shape to federalism in India, which has made the political nation more inclusive, needs to be explored. Nehru's initiative of nuclear programme has helped India to become a weaponised Nuclear State that has enhanced its national power. Nehru used foreign policy to ensure economic development at home which has further proved as a pointer for his successors to use diplomacy as a tool for economic growth.

This book is revisiting some of the issues touched by Jawaharlal Nehru during his tenure as a Prime Minister of India because those issues are very much alive in the contemporary context. These issues range from India's domestic politics to economy and foreign policy. This volume is an outcome of papers invited from scholars working in the different Indian Universities, Institutes and Colleges. I am indeed grateful to all the contributors for their cooperation. It is in fact their endeavours that have made the publication of this volume possible. The editor acknowledges the help rendered by Ms. Neetika Verma, PhD scholar for reading the proofs of this volume. A special word of thanks to Ms. Kalpana Shukla and Mr. Aditya Phogat of Knowledge World, New Delhi for their sincere efforts in bringing out this volume.

Jammu
January 2015

Baljit Singh

Contributors

Ambrish Dhaka is Associate Professor at School of International Studies, Jawaharlal Nehru University (JNU), New Delhi. He gives MPhil Courses on Afghanistan Studies. He specialises in Geopolitics and Ethno-political Studies. Recently, he has introduced Geographical Information System (GIS) for Area Studies as an attempt to congelate Geosciences into the domain of Area Studies. He has successfully supervised 7 PhDs and more than 15 MPhil Dissertations. He has a book published to his credit titled *South Asia and Central Asia: Geopolitical Dynamics.* He has published several papers and articles with national and international publications. His most recent work is "Factoring Central Asia into China's Afghanistan Policy" in the January 2014 volume of *Journal of Eurasian Studies.*

Baljit Singh is Professor in Department of Political Science and Director, Nehru Studies Centre, University of Jammu, Jammu. He did his doctorate in 1997 on Pakistan's Policy towards United States of America during Zia Regime. His teaching career spans over two decades in which he has been actively engaged in teaching and research. Besides co-editing two books on *South Asia: Dynamics of Politics, Economy & Society* in 2006 and *Politics of Identities in Jammu & Kashmir: A Contested Terrain* in 2008, he has published several research papers in journals and books of national and international repute. His current areas of academic interest are Politics in South Asia, Comparative Politics, India's Foreign Policy and National Security.

Debamitra Mitra is Principal, Institute of Leadership, Entrepreneurship and Development affiliated to West Bengal University of Technology, Kolkata. Mitra has done her MPhil in International Relations from Jadavpur University and PhD in History from Calcutta University. She has fifteen years of teaching, research and administrative experience apart from five years work experience in media and journalism. She has authored 3 books, edited 13 books and has more than 50 research articles published in different national and international journals in areas of sociology, political science, political economy, international relations, environmental studies, human resource management, gender studies and cultural studies.

Rajpal Budania is postgraduate in Politics (International Studies) from the School of International Studies (SIS), Jawaharlal Nehru University. He is a former Associate Fellow, Institute for Defence Studies and Analyses, New Delhi, and a recipient of the Jawaharlal Nehru Scholarship. He did his PhD from South Asia Studies Centre, University of Rajasthan, Jaipur. Presently he is Associate Professor in the Department of Political Science at the University of Allahabad, Allahabad. He is the author of the book *India's National Security Dilemma: The Pakistan Factor and India's Policy Response* and published extensively in reputed journals, books and periodicals. His research interest areas include: regional security in South Asia; India's national security issues and relations with Pakistan; international relations.

Ranbir Singh served the Departments of Political Science and Journalism, Kurukshetra University, Kurukshetra in his capacity as Professor and Chairperson. He also served as Dean Social Sciences and Dean Academic Affairs of Kurukshetra University, Kurukshetra. He has published 100 research papers in journal and books of national and international repute. Professor Singh attended and presented papers in more than a hundred national and international seminars/ conferences. He was visiting fellow to Guru Nanak Dev University, Amritsar in 2000 and a UGC Visiting Professor to Himachal Pradesh

University, Shimla in 2001-2. He has also been a resource person at Haryana Police Academy, Madhuban and HIRMI at Kurukshetra. He has been contributing popular articles to *The Tribune* and the *Mainstream*. Presently, he is working as a Consultant at Haryana Institute of Rural Development, Nilokheri.

Ranjit Singh served as an Assistant Professor in the Postgraduate Department of Political Science and Public Administration, Khalsa College, Amritsar. He taught Indian Political System, Indian Political Thought, Politics of South Asia and International Law at the Postgraduate levels. He obtained his PhD from Guru Nanak Dev University, Amritsar in 2004. His teaching career spans over thirteen years, during which he remained constantly engaged in research activities. He has fourteen research publications to his credit. Some of his research papers have been published in renowned referred Journals like *Pakistan Horizon*, *Regional Studies*, *Indian Journal of Federal Studies*, *Siberian Journal of Federal University*, etc. Fifteen students have completed their MPhil degree under his supervision and one is enrolled for PhD. He has presented a number of research papers at international and national conferences and seminars organised by different Universities and Colleges.

Ronki Ram is Fellow and Shaheed Bhagat Singh Professor of Political Science, has been the first incumbent of ICCR Chair Professorship of Contemporary India Studies at Leiden University, the Netherlands (September 2011-June 2013). Currently, he is Dean, Faculty of Arts, Panjab University, Honorary Director, ICSSR North-Western Regional Centre, Chandigarh, and Guardian Professor of Government College, Hoshiarpur. Recipient of various awards both at home and abroad, Prof. Ram has widely travelled in Asia, North America, and Europe on various academic assignments. He has to his credit two solely authored books, several book chapters and research articles in reputed peer reviewed international journals like *Modern Asian Studies* (Cambridge), *Journal of Asian Studies* (Cambridge), *Asian Survey* (Berkeley), *Contributions to Indian Sociology* (Sage),

Journal of Punjab Studies (UCSB) among others. He has several years of teaching and research experience at Panjab University, Jawaharlal Nehru University, Uppsala University (Sweden), Goa University, and Leiden University (The Netherlands).

Saroj Malik has done her MA and MPhil in Political Science from Kurukshetra University, Kurukshetra, Haryana and also qualified UGC-NET examination. She started her teaching career from D. A. V. Girls College, Kosli in 2003 and at present, she has been working as an Assistant Professor in C. R. M. Jat College Hisar, Haryana. She has participated and presented papers in various workshops and national seminars. She has published one article in *Mainstream* and several chapters in edited books. Her areas of specialisation are State Politics and Panchayati Raj institutions.

Simrit Kahlon is an Assistant Professor at the Department of Geography, Panjab University, Chandigarh. Her research interests include Cultural Geography, Urban Geography and the study of Man-Land relations with particular reference to Mountain Environments. She is currently engaged in an ICSSR sponsored research project on Man-Land relations in Lahaul valley of Himachal Pradesh. An avid traveller, she has frequently visited the valley of Kashmir and is widely published on issues of geopolitical and developmental concern with regard to the valley of Kashmir as well as the larger region.

Sukhdev Singh Sohal is Professor in the Department of History, Guru Nanak Dev University, Amritsar (Punjab). He has to his credit four books the latest being *Credit, Rural Debt and the Punjab Peasantry (1849-1947)* published in 2012. He has published about 70 research papers, articles, book reviews and review articles in professional, reputed journals and popular magazines. He has edited *Journal of Regional History*, published by Guru Nanak Dev University Amritsar (2010-13.) He is actively engaged in research as well as research supervision. His areas of interest include social and cultural transformation in the colonial Punjab in particular, and history of the Punjab in general.

Suneel Kumar is an Assistant Professor (Political Science) in the Department of Strategic and Regional Studies, University of Jammu, Jammu. He teaches International Relations Theory, South Asian Politics and Research MetHhods at MPhil and PhD levels. Prior to joining the University of Jammu, he served in the School of Social Sciences, Guru Nanak Dev University, Amritsar; School of Global Relations, Central University of Punjab, Bathinda and Postgraduate Department of Political Science, Lyallpur Khalsa College, Jalandhar. He has published articles in research journals of national and international repute including *International Migration*, *Journal of Punjab Studies*, *Pakistan Horizon*, *South Asian Survey*, *India Quarterly* and *Journal of Central Asian Studies.* He is also Serving as the Consulting Editor of *Journal of Siberian Federal University*, Siberia, Russia. His areas of interest and specialisation are ethnic politics, transnational organised crime, and human security within and across South-Central Asia.

1

Locating Nehru in Contemporary India

Baljit Singh

An idea, institution and leader are products of socio-economic and political contexts, that always consist of certain things relevant in context of time and space but they also carry some elements of universal wisdom, which remains relevant for all time to come. In order to make a fair assessment of their contribution, they are to be placed in the context which shaped them. However, to know their contemporary relevance, the element of universal wisdom embodied in them must be visited in the present context. The same is true of the first Prime Minister of India, Jawaharlal Nehru. He was shaped by the context in which he grew up and worked. Nehru was placed after Indian independence, and did something which has significance even in the contemporary scenario. Nehru is primarily understood through his three books titled *Glimpses of World History* (1934), *An Autobiography* (1936) and *The Discovery of India* (1946), all published before independence. However, they are well thought out and written books, as is obvious from their being continuously in print since their first publication, but they are thus far less pertinent to his statecraft than his writing and speeches after 1947.[1] Therefore, there is need to consult and analyse them for a better understanding of Nehru's idea of statecraft.

I

Nehru is considered as an architect of modern India who has left his mark on every aspect of Indian life including economic, political, strategic, social and technological. Nehru did that because he had some advantages. First, since he was a well read man and educated abroad, Nehru had a fair understanding not only about statecraft but also about various aspects of society. Second, being part of the anti-colonial struggle, Nehru was well-versed with the Indian social, economic and political reality. Third, Nehru got the opportunity to remain at the helm of affairs almost for one and a half decade, when Indian economy and polity were at the formative stage. In the economic domain, Nehru conceived, articulated and executed the mixed economy model/strategy of economic development. He was convinced that India would progress economically if the public sector and private sector coexist. Nehru started the process of modernisation and diversification of Indian economy, which was primarily an agriculture based and backward economy. In his writings, Nehru argued time and again that the production of wealth is essential for economic prosperity. But the distribution is equally important. Nehru articulated that before we think of distribution, there must be production. He was convinced that political freedom will not be able to liberate human beings without economic freedom and argued that the poor whether they are individuals or nations, have little place in this world. He wanted the whole country to become rich, to prosper. To achieve that objective, a lot of hard work and commitment was required. While talking about the crisis of production, Nehru articulated that:

> Now production means hard work, unremitting labour; production means no stoppage of work, no strike and lockout. Now, I am the last man so say that labour should be denied the right to strike, for the weapon of strike has been a much valued weapon by means of which labour had gradually gained a position of strength and eminence in most countries. Nevertheless, there are times when strikes are dangerous, when strikes not only injure the cause of a nation, but also ultimately the cause of the worker himself. We are passing through one of those times and it was for this reason that a

> short while ago, at a conference held in Delhi, the representatives of the Government, labour and industry decided, almost unanimously that we should have a three-year truce during which there should be no strikes or lockouts ... Of course, strikes and lockouts should have no meaning in a properly constituted state, where everyone has his due. Strikes and lockouts are the symbols of something radically wrong in our economic system ... We should remember that this production is not for enriching individuals, but it is to enrich the nation.[2]

To ensure India's economic progress, Nehru opted for the planned strategy of economic development in which five-year plans were formulated and executed and each plan laid emphasis on a particular area/sector as required by economic necessity. For instance First Five-Year Plan had laid great stress on food and agriculture as India was facing the problem of food security. India continued with stress on agriculture but industrialisation was the main focus in the Second Five-Year Plan in which the stress was to set up heavy industries, machine building industries, and steel plants, etc. The philosophy of Second and Third Five-Year Plans, which were launched in Nehru's lifetime, was the development of the Indian economy along socialist lines to achieve rapid economic growth, expansion of employment, reduction in disparities of income and wealth, and promotion of values and attitudes of a free and egalitarian society.[3] Nehru argued that small-scale industries can come up when India begins producing steel and machines in large quantities. Heavy industry forms not only the base of industrial growth but ultimately the substance of economic freedom. From that the small-scale/household industries will grow. Nehru also encouraged the small-scale industries because of their potential to provide employment to a large number of unemployed people, apart from engaging them in a meaningful economic activity. Actually Nehru tried to produce some kind of stable equilibrium between the heavy and small-scale industries. Industrialisation and progress of agriculture sector were critical for producing national wealth. For him wealth does not mean gold and silver but essential consumer goods which are produced from land and industries. Associated with agriculture sector was the rural area which has been housing more than 70 per cent of the population, and Nehru was convinced that without the development of rural area India cannot progress. Although agriculture progress would bring change in the life of rural people, Nehru launched Community Development Schemes aimed at transforming the rural areas and teaching people to change their thinking. He was of the firm opinion that agricultural production is of fundamental importance for the eradication of poverty.[4] Nehru acknowledged the role of human resources for the progress of the nation in his message for *Kurukshetra* Magazine in which he stated:

> People talk of money, and money is, no doubt, useful. But it is the human-being that counts in the end and it is human-beings who have made history and who have advanced the cause of humanity, not money. If we train and prepare the right type of human-beings in India, then the rest is easy.[5]

Nehru was aware of the role of science and technology in the progress of the agriculture and industrial sectors of the Indian economy. That is why he laid emphasis on the development of science and technology in post-colonial India. For a greater increase in agricultural and industrial production which he planned for India, Nehru placed his hopes on science and technology. Influenced by the writings of Russell, Bernal, Haldane and the radical scientists of the 1930s, Nehru saw science as the natural agent of progress and the obvious servant of socialism.[6] Science and technology played a critical role in the modernisation of the Indian economy by developing new tools, techniques and machines. Knowing well the role of energy in the economic progress of the country, Nehru laid emphasis not only on tapping the existing sources of energy but also discovering new sources of energy with the help of science and technology. How to use atomic energy for constructive purposes was a fundamental question that bothered Nehru after the use of the atomic bomb by the US against Japan at the fag end of the Second World War. For that he sought the help of Homi Bhabha, an Indian scientist, and Nehru asked him to prepare a detailed report about atomic energy research. In his letter written to Baldev Singh, Defence Minister in his Cabinet, on February 29, 1948, Nehru stated:

> I have just had a talk with Dr. Homi Bhabha. He has given me a long report about atomic energy research. I am very much interested in this and I am sure that we should seriously start taking steps in this direction ... It will not, of course, bring immediate results. But the future belongs to those who produce atomic energy. Of course, Defence is intimately concerned with this. Even the political consequences are worthwhile ... Homi Bhabha made some suggestions to me about the question of our having a scientific advisor for the Ministry of Defence. I understand that he will be seeing you tomorrow and will explain these proposals in detail. I think they are sound and might well be given effect to. It is not much good our getting a second-rate man from England or elsewhere. It is far better for a real first-rate man to come here from time to time to advise us together with two good men from India, Homi Bhabha himself could be one of them. He is first-rate and highly thought of in the foreign scientific world ... any advice that he may give is therefore worthy of consideration.[7]

The state occupied central stage in Nehru's philosophy and strategy of economic development. His philosophy and strategy of economic growth came under attack in the age of globalisation wherein the state has been replaced by market. Indian state was not only setting the agenda of economic development but also driving the process of economic development since Nehru's period till the introduction of Liberalisation, Privatisation and Globalisation (LPG) reforms in 1991. Increasing state intervention in the economy was considered the cause for the economic crisis India landed in, in 1990. India could have avoided that crisis if the state had become a developmental, instead of predatory or bureaucratic, state in the post-Nehru period. Inherently, there was nothing wrong in using the state as a catalyst for economic development and social justice. What was wrong was not state intervention but the kind of state intervention practised under the Indian planning regime.[8] But the retreat of globalisation since the 2008 financial crisis proved Nehru right when the state was again invited to intervene and save the ailing economy in the United States, which advocated and had been supporting the cause of globalisation during the past couple of decades. In his strategy of economic development, planning was a critical component, which has been retained by India even after neo-liberal economic reforms. Nehru was convinced that India needs a welfare state and he gave shape to that. However, LPG reforms eroded the thrust of welfare state in India since 1991, but initiatives like Mahatma Gandhi National Rural Employment Guarantee Act (MGNREGA), Right to Education Act 2009 and Food Security Act 2013 reinforce the philosophy of welfare state.

Nehru's idea of India was inclusive not only in economic but also in political sense. How to accommodate the diversity of Indian society in the political land space of independent India was a huge question to deal with. However, this hard reality was kept in mind when the framework of governance was drafted, adapted and enacted but India was scared of its diversity as it had already suffered from partition. Of course to ensure the unity of the country was top priority for Nehru but not by demolishing the diversity rather by accommodating it. His idea of unity in diversity and diversity in unity had proved most handy to deal with the issue of unity and diversity simultaneously and quasi-federal arrangement translated that idea into political reality. Nehru faced serious problems when Hindi was declared as a national language with an understanding that it will connect people across the linguistic divisions and thereby would build the political nation, whereas it back-fired when non-Hindi speaking people from South India protested against that and asked for the creation of states on the basis of regional languages. Although Nehru succeeded in accommodating religious diversity through secularism but there was no way out to accommodate the linguistic diversity except by reorganisation of states on language basis. Assertion of regional languages in the public domain was not only a huge political problem but also an internal security threat but Nehru handled it successfully by reorganising the states on the basis of regional languages in 1956. Of course, Andhra Pradesh was the first state created on the basis of language in 1953. Nehru was but reluctant to reorganise states on language basis but he did not take much time to understand the political nuances of assertion of regional languages from South India, and that not only saved the nascent Indian state from disintegration but also helped to build the political nation in the real sense of the term. Nehru's idea of composite culture helped him generate political capital out of cultural diversity to consolidate the Indian nation. While writing letter to Chief Ministers on September 20, 1953, Nehru stated:

> We have always to remember that India is a composite country, composite in many ways, in religion, in customs, in languages, in ways of life, etc. An attempt by the majority group to impose itself on others can only lead to inner conflicts, which are as bad as outer conflicts. The basic problem for us today in India is to build up united India in the real and inner sense of the word, that is, a psychological integration of our people ...[9]

Nehru was against the role of religion in the politics of post-colonial India primarily for three reasons. First, he read a lot about the role played by religion in the politics of Europe. Second, because of the religious diversity in India, the role of religion in national politics could not have done anything good to the body-politic. Third, in 1947, India had already suffered from partition on the basis of two-nation theory, which was articulated on the basis of religion. It was quite obvious that the entry of religion in national politics would lead to communalism. Nehru remained convinced that in a multireligious, pluralist and democratic country like India, a secular framework was imperative. Three years before his death he put the problem in perspective when he conceded that where the great majority of the people in a country belonged to one religion, this fact alone was likely to colour to some extent its cultural climate, but the state itself could remain independent of any particular religion.[10] He recognised that though the Indian Constitution laid down that India was a secular state, it was not wholly reflected in the living and thinking of the people.[11] Instead of religion, the real issues in Indian politics were political freedom, economic equality and social justice. Nehru's vision of India was based on the conviction that it was a composite nation, born of a civilisation which over centuries had drawn from and assimilated the many religious and cultural traditions present on the subcontinent.[12] Therefore, post-colonial Indian state must be secular, not aligned with or identified with any particular religion, but providing for religious and cultural freedom for the many different groups within it.[13]

Nehru articulated India's world view after independence in a highly complex international scenario. His understanding of history, the prevailing global situation and his ability to comprehend future scenario, helped him tremendously to articulate India's position in the comity of nations. While formulating India's foreign policy posture, there were major challenges confronting him, how to keep India away from the alliance politics; how to save India's hard earned independence; how to mobilise financial and technological help from abroad to ensure its development at home; how to construct India's identity in the comity of nations and how India's freedom of action can be retained at the global level. To address them, Nehru articulated non-alignment as a foreign policy posture and strategy of India. Nehru's insights in world history had educated him about the experiences and sufferings of European states as members of various military alliances. He used that experience to save India from the cold-war alliances which were on offer when it got liberated in 1947. Joining military alliances would have multiplied New Delhi's problems which were already causing a difficult situation. Being Prime Minister of India, he knew very well that India's joining of a Western military alliance would not only earn the animosity of the Eastern bloc but would also limit India's sources of economic and technological help which it desperately required for its development. In addition, joining any bloc would have diverted its meagre resources to military modernisation, apart from compromising its credentials as a free nation. Keeping India away from the cold-war alliance politics was Nehru's well-thought decision and went well with India's tradition as a peace-loving nation. He ensured peace for India by maintaining a distance from the Eastern and Western blocs, which helped the newly liberated nation in concentrating on its constructive agenda of development. His strategy of non-alignment saved New Delhi from war but more than that it helped in constructing India's identity in the comity of nations. Nehru articulated India's world view in such a way as to place it as a unique nation at the global level, which did not follow the dictates of any bloc in a bipolar world; rather it charted its own path as required by its national interest. Nehru's non-alignment strategy was quite successful in constructing India's identity as an independent nation when the several newly liberated countries were either joining the Eastern or Western blocs. However, Jawaharlal Nehru told Indian Parliament in 1958:

> "It is completely incorrect to call our (foreign) policy Nehru's policy ... I have not originated it. It is a policy inherent in the circumstances of India, inherent in the past thinking of India ... inherent in the conditioning of the Indian mind." He went on to assert that any other party in power, or any other foreign minister in his place could not have deviated very much from the policy he had pursued.[14]

But B. R. Nanda in his book titled *Jawaharlal Nehru: Rebel and Statesman* argued that Indian foreign policy could hardly have taken the course it did, had Nehru not been at the helm of affairs in the early years of Indian independence.[15] Nehru was humble and right while stating that India's foreign policy was shaped by its circumstances, past thinking and conditioning of the Indian mind. But Nehru's contribution lies in his ability to understand India's past, comprehend the then prevailing scenario and to articulate the best course of action for the future of the nation.

Besides this, Nehru also wanted to construct the Asian identity on the basis of Asian nationalism. He was of the firm opinion that Asian countries under the joint leadership of India and China can shape the destiny of the Asian continent and the future of the world at large. He was aware that if Asian countries work together then the future belongs to Asia. In order to achieve this objective, Nehru convened the Asian Relations Conference in New Delhi in March 1947, a few months before Indian independence. This conference was attended by many Asian countries and they were quite appreciative of Nehru's initiative. While articulating the cause of Pan-Asian identity, Nehru sought to construct the Asian identity to generate political capital amongst Asian states to forge a meaningful cooperation amongst them. Being a student of history, he knew that Asian people played a critical role in the evolution of human civilisation. This dynamic Asia—from which great streams of culture flowed in all directions—gradually became static and unchanging. Other peoples and other continents came to the fore and with their dynamism spread out and took possession of great parts of the world.[16] Colonialism had proved a major setback to Asian dynamism which Nehru wanted to revive and rejuvenate in the post-colonial period. The most dangerous impact of colonialism was the isolation of Asian countries from each other. He wanted to revive the contacts which India used to have with Asian countries from the Northwest, the Northeast, the East and South-East Asia. Because of that, in his book *Glimpses of World History*, Nehru talked about Asian-nationalism. While addressing the Asian Relations Conference, Nehru stated that, "we meet here not to discuss the past history but to forge contacts for the future," apart from clarifying to the Western bloc that Asian solidarity would not be directed against any country, bloc and alliance.

However, despite his best efforts Nehru's urge for Asian solidarity could not become a reality as Asia continued to remain divided due to cold-war constraints, apart from India-China hostility. His initiative that India and China should provide joint leadership to the

Asian states could not see the light of day as hostility between the two Asian giants was set in motion in the 1950s. Nehru successfully managed the challenge of the Cold War to India's foreign policy because neither the US nor the Soviet Union posed any challenge to Indian diplomacy. The major challenge to India's foreign policy was how to deal with People's Republic of China, and how to take the PRC along to evolve the Pan-Asian identity. The major challenge to Nehru's drive for Asian-nationalism emerged from China, which culminated in the India-China conflict from the mid-1950s and the war in 1962. The India-China conflict was also a major setback to India's China policy. Aware of the Chinese threat in advance, Nehru was not prepared to weaken non-alignment or consider military alliances. India's reputation in the world, as he had somewhat complacently assured Parliament,[17] stood high because of her foreign policy; and he had no intention of jeopardising it because of a rebellion in Tibet and Chinese pressures.[18] Vague ideas about searching for allies were a sign of utter weakness of character in an individual and in a nation.[19] It was possible that, hard as India might strive to avoid war, she would be forced into it; but for this the best preparation was self-reliance and the building of industrial strength which could be reflected in the defence forces.[20]

While dealing with the South Asian states, Nehru was successful in bringing some of them like Nepal and Bhutan on the orbit of Indian security through the Treaty of Friendship with Bhutan in 1949 and Treaty of Peace and Friendship with Nepal in 1950, and the same kind of agreement was also signed with Sikkim. The agreements India signed with Nepal and Sikkim in 1950 were more attuned to the challenges that China's control of Tibet posed to the security of the subcontinent. India's December 1950 Treaty with Sikkim reaffirmed its status as a protectorate of India and gave New Delhi the right to deploy troops on its territory.[21] Realism was reflected in Nehru's approach to India's immediate neighbours, as he cultivated the Himalayan states because of their strategic relevance for India's security. Generally, Nehru is criticised for continuing the policy of British Raj towards South Asian states even after independence. India neighbourhood policy during the British rule was shaped by the geopolitics of the Indian subcontinent, and it continued to be shaped by the geopolitics of the South Asian region in the post-colonial period. Criticism of Nehru, that he continued with the policy of the Raj towards the South Asian states even after independence, does not hold any merit because it was the geopolitics and structure of the South Asian region which shaped India's policy perspective about South Asian states. At the same time, Nehru also had a strong realist tendency in his world view that was reflected most acutely in his approach towards security cooperation with the neighbours.[22]

Nehru's conduct of India's foreign relations had created for his country a distinctive, independent international identity. India was seen as an important Asian country located by geography at a significant and sensitive juncture of several areas, by choice within the Commonwealth network of international relationships, and by ideology a major player in a group of non-aligned nations.[23] Nehru's image and international role had undoubtedly advanced greatly when he was at the helm of affairs. Initially, he was seen as a nationalist leader but subsequently he was seen as an Asian figure, a spokesman for Asian aspirations, and broadly as a moderating voice for a more peaceful world order.[24] Nehru wanted to promote internationalism while strengthening the states contrary to the forces of globalisation which have been promoting globalism by making the nation-states weak.

II

In contemporary India, when Nehru is judged as a leader, he is either appreciated for what he has done or blamed for what he could not do or handle properly when he was at the helm of affairs. Most of the time Nehru's performance has been assessed without placing him in a situation in which he performed with all the limitations of a newly liberated state. Therefore, in this volume an attempt has been made to have a fair understanding about Nehru by placing him in the context in which he worked and by also taking into account the limitations of post-colonial India during his time. Contributors for this volume have analysed diverse aspects of Nehru's thinking to understand him keeping in mind the time, space and constraints in which he worked but also to explore the relevance of his ideas in contemporary Indian and global context.

Jawaharlal Nehru's Conception of History is the theme of Sukhdev Singh Sohal's contribution in which he has elucidated Nehru's understanding about history and how it can be used for understanding the present. He stated that for Nehru, history was not only a voyage of discovery and a guide to action but also turns progressive science. Sohal articulates that for Nehru writing of history brings some relief from the weight and burden of the past, and history is a continuous process. This paper argued that Nehru lived in a crucial historical juncture and performed a major role to swim with and tame the tide, and his understanding of history in thought and practice helped him evolve both politically and intellectually. Nehru benefited immensely from history to connect the past to the present for the better understanding of the latter and contemplating the future as well. Sohal concludes by arguing that first, Nehru's historical consciousness delineates his philosophy, his belief in unity in diversity, secularism, democracy, scientific temper keeping individual freedom intact. Second, being an institution-builder, he brought India on the world map. Third, institutions built and nurtured by him are either cracking or crumbling and that has made Nehru relevant in the contemporary scenario.

Nehru's Idea of Federalism and Nation-Building in India is the subject of Ranjit Singh's paper. This paper begins with a formulation that federalism and nation-building are interrelated in a plural society and Nehru understood it well in time. According to the author, Nehru was grappling with two critical issues in India's Constituent Assembly; one was how to accommodate the Indian plurality into its political landscape, and second how to ensure national integration as it had already suffered from partition. To achieve this objective, Nehru was for a centralised federal system, but Nehru stood the test of the time when his government reorganised states on language basis which not only strengthened the Indian federal system but also consolidated the Indian nation. However, Nehru showed reluctance in reorganisation of states on language basis because his mind was preoccupied with national unity, but it has proved a blessing in disguise for nation-building and national integration in India. Singh elucidates that thereby Nehru's commitment to democracy and federalism not only accommodated linguistic, cultural and regional diversity but also built the political nation. However, the goal of national integration was served by the centralised federal system coupled with the planned process of development. He further elaborates that Nehru had a passion for national unity but certainly not for uniformity. Nehru's language policy has also proved useful in strengthening the basis of the Indian nation besides consolidating federalism as a system of governance. Singh winds up his paper by articulating that nation-building in India is still facing certain problems, but the way Nehru handled linguistic diversity by reorganising states in the 1950s built the nation in the real sense of the term, and was also a pointer for his successors to deal with such kinds of political problems in future as well.

Simrit Kahlon's paper titled *Kashmir and Nehru: Contours of a Troubled Legacy*, has examined Nehru's role in the Kashmir problem. This paper starts with the argument that, generally, Nehru is held responsible for the state of affairs prevailing in Jammu and Kashmir. She argues that to have a clear understanding about his role in the Kashmir problem, there is need to take into account the time and space in which Nehru handled Kashmir. To have broader understanding about the Kashmir problem, she has provided the demographic profile of three major regions of the state apart from the chronology of events. While placing the problem in historical context, she has also narrated the circumstances in which Jammu and Kashmir joined the Indian Union in October 1947. She elucidates that because of Nehru's personal attachment with Kashmir, he himself handled the issue of Kashmir, whereas the job on the integration of princely states was entrusted to Sardar Patel. Kahlon articulates that Nehru's handling of the Kashmir problem was marked by indecisiveness and a reactionary rather than a proactive approach; it is also true that when things came to the brink of disaster Nehru did manage to salvage the situation. This paper also elaborates the positive and negative impact of political chemistry and breach of trust between Nehru and Sheikh Abdullah respectively on the Kashmir problem. It is further argued that Nehru not only committed a mistake by taking the Kashmir issue to the United Nations Security Council but also failed to handle it successfully in spite of the fact that he had the expertise and fair understanding of international politics. She concludes her paper with an observation that Nehru partially failed not due to lack of vision but because he could not blend his idealism with realism on the issue of Kashmir.

Suneel Kumar in his paper titled *Communalism, Nehru and National Unity* analyses Nehru's perceptions on communalism as a threat to India's national unity. This paper explores how Nehru handled the communal situation after independence. Kumar argues that secularism was a matter of personal commitment to Jawaharlal Nehru and he made it a point that Indian polity should not derail from the path of secularism. Nehru was a staunch critic of the role played by communal leaders, communal organisations and communal press in spreading communalism in post-colonial India. Nehru further argued that nationalism and communalism are contradictory to each other, thus they cannot coexist. Nehru articulated that nationalism cannot be equated with a particular community, and was opposed to the supremacy of any one community in the public domain as India is a plural society. Kumar further states that Nehru's views regarding communalism have become more relevant in post-Nehru India because of the emergence of communalism as a major threat to its unity and integrity. Kumar concludes his paper while arguing that Nehru's idea of secularism is useful to tame the growing communal identities and reinforce national unity in contemporary India.

Ranbir Singh and Saroj Malik in their paper *Nehru's Paradigm of Panchayati Raj and Its Contemporary Relevance* elucidate the evolution of the Panchayati Raj system besides examining its relevance in contemporary Indian scenario. While clarifying the confusion about the conception of Panchayati Raj in existing literature, they state that Panchayati Raj in India was suggested as a scheme of democratic decentralisation by the Balwant Rai Mehta Study Team in 1957 to achieve the objectives of Community Development Programme (CDP). Being a liberal democrat, Nehru was impressed by this scheme as it served multiple purposes like a device of democratic decentralisation, a tool to effectively implement CDP, apart from realising Mahatma Gandhi's idea of village republic. This paper narrates the various steps taken by Nehru for the institutionalisation of Panchayati Raj system ranging from the creation of a separate Ministry of Community Development, Cooperation and Panchayati Raj at Union level to prevailing upon the Chief Ministers to enact the required legislation in the legislative bodies of their respective states for setting up the Panchayati Raj institutions. Singh and Malik argue that Indira Gandhi pursued the style of de-politicisation and centralisation contrary to Nehru's style of politicisation and decentralisation which culminated in the decay of PRIs. She also abolished the separate Ministry of Panchayati Raj and made it as a part of Ministry of Agriculture. Initiatives to revitalise PRIs came from the States of West Bengal, Karnataka and Andhra Pradesh which were followed by the efforts made by Rajiv Gandhi to strengthen the PRIs. They assert that Rajiv Gandhi followed the style of politicisation and decentralisation instead of the style of de-politicisation and centralisation. Singh and Malik sum up their paper with a finding that the 73rd Constitutional Amendment continued and consolidated the Nehruvian philosophy of PRIs with some modification desired by the changing time and space.

Ronki Ram, in his paper titled *Jawaharlal Nehru, Neo-Liberalism and Social Democracy: Mapping the Shifting Trajectories of Developmental State in India,* has explored the complex relationship between caste, poverty, inequality and neo-liberal market economy in globalised India and its impact on the nature of the Indian developmental state. He argues that mixed economy and social democracy constituted the central philosophy of the developmental state in India during the Nehruvian era. Ram has attempted to address the complex question of how economic liberalisation affects the interrelationship between caste and market on the one hand and its impact on developmental state in globalised India on the other, which has not been addressed adequately so far in mainstream literature. He further states that social democracy calls upon the state to play a positive role for the protection and promotion of the interests of the downtrodden, minorities and other weaker sections of Indian society. But the neo-liberal market economy has called for the rolling back of the state from economic domain which has adversely affected these sections of society and thereby undermined the thrust of social democracy in contemporary India. Notwithstanding the Right to Information Act, the Right to Education Act, Mid-day Meals Programme, Mahatma Gandhi National Rural Employment Guarantee Act, the Food Security Act, the Sarva Shiksha Abhiyan and the Sampoorna Grameen Rozgar Yojana are some significant initiatives aimed at promotion of social democracy. Ram has also pointed out the inherent contradiction between the indigenous institution of caste and the transplanted institution of democracy which got further accentuated due to the neo-liberal economic policies. The central theme of this paper is that neo-liberalism poses a serious challenge to the formation of social democracy in India. Ram argues that to sustain the transplanted sapling of liberal democracy in India, Nehru adopted the mixed economy model of economic development, which has already been replaced by the market-friendly economy in the era of neo-liberalism. However, neo-liberalism is projected as a custodian of enormous opportunities, but what such opportunities are and whom they benefit is a question that directly concerns Dalits. He states that neo-liberalism opens many doors to the haves but it shuts its door for the have-nots—a large majority of whom happen to be low castes, socially excluded, tribals, women, and other vulnerable sections of society. In this context, the Nehruvian perspective of social democracy becomes the most appropriate and promising option for contemporary Indian society.

The interrelationship amongst *Nation-Building, Natural Resources and Regional Development in India* in the Nehru and post-

Nehru eras is the subject of Ambrish Dhaka's paper in which he states that Nehru's approach to nation-building was closely related to his strategy of economic and regional development because Nehru wanted to build an inclusive Indian nation not only in the political but also in the social and economic sense. He acknowledged the role of natural resources including their exploration and utilisation for the economic progress of the country and people at large. Dhaka argues that nation-building was a herculean task for Nehru, and so was the generation of wealth and its equitable distribution for the benefit of every citizen. He further compares Nehru's approach to development with that of Mahatma Gandhi. The former laid more emphasis on heavy industry and capital-intensive strategy, whereas the latter's stress was on rural-based, decentralised and small-scale labour intensive industrial development. Nehru wanted to see India as a self-sufficient economy; Gandhi advocated the cause of village as a self-sufficient economic unit; of course, resources were required for both their strategies, and both of them wanted the indigenisation of development. In his strategy of economic development, Nehru blended capitalism with socialism. Nehru used planning as a tool to ensure economic development and advocated state intervention to ensure distributive justice. Dhaka narrates that while acknowledging the role of natural resources in national growth, Nehru attached greater importance to river-valley projects and minerals, the former were important to generating energy, and the latter equally important for the extension of industrial activity. He winds up his paper by stating that the development projects initiated and executed by Nehru have significantly contributed to nation-building and economic development in contemporary India.

The article titled *Foreign Policy in India's Development Since Nehru Era*, is contributed by Baljit Singh wherein he has discussed the linkages between India's foreign policy and developmental needs. This paper analyses how Nehru used the policy of non-alignment as an instrument to mobilise resources and technology from abroad for facilitating development at home, apart from using it as a strategy to ensure world peace, one of the essential prerequisites for development at the national and global levels. Singh argues that Nehru not only acknowledged the dialectical linkages between developmental aspiration and foreign policy of India when he argued that foreign policy is the outcome of economic policy, but also considered that independent foreign policy depends upon the economic health of a country. Nehru knew that India needs foreign aid for realising its national developmental aspiration, but while accepting aid he did not want to lose India's freedom of action in foreign affairs. As a practitioner of diplomacy, while mobilising foreign aid, Nehru maintained a strategic balance between the developmental aspirations of India and its freedom of action in foreign relations. Nehru avoided aid with strings which could undermine the independent credentials of India's foreign policy. Singh elaborates that Nehru's successors continued with this tendency, besides using diplomacy as a tool to bring desirable change in the international economic order for the benefit of developing countries because they were conscious of the fact that economic change at home is closely tied up with change in the international economic structures. He further explains how change in New Delhi's economic policy since 1991 has changed the thrust of its foreign policy from non-alignment to neo-liberalism which further substantiates Nehru's thesis that the foreign policy of a country is the reflection of its economic policy. Singh concludes his contribution by arguing that in contemporary global economic scenario in which globalisation has been making a retreat, India has been again using multilateral diplomacy from the platforms of G-20, India, Brazil and South Africa (IBSA) and Brazil, Russia, India, China and South Africa (BRICS) to bring about suitable change in International Monetary Fund (IMF), International Bank for Reconstuction and Development (IBRD) and WTO for the larger interests of developing countries and a just economic order at the global level.

Rajpal Budania in his contribution titled *Asian Security Structure and Challenges for India: Efficacy of the Nehruvian Approach* discusses the evolving security structure in the Asian continent in the twenty-first century. He argues that contemporary Asia is the reflection of a complex security scenario because it is not only redefining international security order but is also a complex picture of conflict and cooperation from within. Budania articulates that most of Asia's security problems are China-centric, as a rising China is having problems with Japan and South Korea in the Far East, Vietnam, the Philippines and Malaysia in South-East Asia and India in South Asia. Security has remained a highly contested and competitive phenomenon in Asia and even the dominant player in the Asian security system, that is, the United States of America, perceives threats from non-democratic Asian countries like China, Iran, North Korea and Pakistan. He has also pointed at evolving understanding amongst the democratic countries from Asia like India and Japan with the US and Australia to balance China's hegemonic ambitions, apart from hinting at the arms race going on, including the nuclearisation of Asia. The emerging order in Asia is highly complex wherein states are competing for influence and power and India-China rivalry has acquired the centre stage in Asian geopolitics. The author further argues that ASEAN has emerged as the core of the Asian security and stability as it has accommodated the major powers of the Asia-Pacific region; however, he was not very sure about the emergence of an ASEAN-led Asian order. Budania argues that India can remain oblivious to China's expansionism in Asia and, to be more precise, in South-East Asia and South Asia. India's policymakers have to deal with that at the diplomatic level and in addition have to increase its defence preparedness to meet any eventuality on the ground. India's strategic cooperation with the US, Japan, Australia and South-East Asian states has been taking shape without forming a military alliance. That is the continuation of Nehruvian tradition. For Nehru, the only way to settle differences was negotiation, mutual concessions and accommodation; of course, Nehru made his strategy to deal with security threats more inclusive when he realised the element of defence preparedness after the India-China war of 1962. He elaborates that foreign policy initiatives like Gujral Doctrine, Look East Policy and India's policy towards China are shaped by the Nehruvian world view. The author explains Nehru's aspiration for common India-China perceptions on Asian security and cooperation, which did not materialise during his lifetime. Budania sums up his contribution with an argument that Nehru's vision of cooperative relations in Asia based on Panchsheel is still at the core of India's understanding about Asian security.

Baljit Singh has discussed India's China Policy since Nehru era in his paper titled *Nehru and India's China Policy.* In the first part of this paper, he elucidates how Nehru handled China by following the policy of friendship. Nehru accommodated China on the issue of Tibet but he could not tolerate Beijing on the border issue, to be more precise, its increasing assertiveness across the LAC, which forced Nehru to pursue a forward policy vis-à-vis China. It also demolishes the misunderstanding about Nehru that he could not anticipate the security threat which China was posing during his time. This paper begins with the formulation that Nehru was well aware of the Chinese threat and Indian capabilities to handle that, and through friendly diplomacy he was postponing the threat so that India could improve its capabilities. Nehru's hope that India's goodwill gestures on the issue of Tibet, the Korean War and UNSC membership towards its northern neighbour would generate enough political capital to expand the area of cooperation between New Delhi and Beijing. But during the last round of talks in April 1960, all the friendship had disappeared, and there was a visible chill as Nehru and Zhou Enlai went through the formal courtesies in public. The talks were inconclusive, leading only to the agreement that officials from both sides should sit down and thrash out the details which obviously men like Nehru and Zhou had no time for. Thereafter Nehru decided that China's provocations would have to be countered. In November 1961, the Indian Government ordered implementation of its "forward policy" to augment its position on the border vis-à-vis China. Neither his policy of friendship nor forward defence succeeded in securing India's national interest vis-à-vis China because India and China fought a war in October 1962 and India lost some parts of its territory to China. In the second part, it is argued that estrangement was the defining code of India's policy towards

China till 1976, and diplomatic relations were snapped between the two countries. New Delhi was not ready to engage Beijing till the border dispute was resolved. India revived its diplomatic relations with China during this phase without making any progress because neither New Delhi nor Beijing was ready to accommodate each other's claim on the border issue. India's engagement with China since 1988 is elaborated in next part of this piece. Singh articulates that New Delhi has made a departure from its earlier position vis-à-vis Beijing. From 1988 onward, India agreed to engage China notwithstanding the border dispute; however, they constituted a JWG to negotiate the boundary dispute as well. New Delhi and Beijing signed various agreements to maintain peace and tranquillity along the LAC, apart from making several reciprocal visits by the leadership of both the countries. However the process of engaging China got derailed in 1998 after India's nuclear tests because of Beijing's sharp reaction, but got back on track in 2000 after US President, Bill Clinton's visit to New Delhi. Besides the increasing volume of bilateral trade, an element of strategic competition has also been witnessed in their policies in South, South-East, East Asian regions and the Indian Ocean. New Delhi's engagement with Beijing in the contemporary scenario, knowing well that the latter is a potential threat to its security, is somehow the continuation of Nehruvian China policy. India's engagement with Beijing may be a device to postpone and moderate the Chinese threat and its growing strategic partnerships with ASEAN, Vietnam, Japan and the United States can be the tools to balance China in South-East, East Asia and the Indian Ocean region.

Suneel Kumar in his contribution titled *Nuclear Technology and Nehru's Outlook* argues that Nehru along with eminent scientists and scholars of his times sought the abolition of nuclear weapons to ensure security and peace at the global level apart from advocating the cause of use of nuclear energy for peaceful purposes. Nehru described nuclear weapons as the enemy of humanity and proposed the establishment of atom-free areas around the world. However, regarding India's security, Nehru was not averse to thinking about nuclear options and he was instrumental in laying down the foundation of India's Nuclear Programme. Hence, Kumar finds contradictions in Nehru's philosophy on nuclear technology. It appears that Nehru wanted to keep the nuclear option open for India's security, so long as nuclear weapons exist in the world. The moment the world achieves the goal of universal nuclear disarmament then India does not need nuclear weapons for its security. During his tenure, India's nuclear programme concentrated on the use of nuclear energy for peaceful purposes. He articulates that Nehru's ideas of universal nuclear disarmament and the use of nuclear technology for constructive purposes have contemporary relevance. The former is relevant in the context of the ongoing nuclear arms race and the latter has significance for energy security as the demand for energy is increasing day by day and hydrocarbon sources of energy are already over-exploited across the world. Kumar elaborates that nuclear energy can provide energy security on the one hand and clean energy on the other hand, if the limitations of nuclear power are addressed properly. According to him, India is the beneficiary of Nehru's approach on nuclear technology at the global level and developed nuclear weapons due to the strong infrastructural foundation laid down by him. Kumar concludes that Nehru's nuclear diplomacy proved handy to establish India's credentials as a responsible nuclear state.

In her paper, titled *India's Policy Towards Nepal and Bhutan: Nehru to Present* Debamitra Mitra articulates that Nehru was preoccupied with many critical problems and one of them was how to deal with the Himalayan Kingdoms which had always been crucial to India's security. Nehru viewed these kingdoms as part of India's security perimeter which is considered the continuation of British India's policy towards Himalayan Kingdoms. They were brought into the security orbit of British India through various treaties and agreements. India, under the leadership of Nehru, continued with the same practice when it signed treaties with Tibet, Bhutan, Nepal and Sikkim following almost the same template of the earlier agreements signed by British India with them. Mitra argues that Nehru's reconstruction of the security ties with the Himalayan kingdoms was not a replica of the Raj because he accommodated many of the interests of the kingdoms to encourage them to remain part of the security structure of India's northern frontiers. She further elucidates that in the post-Nehru phase, the strategic significance of Himalayan states for India's security increased manifold as India and China have been competing for influence in South Asia and other parts of Asia. Interplay between "power and principle" has remained a defining code of India's relations with Nepal and Bhutan. Mitra has discussed India's relations with Nepal and Bhutan in detail and argues that Nehru's successors continued India's relations with these two Himalayan states on the same pattern evolved by Nehru, notwithstanding the fact that the special relationship with both the Himalayan buffers evolved by Nehru showed signs of erosion in post-Nehru period.

References

1. Ramachandra Guha (ed.), *Makers of Modern India* (New Delhi: Penguin Viking, 2010), p. 327.
2. Jawaharlal Nehru, Broadcast from Delhi in the Series "Production or Perish," January 18, 1948, AIR tapes, NMML cited in S. Gopal (ed.), *Selected Works of Jawaharlal Nehru*, Second Series, vol. 5 (New Delhi: Jawaharlal Nehru Memorial Fund, 1987), pp. 354-56.
3. B. R. Nanda, *Jawaharlal Nehru: Rebel and Statesman* (New Delhi: Oxford University Press, 2006), pp. 208-9.
4. Jawaharlal Nehru, "Agriculture and Community Development," Inaugural speech at a Seminar organised under the auspices of the Farmers' Forum, New Delhi, March 22, 1957. AIR tapes, NMML. Original in Hindi cited in Mushirul Hasan (ed.), *Selected Works of Jawaharlal Nehru (Feb. 22-April 30, 1957)*, Second Series, vol. 37 (New Delhi: Jawaharlal Nehru Memorial Fund, 1987), pp. 208-11.
5. Jawaharlal Nehru, "Train the Right Type of Human Beings," Message for Kurukshetra on September 5, 1953, Ravinder Kumar and H. Y. Sharada Prasad (eds.), *Selected Works of Jawaharlal Nehru (July 1, 1953-September 1953)*, Second Series, vol. 23 (New Delhi: Jawaharlal Nehru Memorial Fund, 1998), p. 88.
6. Sarvepalli Gopal, *Jawaharlal Nehru: A Biography, Volume III, 1956-1964* (Cambridge: Harvard University Press, 1984), p. 286.
7. Jawaharlal Nehru, "To Baldev Singh on February 29, 1948," cited in S. Gopal (ed.), *Selected Works of Jawaharlal Nehru*, Second Series, vol. 5 (New Delhi: Jawaharlal Nehru Memorial Fund, 1987), p. 420.
8. B. R. Nanda, n. 3, p. 220.

9. G. Parthasarathi (ed.), *Jawaharlal Nehru's Letters to Chief Ministers, 1947-1964,* vol. 2 (New Delhi: Jawaharlal Nehru Memorial Fund, 1985-89), pp. 375-80.
10. B. R. Nanda, n. 3, p. 112.
11. Ibid.
12. Judith M. Brown, *Nehru: A Political Life* (New Delhi: Oxford University Press, 2004), p. 189.
13. Ibid.
14. Government of India, Jawaharlal Nehru, *Indian Foreign Policy: Selected Speeches,* 1946-1961 (New Delhi, Publications Division, 1961), p. 80.
15. B. R. Nanda, n. 3, p.222.
16. Jawaharlal Nehru, Speech delivered at the plenary session of the Asian Relations Conference, March 23, 1947, New Delhi. See, for detail, S. Gopal (ed.), *SWJN,* Second Series, vol. 2 (New Delhi: Jawaharlal Nehru Memorial Fund, 2003), p. 504.
17. Jawaharlal Nehru, *Lok Sabha Debates,* Second Series, vol. 27, March 17, 1959, pp. 6670-93.
18. Sarvepalli Gopal, n. 6, p. 98.
19. Jawaharlal Nehru, Press Conference at Delhi, September 11, 1959; *National Herald,* September 12, 1959.
20. Sarvepalli Gopal, n. 6. pp. 98-99.
21. C. Raja Mohan, "India's Regional Security Cooperation: The Nehru Raj Legacy," ISAS Working Paper, No. 168, March 7, 2013, Institute of South Asian Studies, National University, Singapore, p. 6, available on website: www.isas.nus.edu.sg (accessed on January 16, 2014 at 12.50 pm).
22. Ibid., p.2.
23. Judith M. Brown, n. 12, p. 270.
24. Ibid.

2

Jawaharlal Nehru's Conception of History

Sukhdev Singh Sohal

Jawaharlal Nehru with his cosmopolitan outlook and deep historical consciousness shines like a blazing star in the political firmament of twentieth-century India. India of today is facing new challenges of globalisation. Contemporary contingencies are being pushed through as permanent solutions. In such a situation, there is need to revisit Jawaharlal Nehru, his ideology and political praxis. Jawaharlal Nehru was indeed a great but extraordinarily complex personality and any evaluation of his role in modern history is bound to be equally complex and somewhat controversial.[1] Moreover, he thrived on complexity. He confronted it in the name of diversity in Indian history. In intellectual terms, Nehru spanned the gap between the Indian of the village and the metropolitan, universalist Indian. He kept India together and consolidated its organic integrity.[2] Aristocratic in taste, democratic and egalitarian by conviction, Jawaharlal Nehru comes through as a man with a finely timed artistic sensibility with an increasing curiosity in the world around him never losing his sense of wonder at the marvels of life and the universe.[3] His intellectualism had much to owe to his study of history.[4] Jawaharlal Nehru was "a significant and representative figure." He played a role, deservedly or no, more vital than that of most other persons of his generation in India.[5] In 1939, Rabindranath Tagore wrote to Mahatma Gandhi that he could identify only two "modernists" among India's national leaders: Jawaharlal Nehru and Subhas Chandra Bose. However, both were deeply attached to their country's ancient heritage and both followed anti-colonial stance.[6] M. N. Roy questioned Nehru's "modernism" but the fact of history is that Nehru's modernism mattered.[7] Despite prevailing cynicism about the Nehruvian model of development, to define modern India is to define Jawaharlal Nehru. In difficult times, he looked into history and learned from it. Hence, the present attempt is to delineate Jawaharlal Nehru's conception of history.

I

History is often taken as the study of the past. It is much more than that. Famous philosopher of history, E. H. Carr, delivering the T. B. Macaulay Lecture in Cambridge University in 1961, defined history as "an unending dialogue between the present and the past, a dialogue between the events of the past and progressively emerging future ends."[8] Much earlier, Jawaharlal Nehru followed this methodological principle in his writings and pronouncements. Modest as he was, he never considered himself a "historian or a scholar."[9] He called himself "dabbler in many things."[10]

Born on November 14, 1889 at Allahabad in the house of Motilal Nehru, a prominent lawyer and a Kashmiri Pandit, Jawaharlal Nehru's family had a long and chequered history. The fortunes of the Nehrus had for generations been tied to Muslim patrons. The family took advantage of the conditions and opportunities created by the Raj. In 1919, his tryst with politics began.[11] Nehru thrilled in jail-going and the glow of suffering and self-indulgent sacrifice.[12] In fact, prison became a kind of enforced sabbatical and the most exclusive school in the world. He did reading and writing at this school.[13] The reading and writing in jail kept Nehru "mentally fit" and he forgot about jail surroundings as he lived through the past he was writing about.[14] In his writings, he aimed at describing his motives and appraisal as meticulously as possible. The purpose was not self-justification or rationalisation, but to show the rightness and inimitability of the actions and events in which he was a prime participant. He was a luminous man and his writings reflected the radiance of his spirit.[15] His *Letters from a Father to His Daughter* (1929) shows his strong inclination towards history. He wrote three classic books: (i) *Glimpses of World History* (1934-35); (ii) *An Autobiography* (1936) and (iii) *Discovery of India* (1946). His feel for the flow of human history and his capacity to weave a wide range of knowledge into a meaningful pattern gives *Glimpses of World History* qualities of a high order. What makes it original and unique is its Asian-centred orientation. The lack of balance in historical writing is redressed.[16] In June 1934, he turned to self-analysis and related his own experience of India's struggle for freedom in the celebrated *Autobiography*. In the book, he honestly and stubbornly seeks the truth. He doubts, debates and frankly admits his mistakes. The London *Times* considered it "a book to read."[17] He examined his heritage in the forms of a rambling and discursive history of his native land, social, philosophical, economic, political and cultural. Largely under the influence of M. A. K. Azad and Narendra Dev, he acquired a deep appreciation of the cultural tradition of India and of the influence on his own thought and action. He sought and found the mainsprings of India's struggle for independence with India's historical experience. *The Discovery of India*, written in five months between April and September 1944, throws light on Nehru's new awareness of specifically Indian influences on his character and outlook. In essence, it unfolds Nehru's discovery of his Indian antecedents, and his "mature reflections."[18] It is a text on history in which all sections of our people would find something of their past, a good reason surely why even today this book should be celebrated.[19] However, M. J. Akbar says that its prose is more flat than in *An Autobiography* and history less riveting than in the *Glimpses of World History*.[20] In *Glimpses of World History* and *Discovery of India*, an astonishing sweep in his knowledge and perception of the ongoing drama of Civilisation, in all parts of the world as well as in India.[21] These works are both historical and autobiographical. Bipan Chandra has rightly argued that for "Nehru, history was part autobiography and autobiography part history."[22] This was quite natural, as he tried to find out answers to questions he was confronted with both in his personal life and in history. Logically, he linked the present with the past and the past as a guide to the present. Thus, he regarded history as "a living process."[23]

For Jawaharlal Nehru, history was both "a voyage of discovery and a guide to action." History both formed him and reflected his formation as a political leader and thinker.[24] Furthermore, for S. Radhakrishnan, Nehru's sense of history endowed him with the "vision without which true greatness is not possible."[25] For him, history did not mean heaping facts upon facts in an impersonal, lifeless manner. The past was integrally related to the present and the future.[26] He acknowledged the liberating role of history:

> ... the past is always with us and all that we are and what we have comes from the past. We are its products and we live immersed in it. Not to understand it and feel it as something living within us is not to understand the present. To combat it with the present and to extend to the future, to break from it when it cannot be united, to make of all these the pulsating and vibrating material for thought and action—that is life.[27]

He is conscious of the dangers of studying history for its own sake and hence of becoming a victim of the past. That "is not life" but escapism. He rejects it:

> There is a stillness and everlastingness about the past unaffected by the storms and upheavals of present, it maintains its dignity and repose and tempts the troubled spirit and the tortured mind to seek shelter ... There is peace and security.[28] The past oppresses me or fills me sometimes with its warmth when it touches on the present and becomes, as it were, an aspect of that living present.[29]

Hence, in Jawaharlal Nehru, history turns a progressive science. E. H. Carr rightly says that history can be written only by those who find and accept "a sense of direction" in history itself. The belief that we have come from somewhere is closely linked with the belief that we are going somewhere. History, therefore, acquires meaning and objectivity only when it establishes a coherent relation between past and future.[30] The past carries its own weight. The writing of history is one way of getting rid of the weight of the past. It liberates us from history.[31] Jawaharlal Nehru admitted that the writing of history brings some relief from the weight and burden of the past. The burden of the past is overpowering and sometimes suffocating especially for those who belong to very ancient civilisations like those of India and China.[32] No one writes in vacuum. The purpose is to know the past, one's heritage. He poses a question to himself, "what is my inheritance, to what am I heir?" and answers thus in *Discovery of India*:

> To all that humanity has achieved in tens of thousands of years to all that it has thought and felt and suffered and taken pleasure in ... to that astonishing adventure of man which began so long ago and yet continues and beckons us.[33]

He acknowledges the long, cherished past of India and its heritage. He regards history as "a continuous process." He was deeply impressed with the interaction between India and the outside world since the dawn of history. This helped him in the evolution of his internationalist outlook and simultaneously with the nationalist vision.[34] Not only in historical outlook, in practice also, Nehru was "a good internationalist."[35] His intellectual trajectory moves from "discovery" of the self to "discovery of India" to world history in the historical context. No one reads or writes history in a fit of total absent-mindedness.[36] To enable man to understand the society of the past and to increase his mastery over the society of the present "is the dual function" of history.[37] History without predicting the future can offer some useful guide to it.[38] Historical knowledge is a prevision, an insight to the understanding of future.[39] Nehru, the action-oriented individual, and Nehru, the historian and student of social change, constantly intrude on each other. That is the charm of Nehru's historical writing.[40]

> … it is the action and the thoughts of action that fills me and when action is denied, I imagine that I am preparing for action. The call of action has long been with me; not actions divorced from thought, but rather flowing from it in one continuous sequence ... even now, the call of action stirs strange depths within me and often a brief tussle with thought ... This urge to action, this desire to experience life through action has influenced all my thought and activity.[41]

Jawaharlal Nehru was living in a crucial historical juncture. British Imperialism after World War I was on the back foot, yet boastful. Nationalist sentiments were surging ahead in the Indian subcontinent. The teeming millions were on the march both passively and actively. To contain, control and carry forward the march was the major task of the leaders and intellectuals as well. Jawaharlal Nehru performed a major role at this moment to swim with and tame the tide. His deep understanding of history as a thought and practice helped him evolve both politically and intellectually. The lesson of history is progress. The essence of history, for Nehru, was change which he traces in all aspects—social, economic, intellectual, and cultural.[42]

> What is history indeed but a record of change? And if there had been very few changes in the past, there would have been little of history to write.[43] … a study of history should teach us how the world has slowly but surely progressed … man's growth from barbarism to civilisation is supposed to be the theme of history.[44]

Jawaharlal Nehru's excitement about history made him see patterns in the past, a link between "now" and "then": his knowledge of world politics made him curious about what was happening "there" and not merely "here."[45] He predates R. G. Collingwood that history is "for human self-knowledge."[46]

II

Jawaharlal Nehru based his thinking on his reading of the world history and the Indian history. As a historian, Nehru was particularly interested in the subject of intervention between Asia and the Western world. He notices a particular passivity in Asian history and contrasts it with the "dynamic nature" of European history.[47] Nehru partially accepted the Marxist view of causation in history. In his view, history marched forward through conflict and struggle. Revolutions are common in history. Those who "really matter are the masses."[48] For him revolutions occur:

> Not because any group or person is a lover of bloodshed and anarchy and disorder but because of this desire for greater security for larger number of persons.[49]

He took keen interest in the Revolutions of America (1776), France (1789) and Russia (1917). He saw the French Revolution as marking the beginning of the modern era of liberty, equality and nationalism in human history. He was attracted by the role that ideas and ideologues had played in bringing about the Revolution. He considered the Russian Revolution (1917) "unique in World history" and an example for many revolutions all over the world.[50]

He was highly influenced by the Marxist approach to understand the reality. He admits that "the communist philosophy of life gave him comfort and hope."[51] He defined Marxism as "a way of interpreting history and politics and economics and human life and human desires. It is a theory as well as a call to action. It is a philosophy which has something to say about most of the activities of man's life."[52] He basically adopted the Marxist method which was to be a part of his thinking process for the rest of his life.[53] He writes:

> A study of Marx and Lenin produced a powerful effect on my mind and helped me to see history and current affairs in a new light. The long chain of history and of social development appeared to

> have some meaning, some sequence, and the future lost some of its obscurity.[54]

Nehru's view of Indian history is particularly interesting. He reacts to the Indian past in two distinct ways. As a rationalist, he is not unaware of the weaknesses and strengths of the country and its culture. He speaks of periods of glory as well as decay, of periods when the Indian genius was creative and the influence of Indian culture was felt far beyond her national frontiers. But there were periods when India tended to fall back and "became a bit of a fossil."[55] He searches for the secret of remarkable continuity of Indian civilisation. He traces it in the unity and diversity of India, its deep tolerance and efforts to synthesise divergent elements, its flexibility and adaptability that helped in the absorption of foreign elements, its intellectual freedom and strength of its social institutions.[56] Jawaharlal Nehru in *The Discovery of India* took solace in "the continuity of a cultural tradition through five thousand years of history" which made the 180 years of British rule in India seem like "just one of the unhappy interludes in her long story."[57] He visualises the future of rising Asia:

> History usually works slowly through the Centuries, though sometimes there are periods of rush and burst-ups. Today, however, it is moving fast in Asia and the old continent is waking up after her long slumber. The eyes of the world are upon us, for everyone knows that Asia is going to play a great part in the future.[58]

His emotions had to be stirred and involved before he could react. There was little that was striking about him for the first thirty years of his life. In 1915, the internment of Annie Besant stirred him. Moreover, the Jallianwala Bagh massacre in April 1919 and Mahatma Gandhi's Satyagraha campaign were the turning points. He was revolted not so much by Brig. General Dyer's action as by the widespread British support for Dyer.[59] He became one of Congress's major thinkers, though he was never rigidly doctrinaire. The vision of equality among men and the more equitable redistribution of wealth were for him essential aspects of liberation from imperialism.[60] Nehru lived in the era of state planning. The emphasis on the planning of a modern industrial structure is clearly articulated in *The Discovery of India*: "No country can be politically and economically independent, unless it is highly industrialised and has developed its power resources to the utmost. Nor can it achieve and maintain high standards of living and liquidate poverty, without the aid of modern technology in almost every sphere of life."[61] The appeal of planning for Jawaharlal Nehru was both "emotional and intellectual." The patriot and the historian in him conjured up the vision of something vast—the mighty theme of a nation building and remaking itself. Planning was an answer to alleviate human suffering without infringing human freedom.[62] He chaired the National Planning Committee formed in 1938 which clearly set out the course of action to be followed to usher in socialism after India attained independence.[63] Nehru as an individual has to be set against the currents of history to analyse how far his personality or particular historical circumstances contributed to the significance of Nehru's role in contemporary history.[64]

III

Nehru's theory of history combines three strands: the nineteenth-century belief in perpetual progress; a stress on the role of "the great man" and sociological analysis with a strong infusion of Marxist method. The *leitmotif* of Nehru's thought and action was the global struggle for freedom. Hence, *Glimpses of World History* is a milestone, embodying in its pure form his international idealism.[65] He was fascinated by the great men of history and not necessarily the men of virtue and idealism.[66] He writes:

> … in history, we read of great periods in the life of nations, of great men and women and great deeds performed and sometimes in our dreams and reveries we imagine ourselves back in those times and doing brave deeds like the heroes and heroines of old.[67]

His work *An Autobiography* was at once acclaimed as "as a valuable insight into one of the great contemporary minds."[68] He underwent an intellectual process in the reverse order: he was initially exposed to Western knowledge and Philosophy and at a later stage returned to his own resources.[69] *The Discovery of India* does not compare as a literary achievement with *An Autobiography*, nor its analysis of the past as vigorous and penetrating as that in *Glimpses of World History*. The *Discovery of India* was "an escape into a largely imaginary conception of India's history, which enabled Nehru to keep his spirit afloat."[70] *The Discovery of India*, a gem of renaissance historical writing, provides marvellously fresh vision of the Indian past.[71] He provides "the best account to that date of the impact of colonialism on India and of the rise of the anti-imperialist national movement."[72] Nehru imparted a socialist vision to the national movement and the National Congress a socialist orientation.[73]

Nehru was credited with almost wizard-like qualities of balance combined with idealism of diplomatic adroitness and powers of conciliation. He was a world statesman to whom flowed the admiration and hopes of millions.[74] Through his writings he tries to inculcate "a sense of history."[75] The perils of ignoring history produce "a vagueness of outlook, a divorce from life as it is credulity, a woolliness of mind where fact was concerned."[76] He read voraciously and pondered with a fresh mind the problems which had troubled him.[77] Books fascinated Jawaharlal Nehru. He sought out ideas. He was extraordinarily sensitive to literary beauty.[78] He was the symbol of a new society—liberal, humanist and equalitarian.[79] He clearly saw dangers in Marxism of reductionism:

> ... it is an attempt at reducing human history, past, present and future to a rigid logical system with something of the inevitability of fate or Kismat about it.[80]

He was a Marxist, who rejected regimentation, a socialist who was wholly committed to civil liberties, a radical who accepted non-violence, an international statesman with a total involvement in India and, above all, a leader who believed in carrying his people with him even if it slowed down the pace of progress.[81] While Nehru accepted the Marxist analysis of the past, he was not convinced by the Marxist diagnosis of the future.[82] For Nehru, all thought, including knowledge and study of history was guide to action.[83] History was both "imagined action" and a preparation for future action.[84] His reliance on history was highly interpretative than mere mentioning of facts in a constituent structure.[85] He takes in all shades of history, although his own standpoint is that of judging events from the point of view of humanity at large.[86] Though enamoured of the role of the individual in history, Jawaharlal Nehru, under the influence of Marxism, always saw history as a larger canvas at the systemic level not at individual level.[87] Jawaharlal Nehru symbolised modern India both in thought and action. With Western education and philosophy, he delved deep into the history of the World in general and the Indian subcontinent in particular. He turned to history as a guide. He wrote history in the liberal tradition. Thus, he moved ahead with understanding of the past to comprehend the present. His historical consciousness delineates his philosophy, his belief in unity in diversity, secularism, democracy, progress, scientific temper and urge for planning keeping individual freedom intact. He was an institution-builder. He brought India on the world map. Certainly he was ahead of his time, sometimes acting in haste, ignoring burning issues, which some of us consider his failures. He did the same thing while writing history. He was a renaissance scholar and a leader who inspired generations. Now it is time to remember him more in these testing times when the institutions he built and nurtured carefully seem to be cracking and crumbling!

References

1. Bipan Chandra, *Ideology and Politics in Modern India* (New Delhi: Har-Anand, 2005), p. 1.
2. Arvind N. Das, "Warts and All," *Biblio*, January-February 1997, p. 6.
3. Shyam Benegal, "A Finely Tuned Sensibility," *Mainstream*, vol. 47, no. 48, November 14, 2009, p. 11.

4. Vivek Kumar Srivastava, "Pandit Nehru and His View of History," *Mainstream*, New Delhi, November 18-24, 2011, p. 11.
5. S. Gopal, "The Formative Ideology of Jawaharlal Nehru," *Economic and Political Weekly*, vol. 11, no. 21, May 22, 1976, p. 787.
6. Sugata Bose and Ayesha Jalal, *Modern South Asia: History, Culture, Political Economy* (New Delhi: Oxford University Press, 2006), p. 8.
7. Arjun Sengupta, "Nehru and Indian Socialism," *Mainstream*, vol. 48, no. 47, November 13, 2010, p. 25.
8. E. H. Carr, *What is History?* (Middlesex: Penguin Books, 1987), p. 123.
9. Jawaharlal Nehru, *The Discovery of India* (New Delhi: Oxford University Press, 2004), p. 24.
10. B. G. Gokhale, "Nehru and History," *History and Theory*, vol. 17, no. 3, October, 1978, p. 315.
11. Jawaharlal Nehru, *An Autobiography* (New Delhi: Oxford University Press, 1980); S. Gopal, *Jawaharlal Nehru: A Biography (1889-1947)*, vol. I (Delhi: Oxford University Press, 1976), pp. 16, 17, 35. For a brief biographical sketch, see S. P. Sen (ed.), *Dictionary of National Biography*, vol. III (Calcutta: Institute of Historical Studies, 1974), pp. 253-62. For a critical and controversial account see S. Wolpert, *Nehru: A Tryst with Destiny* (New Delhi: Oxford University Press, 1997).
12. S. Gopal, n. 5, p. 788.
13. M. J. Akbar, *Nehru: The Making of India* (New Delhi: Roli Books, 2002), p. 240.
14. Jawaharlal Nehru, n. 11, p. 352.
15. Indira Gandhi, "Foreword," Jawaharlal Nehru, *Glimpses of World History*, p. v.
16. Michael Brecher, *Nehru: A Political Biography* (London: OUP, 1959), p. 71.
17. A. Gorev and V. Zimyanin, *Jawaharlal Nehru* (Moscow: Progress Publishers, 1982), pp. 182-83.
18. Michael Brecher, n. 16, pp. 116-231.
19. Irfan Habib, *The National Movement: Studies in Ideology and History* (New Delhi: Tulika, 2011), pp. 56-57.
20. M. J. Akbar, n. 13, p. 356.
21. B. G. Gokhale, n. 10, p. 316.
22. Bipan Chandra, *Essays on Indian Nationalism* (New Delhi: Har-Anand, 2005), p. 185.
23. Arvind Gupta, "History, Secularism and Nehru," *Mainstream*, November 24, 1990, p. 23.
24. Jawaharlal Nehru, n. 9, pp. 10-11, and Bipan Chandra, n. 22, p. 185.
25. Quoted in G. S. Jolly (ed.), *The Image of Nehru* (New Delhi: PBS, 1968), p. 1.
26. Satish Chandra, "Nehru the Historian," *Historiography, Religion and State in Medieval India* (New Delhi: Har Anand, 1996), pp. 89-90.
27. Jawaharlal Nehru, n. 9, p. 7.
28. Ibid.
29. Ibid., p. 25.
30. E. H. Carr, n. 8, pp. 123, 130, 132.
31. Benedetto Crore, *History as the Story of Liberty* (London: George Allen and Unwin, 1941), pp. 43-45.
32. Jawaharlal Nehru, n. 9, p. 25.

33. Ibid.
34. Ibid., p. 10. See also, Arvind Gupta, "History, Secularism, and Nehru," *Mainstream,* November 24, 1990, pp. 24-25.
35. Percival Spear, *The Oxford History of Modern India (1740-1975)* (Delhi: OUP, 1983), p. 420.
36. G. R. Elton, *The Practice of History* (Glasgow: Collins-Fontana, 1978), p. 56.
37. E. H. Carr, n. 8 , p. 55.
38. A. L. Rowse, *The Use of History* (London: The English Universities Press, 1946), p. 22.
39. G. R. Elton, n. 36, p. 67.
40. Satish Chandra, n. 26, p. 90.
41. Jawaharlal Nehru, n. 9, pp. 8-9.
42. Satish Chandra, n. 26, p. 91.
43. Jawaharlal Nehru, *Glimpses of World History*, p. 9.
44. Ibid., p. 6.
45. A. K. Damodaran, "A Splendid Partnership," *Mainstream*, vol. 47, no. 48, November 14, 2009, pp. 12-13.
46. R. G. Collingwood, *The Idea of History* (OUP, London, 1973), p. 10.
47. B. G. Gokhale, "Nehru and History," *History and Theory*, vol. 17, no. 3, October, 1978, p. 37.
48. Arvind Gupta, "History, Secularism and Nehru," *Mainstream*, November 24, 1990, p. 25.
49. M. N. Das, *The Political Philosophy of Jawaharlal Nehru* (London: 1961), p. 46.
50. Bipan Chandra, n. 22, p. 187.
51. Jawaharlal Nehru, n. 11, p. 364.
52. Jawaharlal Nehru, *Glimpses of World History*, p. 544.
53. Bipan Chandra, n. 22, p. 186.
54. Jawaharlal Nehru, n. 9, p. 29.
55. S. Gopal, "The Formative Ideology of Jawaharlal Nehru," *Economic and Political Weekly*, vol. 11, no. 21, May 22, 1976, p. 787.
56. B. G. Gokhale, n. 47, pp. 318-19.
57. Sugata Bose and Ayesha Jalal, n. 6, p. 8.
58. Jawaharlal Nehru, *Glimpses of World History*, p. 10.
59. Jawaharlal Nehru, n. 11, pp. 43-44. Satish Chandra, n. 26, pp. 92-93.
60. Judith M. Brown, *Modern India: The Origins of an Asian Democracy* (Delhi: OUP, 1984), p. 232.
61. B. N. Ganguli, *Indian Economic Thought: Nineteenth Century Perspectives* (New Delhi: Tata-McGraw-Hill, 1977), p. 264.
62. Tarlok Singh, "Jawaharlal Nehru: Planned Development and the National Synthesis," in B. R. Nanda and V. C. Joshi (eds.), *Studies in Modern Indian History*, no. 1 (New Delhi: Orient Longman, 1972), p. 67.
63. V. B. Singh, *Nehru on Socialism* (New Delhi: Ministry of Information and Broadcasting, 1977), pp. 103-4.
64. Arjun Sengupta, "Nehru and Indian Socialism," *Mainstream*, vol. 47, no. 47, November 13, 2010, p. 25.
65. Michael Brecher, n. 16, p. 72.
66. S. Gopal, *Jawaharlal Nehru: A Biography*, n. 11, p.175.

67. Jawaharlal Nehru, *Glimpses of World History*, p. 2.
68. M. J. Akbar, n. 13, p. 241.
69. K. N. Panikkar, *Culture, Ideology, Hegemony, Intellectuals and Social Consciousness in Colonial India* (New Delhi: Tulika, 2001), p. 67.
70. S. Gopal, "The Formative Ideology of Jawaharlal Nehru," *Economic and Political Weekly*, vol. 11, no. 21, May 22, 1976, p. 788.
71. David Kopf, "Hermeneutics versus History," *The Journal of Asian Studies,* vol. 39, no. 3, May 1980, p. 496.
72. Bipan Chandra, n. 22, p. 190.
73. Bipan Chandra, "A Total Commitment," *Mainstream*, vol. 47, no. 48, November 14, 2009, p. 11.
74. Percival Spear, n. 35, p. 420.
75. Satish Chandra, n. 26, p. 94.
76. Jawaharlal Nehru, n. 9.
77. Michael Brecher, n. 16, p. 116.
78. Indira Gandhi, "Foreword," Jawaharlal Nehru, *Glimpses of World History*, p. v.
79. Michael Brecher, n. 16, p. 230.
80. Jawaharlal Nehru, *Glimpses of World History*, p. 544.
81. S. Gopal, n. 5, p. 792.
82. Srinath Raghavan (ed.), *Sarvepalli Gopal: Imperialists, Nationalists, Democrats: The Collected Essays* (Bangalore: Permanent Black, 2013), p. 181.
83. Bipan Chandra, n. 22, p. 190.
84. Satish Chandra, n. 26, p. 90.
85. Vivek Kumar Srivastava, n. 4, p. 12.
86. Irfan Habib, n. 19, p. 42.
87. Jawaharlal Nehru, *Glimpses of World History*, pp. 546-47.

3

Nehru's Idea of Federalism and Nation-Building in India

Ranjit Singh

Federalism and nation-building are interrelated in a plural society. Federalism is best suited to a society characterised by wide range of diversities of language, religion, region, etc., as it provides appropriate space to each section claiming to be different from the other strata of society. The Constitution of India contains adequate provisions to make India a federal state as an effort to constitutionally bind the people in a single thread called "nation." The Constitution stipulates equal rights to all including linguistic and religious minorities without discrimination of any type. The state has been proclaimed to be a socialist welfare state with a commitment to secure social, economic and political justice, equality of opportunity, freedom of conscience and worship. Nation-building is an emotional concept implying unity of people sharing common bonds, traditions. Jawaharlal Nehru, one of the founding fathers of the Constitution, laid great stress on building India as a nation, and he used federalism as a strategy to inculcate the sense of belongingness among the people of India. This paper is an attempt to explore the history of federalism in India, Nehru's idea of federalism and nation-building. This paper is divided into three parts: part one discusses the history and constitutional aspect, Nehru's idea has been discussed in part two and part three explains nation-building.

I

The essence of federalism lies not in the constitutional or institutional structure but in society itself. A federal government is a device by which the federal qualities of a society are articulated and protected.[1] Etymologically federalism implies an agreement or a treaty between two sets of government whereby the two agree to share some powers through the Constitution. Federalism comes into existence through centripetal and centrifugal tendencies. In case of the former, already autonomous states decide to surrender some of their powers while retaining some vital powers for the sake of national unity to a new entity called federal government. American federalism is an example of centripetal federalism. Whereas in the latter case, a strong centre unable to manage a plethora of subjects, delegates some of its powers to the constituent units of the state. Indian federalism is an example of centrifugal federalism.

The history of federalism in India can be traced to the third and fourth decade of the twentieth century when nationalists were demanding complete independence, the target set by Indian National Congress at its Lahore Session in 1929-30. In the wake of the civil disobedience movement launched to express discontent against the designs of the imperialist forces to keep India weak by following a policy of divide and rule, the British government convened three Round Table Conferences to find a way out of some crucial issues. The idea of federalism was also debated upon which was rejected by certain quarters till a solution to the communal tangle was found. In such a distressing situation the British Indian government came forward with a new proposal embodied in the Government of India Act 1935, establishing an All-India Federation consisting of Indian states and provinces. Being optional for states and mandatory for provinces to join the federation, this proposal of the Act could not materialise owing to the outbreak of the Second World War and the reluctance on the part of required number of states to join the proposed federation. The existence of a large number of princely states and different nationalities, a set-up was desired wherein they could retain their separate entity while ensuring unity.

The federal form of government was considered more appropriate from this point of view. Therefore, the framers of the Constitution of India carried forward the provisions of the Government of India Act 1935 related to federation, modified and incorporated them into the constitution. But they chose to select the word "Union" instead of "Federation." Article 1 of the Constitution reads: India that is Bharat shall be a Union of States.[2]

The Chairman of the drafting committee vindicated the use of the term "Union" on the ground that the Indian federation not being the result of an agreement amongst the units, they have no right to secede from the union.[3] The features discerning the federal set-up from unitary government are written, rigid, supreme constitution, division of subjects between the union and states, bicameralism, dual administration, double citizenship and independence of judiciary. If an impartial analysis is made bearing in mind the aforesaid features, the Indian Constitution has a unitary bias. The Constitution is written and supreme and administration from top to bottom is carried on in accordance with the directives of the Constitution, not according to the whims and caprices of any ruling elite. The Constitution is based on the principle of rule of law and enjoins upon the state to ensure equality before law or equal protection of law within the territory of India.[4] Barring the provisions dealing with presidential election representation to states in the upper house of parliament, amendment procedure and changes in the seventh schedule, the rest of the Constitution can be amended by the parliament by simple majority for which state's consent is not imperative.

The Constitution authorises the parliament to make laws for the whole or any part of the country and the state legislature for the whole state or part of the state.[5] In administrative field, the executive authority of the centre extends to the subjects mentioned in the union and concurrent list and that of state to the state list, provided that the executive power of every state shall be in compliance with the laws made by the parliament. The union government is empowered to issue directions to the states in respect of matters like construction and maintenance of means of communication, protection of railways falling within the states. Any matter within the executive power of the union can be assigned to the states.[6]

Financially, the Constitution has created a sort of dependency of the states on the centre, which has kept with itself the power to levy important taxes. States have been given the option to seek grants and loans for the upliftment of the weaker sections. The Finance Commission is constituted after every five years to determine the quantum of grants and other financial resources between the centre and the states. The Union government can borrow money from within India and abroad on the security of the consolidated fund of India. States can do so but only within India. While speaking in the Constituent Assembly, B. R. Ambedkar observes that, "legislative and executive authority between the centre and the states are portioned by the Constitution itself ... the states are not dependent upon the centre therein."[7]

No state can have a separate Constitution from that of India except the state of Jammu and Kashmir that was granted this privilege under unusual circumstances. Furthermore, there is no double citizenship. India has dual administration at the union and state level being managed by civil servants. Like any other federal system India adopted bicameralism wherein the Union Parliament consists of two houses, the Lok Sabha (Lower House) and Rajya Sabha (Upper House). The Lower House is elected directly by the people and the Upper House represents the states and is elected indirectly. Unlike other federations, states are not given equal representation in the Upper House. Although the adequate safeguards in the Constitution have made the Indian judiciary independent but its structure is pyramidal in terms of composition and powers. On account of the number of instances of central intervention in the state matters and unitary tendencies, K. C. Wheare describes Indian federalism as "quasi-federalism."[8] While some others like Appleby, Alexandrowicz, Birch and Sawar recognised the federal nature of the Indian Constitution. The Supreme Court of India in its two landmark judgments identified the federal nature of the constitution as a part of the basic structure of the constitution which cannot be altered under any circumstances.[9]

The Indian Constitution lays down an elaborate scheme for the distribution of powers, which is heavily in favour of the centre. There are three lists, the union, state and concurrent. The centre has exclusive control over the union list; the state list is left for the state legislatures. Regarding concurrent matters, both the union and the states have coequal power providing supremacy of union law in case inconsistency exists between laws made by parliament and state legislature, except under one situation when state law has been reserved for the consent of the President. Residuary powers are vested with the centre. Centre can legislate on state matters under Articles 249, 250, 252, 253 and 356. Therefore, parliament enjoys overriding powers in case of legislation. In administrative matters states are not autonomous as they are to obey the directions of the union government. The central dominance is visible in financial matters, as it has appreciable economic resources at its disposal whereas states' sources of income are restricted but liabilities stupendous. Certainly, states enjoy substantive and significant legislative and executive powers but they have been neutralised or rendered ineffective through other devices which are unfederal in character. On numerous occasions the centre has made inroads into the spheres earmarked for the states, and the authority of the states has been circumscribed by the union government. K. Hanumanthaiah put it more clearly, "… it is a peculiar type, it is a 'union' Constitution."[10] Thakur Das Bhargava calls the system of government provided for in the Constitution as "Unitary-cum-Federal."[11] H. V. Kamath aptly described the Constitution as a centralised federation with a facade for parliamentary democracy.[12] Arun Guha has observed "... this Constitution is like a hybrid Constitution, it is a federal Constitution but it has started from the top not from the bottom."[13]

Centralised planning, office of the governor, article 356, all-India services have been a major irritants in the Indian federation. The Planning Commission—constituted on March 15, 1950 by executive resolution—is endowed with the power to formulate plans for the economic development of the whole of India, and is purely a union-dominated body where states are not given due representation. It has been described as a "parallel cabinet" and sometimes a "super cabinet."[14] The grudge of the states against this institution is that it makes plans without taking into consideration the diverse needs of the various states, thereby imposing plans on the states. Notwithstanding the constitutional provisions, there are no specific guidelines to be followed regarding appointment, term and transfer of governor who has played spoilsport. Consequently, the centre has flouted constitutional practices time and again on political considerations. The Sarkaria Commission[15] has suggested to the government to appoint non-partisan individuals to the office of governor so that this office is not drawn into unnecessary controversy. Associated with it are the emergency provisions, especially the constitutional emergency, which has done irreparable damage to the federal structure. This was to be used as a measure of last resort[16] when all other remedial measures have been exhausted to restore law and order in the states. Regrettably, it has become a political weapon in the hands of ruling dispensation at the centre to dissolve opposition-led popularly elected state ministries on political considerations. Its frequent application has destroyed not only the federal fabric but also dented a serious blow to the fundamental rights of the citizen. The Supreme Court has cautioned the government that Article 356 has to be resorted to only to meet the exigencies of special situations[17] and not to settle political scores. States have also complained against the partisan role played by the All-India Services which otherwise play a dynamic role in maintaining national unity. Another thorny issue is the Finance Commission which suggests principles governing the distribution of resources. States allege that the Finance Commission has always acted according to the dictates of the centre ignoring the developmental needs of the state.

II

The discussion in the preceding part exhibits the centralised federalism. Federal system in India bears impact of Nehru's thinking as in the initial years of the working of federalism, the evolution and shaping of structures and processes of federal set-up, the impact of Nehru can be seen. In this regard Nehru was driven by three factors. First, India being a multicultural society, he was aware of the desire to build a strong nation in the midst of divisiveness prevailing in the immediate period following independence. Centralised federalism was the outcome of Nehru's eagerness to foster unity among diversity.[18] In order to maintain national cohesiveness Nehru felt the need for building institutional machinery and psychological means. The second impulse motivating Nehru was his resoluteness to supplement India's political democracy with an economic system to ensure development with distributive justice. Establishment of planning machinery in the form of the Planning Commission by an executive resolution bore the stamp of Nehru's desire to strengthen the centralised federal system. The third impulse was national consolidation and planned economic development strengthened the centralising tendencies in the federal polity wherein a strong centre does not necessarily mean strong constituent units. This demonstrated Nehru's firm commitment to democracy keeping in mind the aspirations of diverse regional, religious and linguistic identities. The objective of national integration coupled with planned development required a centralised federation.

Nehru's political leaning to the left an indelible imprint on the federal set-up that grew out of the deliberations of the Constituent Assembly (CA). The Objectives Resolution moved on December 13, 1946 in the CA, which spoke of residuary powers to the autonomous units, was an effort to appease the Muslim League to maintain unity by avoiding partition. But this proved futile as the proposal of June 3, 1947 proclaimed the government's intention to bifurcate India into two separate independent states. In his letter to the president of the CA, Nehru wrote "... severe limitation on the scope of central authority in the Cabinet Mission's Plan was a compromise accepted by the Assembly much against the judgment of the administrative needs of the country, in order to accommodate the Muslim League. Now that partition is a settled fact, we are unanimously of the view that it would be injurious to the interests of the country to provide for a weak central authority which would be incapable of ensuring peace, of coordinating vital matters of common concerns and of speaking effectively for the whole country in the international sphere … we are clear in our minds that there are many matters in which authority must lie solely with the units and to frame a constitution on the basis of a unitary state would be a retrograde step, both politically and administratively … we have come to the conclusion that the soundest framework for our Constitution is a federation with a strong centre."[19] In a federal framework Nehru was keen for democratic adjustment between the union and the constituent units. Despite his inclination for central control over some subjects like education and health, Nehru did not oppose the state Chief Ministers' attempt to place these subjects either in the state or concurrent list, especially Chief Ministers like B. G. Kher and Govind Ballabh Pant. However Nehru was a great votary of central command in federal matters, but also made some sort of adjustment with regard to the demand for state autonomy provided it has mass support. Consequently, CA was successful in devising a federal system based on the mixture of national power and state autonomy keeping in mind the interests of a plural society of India. This was very much required to maintain national unity and tread the path of planned development to achieve socialistic objectives with distributive justice in a participatory democracy. The major policy decisions which were taken during the Prime Ministership of Nehru were influenced by planned economic development and participatory democracy. The central leadership including Nehru showed reluctance in reorganisation of states on linguistic lines.

Despite a pre-independence commitment to redraw the boundaries of states on language basis, the national leadership was over-cautious in the matter as the partition holocaust was still fresh and in their opinion linguistic reorganisation of constituent units would threaten the very fabric of the republic. Robert D. King remarked that "… within months of independence Nehru began to back-pedal on the issue of linguistic provinces. He felt that their implementation was among the most trifling of the problems facing the country, and because he knew they would bring dissension ... he argued with initial success to postpone dealing with linguistic provinces for as long a time as possible."[20] The report of the Linguistic Provinces Commission called Dar Commission echoed the same sentiment by postponing implementation of linguistic reorganisation of states till the process of integration of princely states was complete and the feeling of nationalism was deeply rooted in India. The Dar Commission in its report submitted on December 10, 1948, concluded that "... no new provinces should be formed for the present. All things considered, the consideration of linguistic provinces should be postponed for ten years."[21] The JVP Committee while ratifying the report of the Dar Commission argued that the "... old Congress policy of having linguistic provinces could only be applied after careful thought had been given to each separate case and without creating serious administrative dislocation or mutual conflicts which would jeopardise the political and economic stability of the country."[22] The Committee further added that "... the primary concern must be the security, unity and economic prosperity of India and every separatist and disruptive tendency should be rigorously discouraged."[23] Subsequently the framers of the Constitution incorporated Article 3 in the Constitution which authorises the union legislature to reorganise, to redraw the boundaries of any state by passing an act with or without the consent of the concerned state. The thought of maintaining national unity instead of reorganisation of states was of prime importance to Nehru. Hence for the sake of the development of the sense of the unity of India, he argued that formation of provinces is an administrative necessity and cannot be done at the cost of the country's interest which is supreme.[24] But despite this commitment Nehru yielded to the popular movement led by Potti Sriramulu for the creation of Andhra Pradesh (AP). AP was created in 1953 as the first linguistic province and State Reorganisation Commission (SRC) was constituted to examine objectively and dispassionately the issue of reorganisation of states of the Indian Union so as to ensure the welfare of the people of each constituent unit and the nation is promoted.[25] The Commission was charged to "investigate the problems, the historical background, and the existing situation ... make recommendations in regard to the broad principles which should govern the solution of this problem ... and submit interim report for the consideration of the government."[26] In case of AP in 1953 and bifurcation of Bombay into Gujarat and Maharashtra in 1960 it was Nehru's democratic disposition which impelled him to concede to popular backed demand for linguistic organisation. The subsequent reorganisation of provinces through the seventh constitutional amendment has established that the fears of Nehru regarding the implications of linguistic reorganisation were exaggerated and linguistically organised states are not a serious threat for the centre. Rather they have well-defined and coherent identities not more difficult to handle for the union than the previous heterogeneous units.

It may be recalled here that national unity was a passion for Nehru, it was not a steamrollered uniformity. This was evident from his attitude towards the official language. Article 343 of the Constitution mandates that, "Hindi shall be the official language of the union and that English would continue to be used as an associate language till January 26, 1965."[27] There was some apprehension about the time limit in the non-Hindi-speaking areas to which Nehru responded on the floor of the Lok Sabha on August 6, 1959 and gave the assurance that there was in fact no time limit and the non-Hindi-speaking states would themselves decide as to when to switch over to Hindi. Nehru observed that "... any attempt to impose a particular form of language has usually met with strongest opposition and has actually resulted in something the very reverse of what the promoters thought."[28] Thus Nehru's move further strengthened the foundations of national unity and consolidated the federal scheme of things through his flexibility of approach and democratic demeanours. Pran Chopra has opined that "... Nehru was a catalyst, no one laboured so hard to open the eyes of each area to what was happening in the rest, this was the effect of his simple repetitive homilies he incessantly preached, so tiring to the cynical intellectuals but for most Indians their first step in learning that they had become parts of a big country." In spite of the fact that Nehru failed to solve all centre-periphery problems like in Nagaland and Mizo areas, federalism under his dynamic leadership had developed strength in absorbing severe strains in centre-state relations and to a considerable extent contained the feeling of separatism. The growth of the trend towards centralisation during the Nehru era from 1950 to 1964 was the complaint which was frequently heard on the part of the states. The grudge was that besides the constitutional overriding authority, the centre had made inroads into the state jurisdiction by way of emergency and other related provisions of the Constitution. C. Rajagopalachari said that "... the independence of the states is being forgotten and a unitary state is being established in India thoughtlessly." One-party dominance coupled with centralised planning provided the space for the encroachment of domains earmarked constitutionally for the states. Financial supremacy of the centre further made the states less autonomous in policy implementation in cases which involved huge funding from the centre. This kind of erosion of state autonomy was more evident in the first one and a half decade of federal relations after independence. The Planning Commission's role in planning and financial matters was so enormous that it had assumed the status of what K. Santhanam called super-cabinet which, despite its extra-constitutional status, had encroached upon the executive autonomy and legislative responsibility of the states. India had thus developed a sort of "paramount federation."[29] Contrarily states had an effective role in the National Development Council (NDC) established in 1952. The NDC was charged with the formal approval of the concept of partnership and cooperation between the union and the federating units over the plans and development. Therefore, despite centralising tendencies in the Indian federalism, there was some sort of cooperation through the medium of NDC. This interdependence has become a significant feature of the federal system the world over including that in contemporary India. Paul H. Appleby appreciated this phenomenon of interdependence between the centre and the states in administrative matters where the centre was dependent on the states.

Over and above, despite Nehru's towering personality, the central leadership was helpless on some occasions in getting its decision enforced at the state level which showed that being one-party dominant system did not imply a completely subservient position of the states to the centre. In 1960 objections of All India Congress Committee to Madhya Pradesh's Land Revenue Code were not accepted by Madhya Pradesh (MP) government. Similarly the failure to swear in K. N. Katju as Chief Minister of MP spoke volumes about the limits of the Central High Command's authority. Even in matters like three-language formula, land ceiling, cooperative farming, the high command's power was restricted in so far as the implementation of these policies was concerned.[30] Notwithstanding a certain degree of centralisation, the relations between the two sets of government were not always in favour of the union. In fact, centre-states relations varied from situation to situation and were determined by the strength of the Chief Minister in comparison to his ministerial colleagues, and internal functioning of the state party organisation. The states were not always at the receiving end. Moreover Nehru's working pattern was a solace to the state against the enforced subordination of states against the centre. Evidently West Bengal Chief Minister B. C. Roy treated Nehru as an equal in matters affecting the interests of West Bengal. Marcus F. Frands aptly sum up the position, "... the central government has not been as strong or as forceful in its relations with West Bengal as the thrust of the Constitution and the dependence of the State on the Centre would seem to make possible."[31] The Prime Minister being the head of the Planning Commission, and head of the ruling party, has an important role to play. Nehru played a key role in shaping and moulding federal relations. However in the initial years of independence emphasis was on national consolidation, hence some degree of centralisation was natural. In the opinion of Nehru a strong federalism was essentially an integral part of overall strategy of democratic nation-building.[32]

III

Federalism was conceived as the workable strategy to infuse among people the sense of belongingness. With the decolonisation process in the twentieth century several independent, sovereign states came into existence on the world map. India played a leading role by getting herself free from the yoke of colonialism and by supporting the freedom movements of numerous states of Asia, Africa and Latin America. Subsequently, in the second half of the twentieth century, a large number of states attained full statehood. After achieving what is called national liberation these nations set on the path of nation-building. However to accomplish the arduous task of nation-building these states including India had to confront a large number of problems. Nehru in his "Tryst with Destiny" speech envisioned independent India with the pledge to convert India into an industrial country. In an attempt to secure state building, social reconstruction and development, strengthening of democracy and ensuring willing participation of the people in the socio-economic reconstruction and development, Nehru and Vallabhbhai Patel showed pragmatism and decided to use the colonial machinery. Undoubtedly this was the testing time for the Indian State and nation which was at an incipient stage of evolution. Even after sixty-six years of independence India is still half way on the road to nation-building which refers to the process of uniting the people into a well-knit unified nation and the transformation of the anti-foreign nationalism into a process whereby free people are engaged in the course of developing a new equitable, egalitarian and developed society. In other words, nation-building is the process wherein the state becomes truly a nation-state and its people become a well-organised, united and cohesive group. It also signifies the process of making the political system autonomous, legitimate and capable of meeting the demands of the people and overcoming threats, crises and other detrimental effects. Nation-building is an involvement of a large number of people from the middle and lower classes from different peripheries and leading social groups through the medium of social communication and economic intercourse. For Nehru, improving agriculture, industry was not merely a prime concern; the social, economic and community aspect was equally important.[33] In a broader sense nation-building refers to the process of welding the people into a nation committed to make subservient all traditional local and parochial loyalties, arrangements and power systems to one overriding power structure, loyalty to the nation, the motherland and to state.

Nation-Building in India

After liberation from colonialism, India started the process of nation-building. The Constituent Assembly (CA) drafted the Constitution which enshrined the objectives of the sovereign, democratic, republic of India. Liberty, equality, fraternity and justice were the goals to be achieved by the state in due course. The Constitution mentions India as a union of states with single citizenship, joint electorate, representative government, federal system with strong centre and a secular state dedicated to all its citizens to ensure the benefits of a welfare state. Fundamental rights are guaranteed to all without discrimination of any kind. The Directive Principles of State Policy, aimed at securing the welfare of all, were incorporated in part four of the Constitution. Under the dynamic leadership of Prime Minister Jawaharlal Nehru the process of nation-building was initiated with the inception of the constitutional, political and legal apparatus which through its operation has penetrated society at various levels and has succeeded in bringing the integration of diversities in national life.

The process of nation-building moves at a snail's pace. In order to achieve independence India had to pay a heavy price, and the task of nation-building is equally cumbersome, perplexing and complex. The reason being that it is easy to bring people on a common platform against foreign imperialist forces, but it is tough to unite them against internal enemies. The Indian response in this regard has been a mixed one. Besides some amazing achievements like meaningful functioning of parliamentary democracy and strenuous efforts against wars with China, Pakistan, the fight against internal vices like poverty, disease, hunger, terrorism, etc., there have been failures to resolve linguistic, regional, centre-state conflicts and the failure to achieve the desired goals of socio-economic development. The Indian nation has been successful in harnessing effectively the efforts in the direction of securing of several elements of nation-building.

First, the drafting and adoption of the Constitution of India conceived by Nehru, Patel and Ambedkar reflects the institutional and legal architecture and its successful implementation can be described as a big stride. The constitution has demonstrated its ability to guide the nation during war and peacetime and has helped the nation to achieve political stability. Government stability is helpful in securing nation-building and has the potential to overcome political crises. Transfer of political power from one party to other has been a smooth affair. Therefore India has the reputation of being the largest and well-functioning democratic state. Zoya Hasan opined that "... our democratic institutions have stood the test of time. They have proved quite robust even surviving the major challenges such as the imposition of emergency in 1975-77 which was reversed by popular electoral vote."[34]

Second, the state has been successful in adopting agreed and accepted national goals. Secularism, socialism, democracy and socio-economic development are accepted by everyone in India. The Directive Principles of State Policy underscores the goals that India has accepted and which are to be achieved through suitable policies. The objective of welfare and state and socio-economic and political justice is a supreme constitutional objective which binds the union as well as states. The goals enumerated in the Constitution are accepted by people as genuine goals of the nation. Currently the state has adopted the goals of democracy, liberalism, market economy, liberalisation, privatisation, globalisation and sustainable development in view of the sweeping waves of liberalisation, privatisation and globalisation.

Third, the Indian nation has displayed an ability to secure desired political change in testing situations through constitutional means. The death of Nehru and Indira Gandhi did not witness any political upheaval, and the transfer of power in 1977, 1989 showed the political maturity of the Indian nation. The way India has accepted and accustomed to coalitions indicates her ability as a liberal democratic system.

Fourth, India has successfully maintained national unity and integrity in the midst of war or warlike situation. During Chinese aggression 1962, Indo-Pak wars in 1965, 1971, the Kargil war 1999 and at other times of natural calamities and disasters, the nation stood like a rock. The change from a one-party dominant system of governance to a coalition system of rule has been smooth and peaceful. In the event of dismantling of monolithic structure of one party the reorientation of relations between the union and the states has reinforced the federal polity instead of weakening it.[35] The nation has been combating vigorously the threat of terrorism which got stronger with an attack on Parliament in December 2001. Despite several crises India has been successful in thwarting the challenges posed to her unity by secessionist movements with ulterior motives. The Nagas, Mizos, Tamils, Manipuris and Gorkhas have been prevailed upon to abandon the path of violence and join the mainstream. Therefore, India has the will, ability, strength and resilience to meet the menace of terrorism.

Fifth, India has been quite successful in building a solid base for technological and industrial development such as development of roads, power generation and communication. Satellites, aircraft, missiles, tanks, ships electronic gadgets, computers, automobiles, railways, airways, waterways, etc., in all these spheres, India has built solid foundations. It has become an industrial developing society. It is now a potential IT superpower. Indian computer software industry has earned for itself a good name, high credibility and has become a source of excellent financial returns. Sixth, India has ensured all-round economic development through planning. Strategic industries have been kept and developed in the public sector and the private sector has been expanded and strengthened. However, the gains of economic development have not been as per expectations but they have been instrumental in ending stagnation and putting the economy on the path of economic growth as its dependence on foreign capital has been reduced considerably. India has successfully avoided the foreign debt trap despite several internal and external constraints and has overcome the economic strains resulting from economic sanctions imposed in the wake of Pokhran II nuclear tests in May 1998.

Seventh, in an effort to initiate the process of socio-economic reconstruction, the policy of special concessions to the weaker sections of the society, India has been successful in integrating the people into the process of development. The Mandal Commission recommendations were accepted to widen the scope of reservation to Other Backward Classes (OBC). In spite of several limitations the step has generated a new consciousness among these people making democracy more inclusive. The state is leaving no stone unturned to secure uplift of women as a result of which women have come to occupy responsible positions in the constitutional and political set-up. All this shows that the process of nation-building has been moving forward, however, at a snail's pace.

Nation-Building in India: Problematic Areas

Notwithstanding these achievements, the process of nation-building still faces problems. First, undeniably the Constitution is a stable and well-functioning document, but frequent amendments and its working as a unitary system can be described as its functional shortcoming. Speaking in the Constitutional Assembly Jawaharlal Nehru said that "... while we want this Constitution to be as solid and as permanent a structure as we can make it, nevertheless there is no permanence in Constitution."[36] Its functioning has led to frequent centre-state conflicts. Political violence, electoral malpractices, political corruption have marred the political stability and development. Proceedings of legislative bodies are stalled at the drop of a hat. Consequently, they have become a platform for settling political scores rather than becoming a forum for discussion and debates.

Second, the state has adopted democracy, secularism, development, equality, liberty, justice and fraternity. Though democracy has taken deep roots in India yet its working has not been up to the mark. Zoya Hasan observed that "... the persistent income inequalities, poverty and mass deprivation point to the absence of substantive democracy."[37] Illiteracy, ignorance, poverty, casteism, factionalism and regionalism have made its working full of loopholes. Despite provisions of secularism in the Indian Constitution, communalism continues to thwart attempts made for nation-building. Secularism pushes religious identities which are pivotal to the lives of the people into the margins and disrespects them.[38] With the adoption of market economy, socialism and welfare state have taken the back seat and the number of people living below the poverty line continues to increase.

Third, personality cult politics has put a question mark over the dynamics of democratic politics. Peaceful political change and constitutional continuance has been the strength of Indian parliamentary democracy. But the process of political socialisation and recruitment has been inadequate. Sons, daughters and family members of political leaders continue to rule the roost as far as composition of political elite in India is concerned. Mass-based political leaders stand nowhere in the political space. Regional political parties are unable to practise the spirit of accommodation and reconciliation in the tension areas between regional issues and national objectives. The manner in which political parties function in parliament has encouraged party bossism and contributed to the development of personality cults.[39]

Fourth, socio-economic imbalances have been another failure on the front of nation-building. The policy of reservation and concessions has not been quite successful in integrating the downtrodden people into the process of social reconstruction and development. They continue to be at the receiving end and outside the ambit of benefits of economic reforms, negating the very objectives of reservation, social justice and economic reforms. It has given rise to reservation and anti-reservation with communal overtones. Analysing the effects of reservation Myron Weiner opined that "among higher-caste Hindus there has developed resistance to reservations most recently in Gujarat, Bihar and Madhya Pradesh ... the backlash is not only against the demand of other backward classes but in some instances even against reservations for scheduled castes and tribes."[40] He further argued that "... reservations [in India] have often left all communities dissatisfied—beneficiaries because they believe the reservations are not satisfactorily administered, and those who are excluded because they view the system as discriminatory."[41] Their integration into Indian society has been unsatisfactory. The policy of reservation has become a tool in the hands of the ruling elite who continue to play with it oblivious of the fact that the benefits have not percolated down to the deserving. Since upliftment of the downtrodden has become a political weapon, no political party has come forward to scrap caste-based reservation and introduce economic-based policy.

Nation-building in India is a problematic process owing to the presence of numerous hindering factors. Firstly, the population explosion impedes the drive towards nation-building. Notwithstanding family planning measures, the population continues to grow at a much faster pace. A rapidly growing population makes increasing demands on resources for unproductive purposes and this hinders capital accumulation.[42] With limited resources India has been unable to meet the basic needs of an ever-growing population. Secondly, mass poverty is also a significant impediment on the way to nation-building. Those who live below the poverty line have the feeling that the state does not care for their needs, alienating them further from the mainstream. Slow and inadequate economic growth, despite economic reforms, has not improved the plight of the miserable. Structural adjustments in the economic domain have benefited the educated section belonging to the upper strata of society, whereas the situation has worsened for the majority of the rural population.[43] They continue to suffer economic deprivation. Poverty is thus a denial of choices and opportunities for living a tolerable life.[44] Thirdly, widespread regional imbalances coupled with uneven economic growth, growing economic inequalities, increasing gap between rich and poor, unemployment, underemployment have limited the progress of socio-economic development. The BIMARU states present a dismal picture as far as economic development and regional imbalances are concerned. Political parties have failed to prioritise the urgency of meeting the barest needs, welfare and livelihood issues of the people.[45] Fourthly, socio-economic problems like regionalism, communalism, centre-state tensions, interstate disputes, corruption, lack of commitment to work, etc., have weakened the roots of the nation and adversely affected the process of nation-building.

To conclude, it can be argued that federalism and nation-building are interrelated in India. During Nehru's phase the emphasis was on national consolidation and national integration to build a political nation in post-colonial India, and federalism has proved an effective tool to realise it. Although Nehru was reluctant to reorganise states on language basis in the 1950s, he ultimately took a decision to this effect which has actually built the nation in the real sense of the term. In the post-Nehru period governments kept on accumulating powers at the cost of state autonomy which resulted in the demand for autonomy from different parts of the country. Subsequently, federalism entered a new phase of cooperation between the centre and the states. The phenomenon of coalition politics has strengthened the foundations of federalism and nation-building by providing representation to all sections of society by way of representation in the coalition government. Still there are a number of challenges like communalism, rising income inequalities, corruption, criminalisation of politics, etc., confronting the nation. The need of the hour is to fight these challenges to the nation. The values of Indian culture, love for peace and non-violent means, harmony, universal brotherhood, secularism, cultural pluralism, toleration, service before self, love for motherland can provide a solid foundation for nation-building. All Indian religions uphold these values and can provide sufficient space and strength to the process of nation-building. The history of the freedom struggle, the values of the national movement combined with the ideas of Nehru, Gandhi and Tagore can stand India in good stead and help the invigoration of the process of nation-building.

References

1. William S. Livingstone, *Federalism and Constitutional Change* (Oxford: Clarendon Press, 1956), p. 2.
2. S. C. Jain, *The Constitution of India* (New Delhi: Taxmann, 2000), p. 7.
3. *Constituent Assembly Debates,* vol. VII, Col. 43.
4. Jain, n. 2, p. 19.
5. Ibid., p. 199.
6. Ibid., pp. 204-5.
7. *Constituent Assembly Debates,* vol. XI, Col. p. 976.
8. K. C.Wheare, *Federal Government* (London: Oxford University Press, 1963), p. 27.
9. *Kesavananda Bharti vs. Union of India* 1973, *S. R. Bommai vs. Union of India*, 1994.
10. *Constituent Assembly Debates,* Col. 616, 618.
11. Ibid., Col. 683.
12. Ibid., Col. 689.
13. Ibid., Col. 728.
14. *Administrative Reforms Commission Interim Report on the Machinery of Planning,* New Delhi: 1967, para, 15.
15. Government of India, *Commission on Centre State Relations Report, Part I* (New Delhi: Publications Division, 1987), p. 121.
16. *Constituent Assembly Debates,* vol. IX, Col. 177.
17. *S. R. Bommai vs. Union of India*, 1994.
18. V. T. Patil (ed.), *Explorations in Nehruvian Thought* (New Delhi: Inter-Indian Publications, 1988), p. 269.
19. Ibid., p. 270.
20. Robert D. King, *Nehru and the Language Politics of India* (New Delhi: Oxford University Press, 1997), pp. 97- 98.
21. *Report of the Linguistic Provinces Commission,* Government of India, 1948.
22. Ministry of Home Affairs (Govt. of India), Report of the States Reorganisation Commission, New Delhi: Publication Division, 1955, pp. 16-17.
23. Ibid.
24. Jawaharlal Nehru, Speech at Public Meeting in Ludhiana, November 8, 1953.
25. Robert, n. 20, p. 118.
26. *State Reorganization Commission*, Government of India, p. i.
27. P. M. Bakshi, *The Constitution of India* (New Delhi: Universal Law Publishing Company, 2009), pp. 286-87.
28. *Lok Sabha Debates*, July 7, 1952, Linguistic States, *Speeches,* 1:37.
29. Patil, n. 18, p. 276.
30. Ibid., p. 277.
31. Marcus Franda, *West Bengal and the Federalising Process in India* (Princeton: Princeton University Press, 1968).
32. Patil, n. 18, p. 270.
33. Judith M. Brown, *Nehru: A Political Life* (New Delhi: Oxford University Press, 2003), p. 190.
34. Zoya Hasan, "Indian Democracy and Social Inequalities," in Rajesh M. Basrur (ed.), *Challenges to Democracy in India* (New Delhi: Oxford University Press,

2009), pp. 130-31.

35. Balveer Arora, "The Indian Parliament and Democracy," in Ajay K. Mehra and Gert W. Kueck (eds.), *The Indian Parliament: A Comparative Analysis* (New Delhi: Konark, 2003), pp. 22-23.
36. Jawaharlal Nehru, *Constituent Assembly Debates*, New Delhi: Lok Sabha Secretariat, Reprint 1999, vol. 7, p. 322.
37. Zoya Hasan, n. 34, p. 128.
38. Asish Nandy, "The Politics of Secularism and the Recovery of Religious Toleration," in Rajeev Bhargava (ed.), *Secularism and Its Critics* (New Delhi: Oxford University Press, 1998), pp. 321-44.
39. Neena Vyas, "The Personality Cult in Indian Politics," Arvind Sivaramakrishanan (ed.), *Short on Democracy: Issues Facing Indian Political Parties* (Gurgaon: Imprint One, 2007), p. 143.
40. Myron Weiner, "India's Minorities: Who Are They? What Do They Want?" Partha Chatterjee (ed.), *State and Politics in India* (New Delhi: Oxford University Press, 1997), p. 487.
41. Ibid., p. 488.
42. S. K. Mishra and V. K. Puri, *Indian Economy: Its Development Experience* (New Delhi: Himalaya Publishing House, 2012), p. 115.
43. Jayati Ghosh, "Income Inequalities in India," *People's Democracy*, February 17, 2004.
44. United Nations Development Programme, *Human Development Report 1997*, New York, 1997, p. 16.
45. D. L. Seth, "The Crisis of Political Authority," in Rajendra Vora and Suhas Palkishar (eds.), *Indian Democracy* (New Delhi: Sage Publications, 2004), p. 87.

4

Kashmir and Nehru: Contours of a Troubled Legacy

Simrit Kahlon

The issue of Kashmir and the persona of Jawaharlal Nehru have for long remained inextricably linked to each other. Every discussion on Kashmir begins with a reference to Nehru's deeds of omission and commission in the context of this region. Nehru is largely held to be responsible for the difficult situation that India is in with respect to this troubled State. The present paper seeks to deconstruct the events that took place around the time of the partition of the subcontinent, Jammu and Kashmir's accession to the Indian Union and the subsequent course that history took with regard to this State. While Nehru's handling of the Kashmir problem was marked by indecisiveness and a reactionary rather than a proactive approach, it is also true that when things came to the brink of disaster, Nehru did manage to salvage the situation. Nehru's perspective on the Kashmir issue was coloured by his idealistic and romantic construction of the land of his ancestors while his dealing with Kashmir—particularly so at the international level—was dictated by his utopian notions of a level playing field where he chose to take the moral high ground. As a result, he made promises that he could not fulfil and placed his faith in individuals who did not deliver when it came to the crunch. In essence Nehru fumbled on the Kashmir issue not due to a lack of vision or intent but due to his inability to temper his idealism with the steel of pragmatism.

Introduction

Among the most contentious legacies of the Nehru era that still irks Indian polity and places it on the back foot at all international forums is the Kashmir issue, as it is normally addressed. Whereas his own party has veered away from most of his policies, economic as well as diplomatic, and remains apologetic on the count of Kashmir, most right-wing political thinkers and practitioners herald it as one of the major follies of the man. The Jammu and Kashmir government most often turns the situation to its advantage using his promises as a bargaining chip and the Pakistan supported separatists use the issue to malign the country at every international forum. It is not without reason that Nehru is associated with the Kashmir issue. He was the face of India during the period that the Kashmir dispute took root. Even though the task of amalgamating the 565 independent princely states with the Indian Union at the time of independence was apportioned to Sardar Vallabhbhai Patel, Deputy Prime Minister, Kashmir was one issue that was personally being looked into by Jawaharlal Nehru.[1] A number of questions arise in the context of the whole situation, the chief among them being: What is it that made Kashmir an issue or a problem unlike more than 500 princely states that acceded to the Indian Union? What was the role of Jawaharlal Nehru in the situation as it emerged and evolved? What were the possible factors that influenced his decisions? What were the ramifications and results of his handling of the Kashmir situation? What has been the impact of his actions and lack of action on the present situation in Kashmir? What shape is the Kashmir issue going to take in time to come? The present paper seeks answers to all these questions through a perusal of available writings on Nehru, by analysing the contents of his speeches and critical assessment of Nehru and his handling of the Kashmir issue. Literature both on Nehru, by Nehru, and on the Kashmir issue is extensive. The present paper does not claim an access to all such sources; rather, it has made an effort to present a balanced view by accessing a variety of perspectives.

Chronology of Events

The princely state of Jammu and Kashmir though ruled by the Dogra ruler Maharaja Hari Singh was populated by a predominantly Muslim population. More the result of a quirk of fate rather than a shared cultural and historical experience, it comprised three distinct physiographic divisions. The sub-montane Jammu region, including the mountainous areas south of Pir Panjal, was essentially a valley carved out by the Chenab river. North of the Pir Panjal and south of the Greater Himalayan range lay the valley of Kashmir, this was a lacustrine plain. The third distinct physiographic region lay beyond the Greater Himalayas and included the Ladakh and Baltistan area. All three regions had distinct cultural traits as well, with the Jammu region being populated predominantly by Hindu Dogras and a small number of Sikhs, the Kashmir valley by Sunni Muslims and Kashimiri Pandits and the trans-Himalayan regions by Shia Muslims, Buddhists and Aryan tribes of Nubra. Political and economic clout in this heterogeneous kingdom rested in the hands of the minority community of Kashmiri Pundits who owned most of the land and held most of the important offices in this kingdom. Tyndale Biscoe in his autobiography writes:

> When I arrived at the S. M. S. School in Srinagar I found it full of the sons of Hindu ruling class, the top dogs in this Mohammedan country. Over 90 per cent of the Kashmiris are Mohammedans … (They) did not send their sons to schools as all government service was closed to them.[2]

This was the situation that prevailed in the state of Jammu and Kashmir just prior to independence. With the partition of British India on the anvil, the Maharaja had to decide which way to go. Of the three options he had, the Maharaja would have preferred to stay independent of either of the two dominions. He had no sympathy for Nehru who was openly supporting the "Quit Kashmir" movement that Sheikh Abdullah and his National Conference had initiated. Being a Hindu, joining Pakistan was also not an option he savoured. Pakistan on the other hand expected the accession of Kashmir to the dominion of Pakistan on account of its population being predominantly Muslim. The Maharaja realised that a landlocked Jammu and Kashmir needed to maintain friendly relations with both India and Pakistan. With this thing in mind he adopted delaying tactics and began to have parleys with both Indian and Pakistani emissaries. He was even able to negotiate a standstill agreement with Pakistan on the issue of accession, however India did not oblige.

Things came to a head on October 21-23, 1947 when Pakistan, fed up with waiting, sent in some 5,000 Afridi and Waziri tribesmen to try and capture Kashmir. The Maharaja had no option but to turn to India for help. After frantic parleys that involved Jawaharlal Nehru, Sardar Patel, Baldev Singh, V. P. Menon and Mehar Chand Mahajan wherein Nehru insisted on bringing Sheikh Abdullah on board,[3] the Instrument of Accession was signed by the Maharaja on October 27, 1947. Consequent upon that the Indian forces began to be flown into Kashmir. The war lasted more than a year during which Maharaja Hari Singh abdicated in favour of his son Karan Singh and at the behest of Nehru appointed Sheikh Abdullah the head of the caretaker regime. Jawaharlal Nehru in the meanwhile took the matter to the United Nations where he committed to holding a plebiscite in Kashmir to know the preference of the people once the Pakistani forces had withdrawn from the territory that was under their occupation. The United Nations set up a committee to look into the issue. This was the step that led to the internationalisation of the Kashmir issue. The plebiscite of course was never held because the conditions laid down for the conduct of plebiscite did not materialise, apart from the other reasons. In the meanwhile Sheikh Abdullah—proof of the Kashmiri desire to be with the Indian Union—had begun to send out conflicting signals. On the one hand he became hero among the Muslims in the valley by instituting land reforms that led to the redistribution of agricultural land to the benefit of the Kashmiri Muslims. On the other hand, his growing popularity among the Muslims in Kashmir put the Union

Government on the back foot resulting in Sheikh's extraction of a number of concessions from New Delhi without corresponding commitments and results.

Sheikh succeeded in getting a special status for the state of Jammu and Kashmir through the enactment of Article 370 and what was termed as the July Agreement in 1952 wherein the state of Jammu and Kashmir would have its own constitution, a separate flag and the head of the government would be known as Prime Minister and the head of the state as the President. This sent the Jammu division up in flames and the Praja Parishad launched a protest movement under the slogan *Ek Pradhan, Ek Nishaan, Ek Savidhan*. Things finally came to a head in 1953 when Sheikh had to be dismissed as head of government and replaced by Bakshi Ghulam Mohammad. He was placed under arrest and was to remain so for the next eleven years. For long the situation in Kashmir remained at a kind of status quo with the regional parties from the valley forming the government and the Congress party having something of a footprint in the state at most times. Towards the end of the 1980s, the international and regional scenario changed as the erstwhile Soviet Union disintegrated leaving behind a much weaker Russia that no longer posed a threat to the USA. Consequently, the Mujahideen who had been trained to fight the Soviet forces in Afghanistan were now free and they were directed towards Kashmir. Within the state rampant corruption and a high rate of unemployment alienated the youth who were ripe for conversion to the dreams of "azaadi and jihad." The Kashmir valley saw a virtual ethnic cleansing and a mass exodus of the Kashmiri Pandits from the valley in the late 1980s. This was followed by strikes, clamp downs and media bashing. A dysfunctional civil administration had no means of dealing with such an uprising and the army had to be called in to control the situation in the valley. Pakistan has once again succeeded in giving the Kashmir problem an international exposure. From a simple landlocked princely state like numerous others which got timely amalgamation with the

Indian or Pakistani Union, Kashmir has deteriorated into the "Kashmir Imbroglio." Where did Nehru go wrong in the handling of this issue? What prompted him to take decisions that, viewed with hindsight, seem almost like committing diplomatic *hara kiri*. One needs to delve beyond the obvious. The successive acts of the Kashmir drama were played out at a variety of forums, regional, national and international, and involved a variety of personalities and incidents all of whom left their imprint on this problem, the chief among them being Jawaharlal Nehru and Sheikh Abdullah. The attitudes and roles of each and the dynamics of their mutual interaction and association need to be deconstructed and reviewed for a proper understanding of the situation.

Nehru and Kashmir

At the time of independence the division of administrative duties in the country was very clear. Whereas Nehru as Prime Minister was in charge of carving out the developmental road map of the newly independent country, Sardar Vallabhbhai Patel, as Minister for Home Affairs, was entrusted with the responsibility of integrating the large number of princely states that had simultaneously become free, into the Indian Union. In this regard the "Sardar" functioned with complete autonomy. Strangely, in the case of Kashmir, the Sardar was kept at a distance. In fact from the day that the Indian forces landed in Srinagar on October 27, 1947, Nehru had taken charge of Kashmir and others were seldom consulted with regard to its policies, particularly those pertaining to its internal developments.[4] He was known to consider it as the one feather in his cap for which he alone must have all the credit.[5]

Nehru's fondness for Kashmir is evident in his writings. There must hardly be any other place that he mentions with greater nostalgia and affection than Kashmir. In official as well as personal correspondence Nehru kept coming back to what he himself described as his "partiality for Kashmir."[6] He often narrated its praises to his daughter, Indira Gandhi:

> Kashmir is a place well worth visiting and as you know it is our old homeland ... Long long ago we left it and since then the whole of India has been our home. But the little corner of India which is Kashmir draws us still both by its beauty and its old associations.[7]

Till the year 1940, when he visited the valley after a hiatus of almost twenty-four years, once there, he felt "excited and moved." Nehru wrote to Indira Gandhi:

> I find Kashmir exhilarating and I have a sense of coming back to my own—it is curious how race memories persist or perhaps it's all imagination.[8]

Either from inherited memories or by virtue of his imagination, Nehru's love affair with that poor Himalayan state ... blossomed.[9] He compared it favourably with Europe where he had spent most of his boyhood and youth, while stating that:

> I am convinced that it (Kashmir) is superior to Switzerland and, I would say, healthier ... I wish I myself could go there for two months every year ... that would be an ideal life.[10]

Even in official correspondence whether with the Maharaja of Kashmir or his Prime Minister or Sheikh Abdullah or even his wife, Nehru time and again reiterated his personal love for and interest in Kashmir. In a letter to Sheikh Abdullah's wife he writes:

> Kashmir is dear to me ... Being a Kashmiri I can never forget it and I am passionately attached to its mountains and ... Scenery ... Kashmir and its people ... will ever remain a first priority with me.[11]

Later, very close to the accession of Kashmir, Nehru wrote to both Sheikh Abdullah and Meher Chand Mahajan in the same vein: "for me Kashmir's future is of the most intimate personal significance."[12] Further, while writing to Mehar Chand Mahajan, Nehru stated that,

"... for me it is both a personal and public matter. It would be a tragedy, so far as I am concerned, if Kashmir went to Pakistan."[13] In fact so inexplicable and irrational was Nehru's obsession with Kashmir that even on the eve of independence, when the whole country was in a state of flux, Nehru wanted to put everything on hold and visited Kashmir ostensibly to help the Kashmiri people's struggle for independence. Mountbatten had to remind him that he would soon be the Prime Minister "... ruling at least two hundred and fifty million and I would consider it highly reprehensible of him to desert his most important duties at the Centre to interest himself on behalf of four million who might very well be going to join Pakistan."[14]

After becoming Prime Minister of India, Nehru focused all of India's might and his own time and attention on Kashmir.[15] How does one explain Nehru's keen interest in Kashmir? The son of a successful anglophile lawyer, educated at Harrow and Trinity, Nehru was deeply influenced and impressed by all things European, including the ideas of socialism and nationalism. This fondness was extended to the temperate climate and rolling topography of the continent as well. On his return to India and his involvement in the Indian National Movement, he made an effort to discover India and strengthen his Indian roots, and the discovery of his Kashmiri ancestry was a natural fallout of that. The fact that Kashmir reminded him of Europe was a very happy coincidence. It was no wonder then that Nehru felt that he had a personal stake in the integration of Kashmir within the Indian Union. At the same time, for all the attachment that Nehru might profess for Kashmir, his long-lost homeland, it is fairly apparent that the desire was to appropriate and command the physical beauty of Kashmir. There was no visible cultural affinity for the place as Nehru was always more at home in his Savile Row suits and Western milieu.

The love that Nehru had for Kashmir, whether real or imagined, did not encompass the whole state of Jammu and Kashmir. It was restricted to the valley of Kashmir. In the process of handling the Kashmir issue, Nehru almost alienated the Jammu and Ladakh regions. In fact at one point when Mountbatten hinted at the partition of the State with Jammu coming to India and the rest, including the valley of Srinagar, going to Pakistan,[16] Nehru insisted that it was "totally unacceptable to us" although "... if the worst comes to worst, I am prepared to accept Poonch and Gilgit area being partitioned off ..."[17]

Through the amalgamation of Kashmir with the Indian Union, Nehru found an opportunity for the fructification of his secular, nationalist and socialist dreams. By retaining control of predominantly Muslim Kashmir, Nehru hoped to prove to the world that India was a truly secular union of peoples of many faiths and not just a Hindu state.[18] Even in supporting and building up Sheikh Abdullah, a poor shawl weaver's son, Nehru was no doubt satiating his socialistic pretensions. Thus, for Nehru, Kashmir was in the nature of a personal crusade and a private ambition to achieve which he walked many an extra mile and made many a compromise including dealing with the difficult and ambitious Sheikh Abdullah, and putting at stake his ambitions in the arena of international politics.

Handling Sheikh Abdullah

Sheikh Abdullah was the son of a Kashmiri shawl weaver/vendor. He epitomised the poor Kashmiri Muslim languishing under the rule of the Dogra rulers and the Brahmanical elite in the 1930s. Under the influence of the Indian National Movement that was gaining momentum in other parts of the subcontinent the Sheikh formed the Reading Room Party whose radical views were regarded by the Maharaja as seditious. Sheikh was put in jail. Nehru, who had developed a personal interest in Kashmir as part of his discovery of his Indian roots,[19] saw in Sheikh's personality the ideal person to embody his dreams of Kashmir nationalism as an affiliate of Pan-Indian nationalism, and thus to thwart the two-nation theory of Jinnah. Not only did he promote and build up Sheikh Abdullah as a democratic alternative to the Maharaja, he even wielded a considerable influence on the drafting of the core concern of Sheikh's political outfit, and got its name changed from Muslim Conference to National Conference. He openly supported Sheikh in his "Quit Kashmir" movement against the Maharaja and was placed under arrest. Later Nehru insisted on bringing Sheikh on board before he sent Indian Military aid to Kashmir against the tribal invasion.

Once Sheikh was put in charge of the caretaker administration and later made the Prime Minister of the State on March 5, 1948, Nehru showcased him as the voice of the people of Kashmir at international forums like the United Nations. At home he executed the land reforms which involved redistribution of land holdings from the Kashmiri Pandits to the landless Muslims, thus establishing himself as the unchallenged leader of Kashmiri Muslims. However after the first flurry of land reforms Abdullah was not able to offer anything more to Kashmiris than his formidable rhetoric and the glamorous myth of the prisoner of conscience.[20] In order to build his image and also to save his political constituency he started making contradictory statements. Whatever his assertions in Delhi and Lake Success, in the valley he had been reiterating that the issue of accession was still not final.[21] He also annoyed the residents of Jammu, many of whom were still loyal to the Maharaja, with his pro-Muslim and anti-Dogra polices. When rumblings of discontent from the state reached New Delhi, the Prime Minister was questioned in Parliament. Nehru however stoutly defended the Sheikh. In a speech delivered on August 7, 1952 in Parliament, he said:

> ... you can criticise Sheikh Abdullah ... (But) he is a brave man and great leader of his people. That is a big enough thing ... If he has failings, if he has made a mistake here and there, if he has delivered a speech we do not like, what of that? Bigness is bigness in spite of a hundred mistakes.[22]

In the hope that the Sheikh would come round and that his friendship and influence would prevail, he made one concession after another ... and in the process allowed Sheikh to push New Delhi from one position to another without corresponding commitments and result.[23] It started with a wish to have a separate constitution unlike any other state that had joined the Indian Union. The idea of setting up a Constituent Assembly was to help evolve the structure of internal government that was compatible with the national ethos and forge a formal constitutional relationship with the Indian Union. Instead Sheikh gave the people in Kashmir the impression that Kashmir was to be a sovereign unit within the large sovereign India. This again was defended by the Prime Minister in the Parliament thus:

> It is necessary to consider the case of J&K state on a somewhat different footing from the other states in India. This is inevitable because Kashmir has become an international issue in the last few years. A different footing does not mean any special right or privilege except in the sense that it may mean a greater measure of internal autonomy.[24]

For the benefit of Kashmir and to appease the Sheikh, Article 370 was included as a temporary provision in the Constitution of India. The article provides special status to the state of Jammu and Kashmir and has been heralded by many thinkers on Kashmir as being divisive and inimical to integration. The article has resulted in the State being the only one within the Indian Union that has its own constitution. Though considerably eroded by subsequent amendments, the Article continues to remain a sore point between the Kashmiri and pan-Indian thinkers. The Kashmiris' harangue has to do with the disrespect shown to it while the Pan-Indian thinkers consider its existence as the root cause of the problem of Kashmir.

While debate on the sanctity and the necessity of the Article continues to rage to this day, and shall probably remain alive for many more years to come, Nehru had to eat humble pie as far as his protestations in favour of Sheikh and his policies were concerned, much sooner than anyone had anticipated. In the autumn of 1953, Sheikh Abdullah was summarily dismissed from the Prime Ministership of Jammu and Kashmir, brought to New Delhi, placed under arrest and replaced by Bakshi Ghulam Muhammad. It is argued that the arrogant and contrary behaviour of the Sheikh and his inability to take his own Cabinet along with him had necessitated this step both in the interest of the state as well as the Indian Union; however, the fact remains that this act coloured the perceptions of the people in the State towards the Union governments for all time to come. Further it exposed Jawaharlal Nehru not only as a man who placed more faith on personalities than ideologies but also as one who was a poor judge of personalities. While this one act of Nehru's raised Sheikh's personality to iconic levels in the eyes of his people, it greatly diminished Nehru's status amongst his detractors.

Handling International Opinion

One of the most embarrassing facets of the Kashmir problem has been its internationalisation and the failure of the Indian diplomatic machinery to garner support at the international forum. This facet gains greater relevance in the context of the fact that External Affairs was a ministry that was directly under Nehru and he is known to be the architect of India's foreign policy. Nehru had an abiding interest in world affairs no doubt fostered by his exposure to the international milieu at an early age. The Brussels Congress of Oppressed Nationalities in 1927 was his first step in this direction. Even after returning to India and becoming deeply involved in the Indian National Movement he continued to take an interest in international politics. As Maulana Azad said, "Jawaharlal has always been more moved by international considerations than most Indians. He looked at all questions from an international rather than a national point of view." Even after independence Sardar Vallabhbhai Patel ran India's administration, while Nehru indulged mostly in foreign affairs and high Himalayan adventure.[25]

Despite his avowed interest and expertise in this field Nehru clearly blundered in the handling of the Kashmir problem at the international level. His initial mistake lay in taking the issue to the United Nations Security Council and agreeing to a ceasefire despite being in a position of strength and being sinned against by Pakistan whose forces had transgressed onto Indian territory. His second mistake lay in promising to hold a plebiscite in Kashmir and that too under the auspices of the United Nations. His third mistake lay in not being able to get the plebiscite conducted at a time when the local population was inclined in favour of integration with India. Thus it is that while almost one-third of the state of Jammu and Kashmir still remains under the occupation of Pakistan, it is India that is accused of illegal occupation of Kashmiri territory and denial of the right to self-expression to the people of Kashmir.

Nehru often let idealism overpower pragmatism as far as international affairs were concerned. Despite the fact that in this dispute it was India that was the aggrieved party, world opinion was sympathetic towards Pakistan. This resulted in part from Nehru's efforts to promote the policy of Non-alignment and organise the newly independent erstwhile colonised countries at the international level. Pakistan, on the other hand, actively sought and received patronage and support both in cash and kind from the US-led NATO bloc. This made India dependent on the Soviet Union for a veto on the issue of international intervention in Kashmir. As a result Nehru's policy of Non-alignment could not become a reality or an agency to be reckoned with on the global scene. It was a legacy of the mishandling of the Kashmir issue that even after winning the 1965 war, Shastri was pressurised by the Soviet Union to return all occupied territories to Pakistan. The regional security scenario emerged after the 1971 war forced India to sign Treaty of Peace and Friendship with the Soviet Union, which had reflected on the non-aligned credentials of its foreign policy. Further, the loss of Gilgit and Baltistan to Pakistan and their subsequent transfer to China means that India has lost access to the republics of Central Asia that were once a part of the erstwhile Soviet Union. These include large reservoirs of untapped energy sources including petroleum, natural gas and uranium. This has caused serious harm to the future of India's energy and economic interests. India's doyen of foreign policy, while handling the Kashmir issue, slipped up and failed to protect the country's strategic and economic interests.

Conclusion

Kashmir today remains a festering sore both in economic and political terms for India. Whereas more than 560 princely states were successfully amalgamated into the Indian Union the integration of Jammu and Kashmir—despite its ruler too having signed an Instrument of Accession—still remains in doubt from a number of quarters not a few of them international in status. Coincidentally this was the only state whose accession was being handled directly by Nehru. It would seem only right that one accepts Nehru's failure to successfully bring the state into the Indian fold. However, one must also acknowledge that despite a couple of fatal errors—in agreeing to a ceasefire at a time when the Indian forces were in a winning position, and in promising a plebiscite that never got held—Nehru did manage to deliver in situations when we tottered on the brink of disaster: one, in getting the Instrument of Accession duly signed, and two, in dismissing Sheikh when he began to get out of hand. If at all Nehru is to be blamed it would be due to his partiality to individuals—be it Mountbatten, Sheikh or Krishna Menon—over hard-core political insight, and his idealistic and romantic attitude towards Kashmir.[26] It seems that Nehru's own description of Kashmir was to prove prophetic: "... it seemed to me ... like the hopes and desires that fill us and so seldom find fulfilment."[27] Indeed, Kashmir was a dream for Nehru the complete fulfilment of which remains elusive, the brunt of which the State and people of both Jammu and Kashmir and the rest of the country have borne and will continue to do so at least in the foreseeable future.

References

1. Bal Raj Madhok, *Portrait of a Martyr: A Biography of Shyama Prasad Mookherji* (New Delhi: Rupa & Co., 2001), p. 182.
2. Tyndale Biscoe, *Tyndale Biscoe of Kashmir: An Autobiography* (London: Seeley Service, 1951).
3. B. N. Sharma, *India Betrayed: The Role of Nehru* (New Delhi: Manas Publications, 1997), p. 316.
4. Bal Raj Madhok, n. 1, p. 180.
5. Ibid., p. 181.

6. Pankaj Misra, "The Birth of a Nation," *The New York Review of Books,* vol. 47, no. 15, 2000.
7. Nehru to Indira, March 30, 1934, S. Gopal (ed.), *Selected Works of Jawaharlal Nehru*, vol. 6 (Delhi: B. R. Publishing Corporation, 1972), p. 246.
8. Nehru to Indira, Kashmir, May 29, 1940, Sonia Gandhi (ed.), *Two Alone, Two Together: Letters Between Indira Gandhi and Jawaharlal Nehru, 1940-1964* (London: Hodder & Stoughton, 1992), pp. 63-64.
9. Stanley Wolpert, *Nehru: A Tryst with Destiny* (New York: Oxford University Press, 1996), p. 272.
10. Jawaharlal Nehru to Indira, June 16, 1940 cited in Sonia Gandhi (ed.), *Two Alone, Two Together,* p. 65.
11. Jawaharlal Nehru's Letter to Begum Abdullah, June 4, 1947, S. Gopal (ed.), *Selected Works of Jawaharlal Nehru*, Second Series, vol. 3 (New Delhi: Jawaharlal Nehru Memorial Fund, 1985), p. 197.
12. Jawaharlal Nehru to Sheikh Abdullah, October 10, 1947, S. Gopal (ed.), *Selected Works of Jawaharlal Nehru,* Second Series, vol. 4 (New Delhi: Jawaharlal Nehru Memorial Fund, 1986), pp. 270-71.
13. Jawaharlal Nehru to Mahajan, October 21, 1947, S. Gopal (ed.), *Selected Works of Jawaharlal Nehru,* Second Series, vol. 4, pp. 272-73.
14. Mountbatten's Interview with Nehru on June 24, 1947, cited in N. Mansergh and E. W. R. Lumby (eds.), *The Transfer of Power, 1942-47,* vol. 11 (London, 1983), pp. 591-92.
15. Stanley Wolpert, n. 9.
16. Ibid., p. 435.
17. Jawaharlal Nehru to V. K. Krishna Menon, February 20, 1948, S. Gopal (ed.), *Selected Works of Jawaharlal Nehru*, Second Series, vol. 5 (New Delhi: Jawaharlal Nehru Memorial Fund, 1987), p. 223.
18. S. Wolpert, n. 9, p. 417.
19. Pankaj Misra, n. 6.
20. Ibid.
21. Harbans Singh, "When the Sheikh was Shown the Door," *The Jammu Height,* vol. 1, no. 11, 2013, p. 7.
22. Jawaharlal Nehru, "The Fundamental Unity of Kashmir with India," S. Gopal (ed.), *Selected Works of Jawaharlal Nehru,* Second Series, vol. 19 (New Delhi: Jawaharlal Nehru Memorial Fund, 1996), pp. 297-98.
23. Harbans Singh, n. 21, p. 6.
24. Jawaharlal Nehru, "Friendly and Affectionate Union," Speech while moving motion regarding Jammu and Kashmir State, August 7, 1952, cited in S. Gopal (ed.), *Selected Works of Jawaharlal Nehru*, Second Series, vol. 19, p. 294. Also see for detail, *Parliamentary Debates* (House of People), vol. IV, Part II, Cols. 5775-5785.
25. Stanley Wolpert, n. 9, p. 433.
26. Amitabh. Mattoo, "Understanding Article 370," *The Hindu,* December 6, 2013.
27. Uma Iyengar (ed.), *The Oxford India Nehru* (New Delhi, Oxford University Press, 2007), p. 700.

5

Communalism, Nehru and National Unity

Suneel Kumar

Since its liberation from British colonialism, the Indian state has faced various overt and covert threats such as communalism extremism, separatism and secessionism, which are posing a question mark to the survival of the country. Amongst these threats, communalism had affected Indian politics adversely in the colonial as well as the post-colonial periods. Communalism, which can be termed as a blind loyalty to one's own religious community, has often been used as a tool by the community elite for its own political objectives leading to bitterness, anxiety and even violence amongst different religious communities. Both in the colonial and post-colonial periods, Indian society has had to face the anxiety of communal violence instigated by the vested interests. Understanding the dangerous consequences of communalism as a political instrument in India, during the anti-colonial struggle, national leaders such as Mahatma Gandhi, Maulana Abul Kalam Azad and Jawaharlal Nehru had practised, promoted and propagated secularism as the national ideology. Analysing the gravity of communalism, as the first Prime Minister of India, Jawaharlal Nehru had tried to evolve a humane, inclusive, comprehensive and liberal political culture in the country. Secularism was a matter of personal commitment to Jawaharlal Nehru. He always spoke highly of secular and democratic credentials. Thus, in the light of Nehru's writings, speeches and communications, the present paper analyses his perceptions and vision on the question of communalism and national unity of India. Furthermore, an attempt has also been made to explain to what extent Nehru's approach is relevant in the contemporary era for the unity of the country.

Communalism and Nehru's Outlook

Jawaharlal Nehru, under whose stewardship India became united and confident of itself, relentlessly fought against disruptive communal forces. The British colonialism sowed the seeds of communalism in India for its own political ends. They identified the differences in Indian society and amplified those differences. Thus communalism originated and flourished during the colonial period. This led to the surfacing of various communal organisations, such as All-India Muslim League, Hindu Mahasabha, Rashtriya Swayamsevak Sangh (RSS) and Shiromani Akali Dal (SAD), and caused various communal riots. Communalism reached its peak in 1947 when India faced communal violence and its partition into two separate countries. Long before the partition and independence of India, Nehru had visualised the harsh realities of communalism. He had not only witnessed the communal riots that occurred at regular intervals in India but also seen its ugliest face during the partition of the country when thousands of Hindus, Muslims and Sikhs had been butchered. Therefore, since the beginning, having a scientific and secular outlook, Nehru had shown his determination to fight against communalism.

Nehru considered communalism a myth having no link with reality and an upshot of anger and passion which would disappear as and when people regained their tempers.[1] He emphasised secular politics. He visualised religion as the fountainhead of authoritarianism and the method used universally to secure the submission of the oppressed.[2] According to him, alliance of religion and politics which in the narrowest sense of the word results in communal politics is a most dangerous alliance. This nexus, he argued, would no doubt be harmful to the country as a whole, and to the majority community as well. But in all likelihood it would prove most injurious to minority communities, those who seek to gain some advantage from the politico-religious nexus. He argued that if a minority community in an independent country seeks to isolate and separate itself, it does some damage to the country and most of all injures its own interest. The reason being that by doing so, that particular minority community inevitably puts a barrier between itself and the others and is thereby unable to have intercommunity economic cooperation.[3] Thus, Nehru suggested that no community should try to take the advantage of communal politics as that would backfire on itself. He opined that people in India have their religion and they have a right to hold firmly to it. But they should not import religion into politics. He argued that politicisation of religion was held in Europe resulting in disastrous consequences. And a similar situation could exist in India if politicisation of religion was not prevented. Considering communalism a "badge of a backward nation, not of the modern age," Nehru advised individuals and communities to adopt a scientific outlook and temperament for their own and the country's betterment. Each individual, according to him, whether he belonged to the majority or minority group, must function in a way to gain the goodwill of the other group of individuals.[4]

Nehru held the British, the communal leadership, economic disparity and the middle class as factors responsible for the origin and expansion of communalism in India. Although he did not state blatantly that the communal divide in India—especially the Hindu-Muslim divide—had been created by the British, he explained that after the uprising of 1857, the British Government made continuous efforts to instigate this communal divide. They endeavoured to discourage unity and cooperation between the two communities. Even during the non-cooperation movement, when Hindu, Muslim and other communities came together against the colonial regime, the British government tried to weaken communal unity by exploiting the backwardness of the people. The British police and secret service sent secret agents as sadhus and fakirs and encouraged communal violence. This policy of the British government succeeded as there were rifts and cleavages in Indian society.[5] Alongside the British government, the communal leaders of the two communities also instigated communal tension. They exploited the religious sentiments of the masses for their own vested interests. The middle class and the economic disparity between the two communities—Hindus and Muslims—also were the reasons for communal hostilities. As Nehru writes:

> The unemployed middle-class Muslim felt that the Hindu monopolised all the jobs and stood in their way. They demanded, therefore, separate treatment and separate shares in everything. Politically, the Hindu-Muslim question was essentially a middle-class affair, and a quarrel over jobs. Its effect, however, spread to the masses.[6]

Therefore, the combination of these factors, as Nehru observed, enhanced the communal bitterness between the two major communities of India, which strengthened the Muslim nationalism that looked to the community rather than to the country.[7] As a result of this, throughout the anti-colonial struggle, these communities looked at nationalism and patriotism in the light of their own communal interests and not national interests.[8] Nehru was of the opinion that each community wanted far more than its share, which inevitably created conflicts. As intercommunal bitterness increased, the more extreme leaders of each group came to the front, for, in moments of anger, each group chooses as its representative the person who pitches its demands highest and curses the others most. Communal conflicts were aggravated by the British Government by encouraging the extremist leaders. So the poison of communalism continued to spread creating a "vicious circle" resulting in numerous communal clashes and ultimately led to the partition of the country.[9]

Likewise, communalism continued to haunt the country in different forms even in the post-independence era. Various communal organisations, political parties and communal leaders continued to spread communal detestation and swindle the people for their own political ends. Nehru even noticed the involvement of some of newspapers in spreading communalism. In his words:

> ... often it is the newspapers ... I shall not name them, which are responsible for spreading communalism. They proclaim their nationalism very loudly but are in fact saturated with communalism and do great harm to India.[10]

Nehru criticised the role of communal leaders, communal organisations and communal press for spreading communalism amongst the common masses and argued that nationalism cannot coexist with communalism. He argued that nationalism in India cannot be identified with a particular community. Thus all the citizens of the country should keep themselves away from the communal forces and discourage the communal organisations such as Jana Sangha, Hindu Mahasabha and Ram Rajya Parishad. He argued that such entities foment disunity amongst the people and are a hurdle in the way of India's becoming a modern, progressive and welfare state.[11] Thus, Nehru tried to create the opinion and institutions to weaken and eradicate communalism and communal forces.

Religious Minorities and Group Rights

As communal forces continued to spread communal hatred in post-colonial India, as a secularist leader Nehru also continued to demonstrate his commitment for the establishment of a secular political system. He was opposed to the supremacy of any one community in the country. When the minorities had started to perceive that India would be transformed into a Hindu state then, Nehru assured them that:

> As long as I am at the helm of affairs India will not become a Hindu State.[12]

As a true nationalist, he was able to stall the establishment of Hindu theocracy. His concern for the minorities was far greater than that of any other Congress leader of his time. His major worry was the creeping of communal sentiments into the Congress fold. He condemned the vote bank politics and never permitted compromises to be made in the name of religion. Wherever Nehru found the Congress leadership faulting, he castigated it in strongest terms and criticised their theocratic tendencies because they were anti-democratic. He knew that majority communalism was very dangerous but he was equally aware of the dangers inherent in minority communalism. He also assured the religious minorities that:

> ... we are all anxious to see that full justice is done to all communities in India, ... and that their legitimate demands for protection, in so far as they are consistent with national interests, are met. It follows, therefore, that we cannot be a party to any arrangement which is patently unfair to any community. We are convinced that India as a nation cannot progress and fulfil her destiny, unless every group and community has the fullest freedom and opportunity to progress and develop itself.[13]

Moreover, he consistently emphasised the development of India as a democratic secular state where neither any religious community would be favoured nor discriminated against. Having the awareness of the existence of cultural diversity in India, he sought to protect the cultural interests of the different communities. He opined that cultural minorities in every country should have the "fullest autonomy" in their cultural affairs. Such cultural communities should be given freedom and, furthermore, be encouraged to preserve and cultivate their culture. This would help India to build up a rich, varied and yet a common culture for India. He argued that if sufficient safeguards are provided to the minorities, then communalism would disappear.[14] Although Nehru recognised the group rights of religious minorities and made sufficient provisions in the Indian Constitution to save them, yet he never supported the idea of separate electorates on religious grounds. He envisaged separate electorates on communal basis as a peril not only to the national unity but also to the interests of minority communities. He said:

> ... separate electorates, which are meant to protect the interests of minorities, really injure them and reduce their effective power in the state. If anybody should be against that, it is the minority. But such is the power of a myth that many of us have come to believe that separate electorates are a "valued privilege" to which we must cling on.[15]

Irrespective of the opposition to separate electorates, Nehru stood for the rights of the minorities, particularly Muslims, but also the rights of Sikhs and Christians. He assured the Christians of full freedom for evangelical work so long as it did not impinge on politics, and giving Muslims special attention, encouraged their recruitment to the armed and civil services, particularly the police, their employment in the private sector. Recognising that Urdu, while spoken by both Hindus and Muslims, had become a symbol of Islamic culture, he provided that its use and teaching were given priority especially in Delhi and Uttar Pradesh.[16]

Nehru considered that it is the primary responsibility of the majority to satisfy the minorities in every matter. His argument was that the majority community, having its own strength, does not entail any protection. However, such statutory protection is required to minorities. And therefore, according to Nehru, the majority community is responsible to give particular consideration to the demands and interests of the minorities. He was of the view that if the Hindus as the majority community showed generosity towards the minorities, it would remove the existing fear and suspicion of minorities.[17] The Objective Resolution moved by him was a signpost for the Constituent Assembly to establish as a democratic secular state that could ward off the disintegrating and divisive forces, and where minorities could also flourish. Since its inception, the Indian National Congress had also favoured equal rights and opportunities for the people of India irrespective of distinct religious and racial backgrounds. Nehru agreed that the community rights of the minorities should be recognised and emphasised to provide due space for respective minority communities in the political arena of the country. And, on the other, he warned the people to be aware of the communal forces that would be destructive for India. His major worry was the creeping of communal sentiments into the Congress fold. He condemned the vote bank politics and never permitted compromises to be made in the name of religion. Wherever Nehru found the Congress leadership faulting, he castigated it in strongest terms and criticised their theocratic tendencies because these were anti-democratic.

Communal Diversity and the Question of National Unity

Since communalism was damaging the social fabric of the country in the post-independence period, Nehru asked the people of India to remember the lesson of unity taught by the anti-colonial struggle. Although the religious differences were shallow and not deep-rooted, lumpen elements were instigating and sharpening these differences for their vested interests.[18] To save the country from such elements, Nehru had expressed strong zeal for the unity amongst the people of diverse backgrounds. He emphasised the integration of all parts of the country irrespective of language, regional or religious differences. As he writes:

> Whether you go to Kashmir or Ladakh where Buddhism is to be found, they are all part of our country. Or, if you go to the South, to Kanyakumari, near Ceylon, there may be differences in language, etc., but they are all parts of India. We have to integrate all of them together because if they are regarded as separate parts, we shall be overtaken by weakness.[19]

Nehru was cognisant of the prevailing social, religious, cultural and geographical diversity of India, and was supportive of accommodating that prevailing diversity. On the basis of the diversity, he never recognised anybody's right to say to anybody else that "we are a part of India or that they are not." Due to such differences, according to Nehru, nobody had even the right to impose his will on others.[20] Hence, he strongly advocated the preservation of the diversity of India. In his words:

> There is great diversity among the people living in the North, near the borders, or in Kashmir or Ladakh or Assam, near Tibet and Burma, and the people in the South, in Malabar, etc. The climate is wholly different. In some area, there is snow and it is bitterly cold and in the other, it is always hot. There is difference in dress, food, living habits, etc. ... and all of it together goes into the making of this country. The grandeur of this country lies in its diversity but it will become dangerous if it is not securely bound by unity. So we must preserve both the diversity and the unity of the country.[21]

When there were voices for "complete uniformity," Nehru had not felt its requirement for the country. He argued that the "beauty of India" lies in its diversity.[22] He sees nothing wrong in serving one's province, its special culture, literature and traditions. In fact he argued that the Indian people must preserve their provincial, regional and religious heritage. At the same time, they should also work for the progress of the country.[23] Moreover, their demands should not be contrary to the national interests. Nehru suggested every Indian to ask himself the question:

> What do I want to make of India, one country, one nation or 10, 20 or 25 nations, a fragmented and divided nation without any strength or endurance, ready to break to pieces at the slightest shocks? Each person has to answer this question. Separateness has always been the weakness of India. Fissiparous tendencies, whether they belong to Hindus, Muslims, Sikhs, Christians or others, are very dangerous and wrong tendencies. They belong to petty and backward minds. No one who understands the spirit of the times can think in terms of communalism.[24]

Nehru also conveyed the message of unity and true citizenship to the defence services of India. He asked them to bring honour and glory to the country. During an address to the Defence Services, Nehru said:

> We must constantly remind ourselves that whatever our religion or creed, we are all one people. I regret that many recent disturbances have given us a bad name. Many have acquiesced to the prevailing spirit. This is not citizenship. Citizenship consists in the service of the country. We must prevail on the evil-doers to stop their activities. If you, men of the Navy, the Army and the Air Force, serve your countrymen without distinction of class and religion, you will bring honour to yourselves and to your country.[25]

In brief, visualising unity in diversity, Nehru opposed the demand of complete uniformity in the country. For him, communal diversity was a positive feature and not a threat to national unity. He supported the communities to preserve their distinctive cultural identities and suggested to them to remember the lesson of unity and to be aware of the destructive forces.

Contemporary Relevance

Nehru's outlook regarding communalism seems more relevant in the post-Nehruvian period. As is clear, due to his secular and scientific outlook, Nehru attempted to eradicate the communal competitiveness and hostility which surfaced during the colonial period and was aided and abetted by colonial power. Even post-independence, communal parties and extremist leaders attempted to use the communal divergence for their own narrow interests. However, at that time, it was Nehru's commitment to secularism that minorities in India were protected with all state might. Nehru wisely and strongly warded off attempts at aborting democracy and secularism. As a true nationalist, he was able to stall the establishment of Hindu theocracy and to provide adequate protection to the minorities. Despite all that in the post-Nehruvian period, communal forces became stronger as politics in India continued to get more and more communalised. Communal identities of the common masses were exploited by the opportunist political leaders and political parties leading to communal massacres, like the anti-Sikh riots of 1984, Bombay riots of 1992 and Gujarat riots of 2002. Because of communal hostility between 2005 and 2009, 4,030 incidents of communal violence occurred, in which 648 people were killed and 11,278 were injured. It was noticed that during this period annually an average of 130 people had been killed and 2,200 people were injured.[26] In 2012, 93 persons were killed and 2,067 were injured in 640 communal incidents.[27] Due the same reason, in 2013, 107 people died and 1,647 were injured in 479 communal clashes.[28] In the post-Nehruvian period, various political leaders have emphasised secularism while criticising communalism; however, all that has been done merely to secure the vote bank of a particular community. In a practical sense, they have not done anything to eradicate communalism or to promote communal harmony. Hence, the exploitation of communal divergence has continuously become a threat to the national unity of India. Nehru's outlook needs to be perused in contemporary times to marginalise the communal forces and eradicate communalism.

References

1. Jawaharlal Nehru, "The Sword Arm of India," Presidential Address at the Punjab Provincial Conference held on April 11, 1928, published in Jagat S. Bright (ed.), *Important Speeches of Jawaharlal Nehru (From 1922 to 1946)* (Lahore: The Indian Printing Press, nyp), pp. 139-40.
2. S. Gopal, "Nehru and Minorities," *Economic & Political Weekly*, vol. 23, no. 45/47, November 1988, p. 2463.
3. Jawaharlal Nehru, "Tolerance and Communal Harmony," Speech Delivered in the Constituent Assembly on a Resolution on the Elimination of Communal Organisations, April 3, 1948 published in Mushirul Hasan (ed.), *Nehru's India: Select Speeches* (New Delhi: Oxford University Press, 2007), p. 138.
4. Jawaharlal Nehru, "Communalism, A Badge of Backwardness," Speech Delivered at Srinagar, July 19, 1961, published in Mushirul Hasan (ed.), *Nehru's India: Select Speeches* (New Delhi: Oxford University Press, 2007), p. 141.
5. Jawaharlal Nehru, *Glimpses of World History* (New Delhi: Penguin Books, 2004), pp. 837-38.
6. Ibid., p. 838.
7. Ibid.
8. Ibid., p. 839.

9. Ibid., pp. 839-40.
10. Jawaharlal Nehru, "Hurdles in Building a New India," March 26, 1954, *Selected Works of Jawaharlal Nehru*, vol. 25 (New Delhi: Oxford University Press), p. 10.
11. Jawaharlal Nehru, "Equal Opportunities for All," Speech Delivered in a Public Meeting at Kozhikode, Kerala, February 25, 1957 published in Mushirul Hasan (ed.), *Selected Works of Jawaharlal Nehru*, Second Series, vol. 37, 2006, p. 50.
12. Jawaharlal Nehru, "India Will Not Be a Hindu State," An Address to Mill Workers and Labourers in Delhi, September 30, 1947 published in S. Gopal (ed.), *Selected Works of Jawaharlal Nehru*, Second Series, vol. 14 (New Delhi: Oxford University Press), p. 108.
13. Jawaharlal Nehru's Letter, "To Tara Singh," May 10, 1949 (New Delhi: Jawaharlal Nehru Memorial Fund, 1991), p. 235.
14. Nehru, n. 1, p. 140.
15. Ibid., p. 140.
16. Gopal, n. 2, p. 2466.
17. Ibid.
18. Jawaharlal Nehru, "Unity in Diversity," published in Ravinder Kumar and H. Y. Sharada Prasad (eds.), *Selected Works of Jawaharlal Nehru*, Second Series, vol. 22 (New Delhi: Jawaharlal Memorial Fund, 1998), p. 39.
19. Ibid., pp. 39-40.
20. Nehru, n. 10.
21. Ibid.
22. Jawaharlal Nehru, "People's Cooperation in Progress," April 10, 1954 published in *Selected Works of Jawaharlal Nehru*, Second Series, vol. 25 (New Delhi: Oxford University Press), p. 17.
23. Ibid.
24. Nehru, n. 4.
25. Jawaharlal Nehru's Radio Address to the Defence Services, December 1, 1947.
26. Rohit Kumar, "Vital Stats: Communal Violence in India," *PRS Legislative Research* (New Delhi: Centre for Policy Research, 2011) (online edition).
27. Bharti Jain, "Government Releases Data of Riot Victims Identifying Religion," *Hindustan Times*, September 24, 2013.
28. Ibid.

6

Nehru's Paradigm of Panchayati Raj and Its Contemporary Relevance

Ranbir Singh and Saroj Malik

There exists a widespread ambiguity and great deal of confusion regarding the concept of panchayati raj among the social scientists, policymakers and administrators. Some of them perceive it as an attempt to revive the system of traditional panchayats that had been in existence in India since ancient times. Others see it as an attempt to realise the Gandhian vision of Gram Swaraj which was based on the belief that India should be a commonwealth of politically independent and economically self-sufficient villages. A few of them view its introduction as the fulfilment of the promise of creation of gram panchayats as institutions of self-government that had been made in Article 40 of the Indian Constitution. The remaining among them view panchayati raj as an extension of the scheme of federalism established by the Constitution of India beyond the state level to the district, block and village levels. However, all these conceptions are fallacious. In fact, panchayati raj is the scheme of democratic decentralisation suggested by the Balwant Rai Mehta Study Team in 1957 and implemented in 1959. The Team suggested the creation of a three-tier structure comprising Gram Panchayats at the village level, Panchayat Samitis at the block level and the Zila Parishad at the district level. It also recommended that the block level body, the Panchayat Samiti, should be given the key role in it instead of the district level body, the Zila Parishad, because the block is neither as small as a village nor as large as a district and has an optimum size for devolution of powers. Moreover, there existed a team of extension officers of line departments under the leadership of Block Development Officer (BDO) at the block level for undertaking the task of planning and its implementation. Moreover, the very word "block" has in the rural psyche begun to be associated with development.[1] Such a scenario leads us to a series of questions. What were the considerations that made Nehru opt for this scheme? What did he do to institutionalise it? How far was he successful in this context? What led to the subsequent stagnation and ultimate decay of Panchayati Raj Institutions (PRIs) in the post-Nehru era? What efforts had been made in 1977 to revitalise PRIs and why did those efforts fail? How did the revival of Indira Gandhi's dominance in the 1980 parliamentary elections adversely affect the PRIs? How far did the second-generation panchayats created in 1980s correspond to Nehru's paradigm of PRIs? How far did Rajiv's vision of panchayati raj resemble that of Nehru? Does the panchayati raj system set up by the 73rd Amendment to the Indian Constitution (1993) differ from that of Nehru? What is the relevance of Nehru's paradigm of panchayati raj in the era of Liberalisation, Privatisation and Globalisation (LPG)?

Nehru and Panchayati Raj Institutions

Nehru opted for Panchayati Raj because of various considerations. First, he had great faith in the ideology of liberalism which he had imbibed during his stay in England for education and also on account of the influence on him of his father, Moti Lal Nehru, who was deeply committed to this ideology. Although Nehru subsequently got influenced by Marxism even this could not dilute his adherence to liberalism. Since liberalism considers democratic decentralisation essential for the institutionalisation of democracy, Nehru was bound to be fascinated by the scheme that had been suggested by the Balwant Rai Mehta Study Team. Second, Nehru's option for panchayati raj could also be traced to the influence of Mahatma

Gandhi on him. It is pertinent to mention that the Mahatma had declared Nehru as his political heir. He had also proclaimed that Nehru would speak his language after his demise. Although Nehru did not share Gandhi's romantic view of village communities and did not accept his suggestion for a partyless democracy, he did feel the need for some sort of participatory democracy for strengthening parliamentary democracy. Hence he at once supported the scheme for democratic decentralisation envisaged through the Gram Sabha. Third, Nehru's choice for panchayati raj was also influenced by his quest to make the Community Development Programme (CDP) successful in India. The CDP was launched on October 2, 1952 for bringing a silent revolution in rural society by awakening the dormant forces of progress in it. However, it proved to be the proverbial God that failed because of the bureaucratic mode of its implementation. Nehru considered panchayati raj as a basic prerequisite for the mobilisation of human and material resources for the success of the CDP. Fourth, Nehru's decision to introduce panchayati raj in all the states of Indian Union was also influenced by his model of nation-building which sought to ensure penetration of the Centre into the periphery, and Balwant Rai Mehta's scheme of democratic decentralisation could be a useful device. It not only democratised the district and sub-district administrations but also the village administration.[2] Fifth, as Paul Wallace observed, Nehru's style was that of politicisation and decentralisation, and panchayati raj ensured both. On the one hand, it politicised the rural masses by providing them the opportunity of participating in the elections of Gram Panchayats, Panchayat Samitis and Zila Parishads; on the other, it decentralised power from the State to the District, Block and Village levels.[3]

As the Prime Minister of India and supreme leader of the Congress Party from 1947 to 1964, Nehru took various steps for the institutionalisation of panchayati raj system in India. First, he got the scheme of democratic decentralisation suggested by the Balwant Rai Mehta Study Team—which was appointed by the Committee on Plan Projects of the Planning Commission of India in 1957—

approved from the National Development Council (NDC) in 1957 and by the Conference of Ministers of Local Self-Government of various States held at Hyderabad in 1958. It was in these that a consensus was reached that the scheme of democratic decentralisation be introduced by various states by customising it as per their specific needs. However, they must ensure that the panchayati raj bodies are democratically elected and organically linked. Moreover, there should be genuine devolution of powers to them.[4] Second, Nehru created the Ministry of Community Development, Cooperation and Panchayati Raj in the Government of India in 1959 and appointed S. K. Dey, the chief administrator of CDP, as the first Minister. He was selected for heading this ministry because of his deep commitment to the concept of panchayati raj. He was assigned the task of ensuring that the panchayati raj system was institutionalised in all the states of the Indian Union.[5] Third, he prevailed upon the chief ministers of all the states to get the statutes enacted from their respective state legislatures for the setting up of the panchayati raj systems. This was essential because local self-government was a state subject. He also prevailed upon them to set up training Institutions in their respective states for the capacity building of the elected representatives and official functionaries.[6] Fourth, Nehru also set up a national level institution of community development and panchayati raj for supervising and coordinating training programmes in various states and also for the capacity building of stakeholders in panchayati raj system. This institution was subsequently converted into National Institute of Rural Development, Hyderabad.[7] Fifth, Nehru also favoured a healthy interface between the panchayati raj Institutions and the cooperatives bodies. According to him, it will ensure both political democracy and economic democracy. It is pertinent to mention that Panchayati Raj Act of some states provided for the representation of the cooperative societies and market committees in the Panchayat Samitis.[8] Sixth, Nehru also prevailed upon the Indian Institute of Public Administration (IIPA), New Delhi to make the study and research on panchayati raj a priority area. That is why the Institute was able to bring out various publications on panchayati raj which were able to identify the weaknesses in the system and also to make concrete suggestions for strengthening the PRIs. *The Indian Journal of Public Administration*, which is published by the Institute, carried articles on Panchayati Raj in various issues. It also published a special issue on panchayati raj in 1964.[9] Seventh, he also got appointed many study teams for the evaluation of panchayati raj system in various states which made significant recommendations for strengthening Gram Sabha and other institutions of panchayati raj. They also highlighted the problems such as conflict between the officials and non-officials in the PRIs and the need for strengthening the Gram Sabha. Valuable suggestions had also been made by them for tackling this problem.[10]

Jawaharlal Nehru was successful in the institutionalisation of panchayati raj system in almost all the states; however, the PRIs institutions were not equally strong in all of them. First, whereas states like Maharashtra and Rajasthan were able to set up vibrant systems of panchayati raj, those like Punjab and UP could not do so because of the lack of commitment to the concept of democratic decentralisation of their chief ministers.[11] Second, Nehru failed to change the mindset of the bureaucracy which continued to maintain a hostile attitude towards these institutions of grassroots governance.[12] Third, despite sincere efforts, Nehru could not change the mindset of political leadership. The MPs and the MLAs kept on considering the leaders in PRIs, particularly the chairpersons of the Zila Parishads and Panchayat Samitis, as their political rivals. They not only began to play an important role in the elections of chairpersons of Zila Parishads and Panchayat Samitis but also persisted in undue interference in their day-to-day administration.[13]

It is pertinent to mention here that Nehru could foresee that attempts may be made to undermine the Panchayati Raj System after his death. This is evident from the fact that he gave a late night call to S. K. Dey to enquire about the future of PRIs after him. Dey told him that it cannot be destroyed in Maharashtra and Gujarat where strong PRIs have emerged. But it could be destroyed in northern states where Panchayati Raj remained weak. He implored Dey to make early efforts for strengthening PRIs. Nehru also warned him that he has very little time for this purpose and hence there should be no delay in this context.[14]

Panchayati Raj System after Nehru

The Ashoka Mehta Committee Report (1978) pointed out that the panchayati raj system had been pushed into stagnation after Nehru's death. First, this happened because Nehru's successor, Lal Bahadur Shastri, did not share his enthusiasm for panchayati raj. Second, the country had to fight a war with Pakistan in 1965 and hence the issue of PRIs was put on the back burner. Third, India faced an acute shortage of food grains at that point of time. Consequently, agriculture production got priority over democratic decentralisation. The Government of India not only introduced Intensive Agriculture Areas and Intensive Agriculture District Programme for this purpose but also set up Agriculture Production Committees headed by the Deputy Commissioners/Collectors at the district levels. The BDOs were also involved in the task of increasing agriculture production. They were put under the control of agriculture department for this purpose. This did help in bringing about self-sufficiency in food grains. However, its logical outcome was decline in the role of PRIs in rural development. This led to stagnation in panchayati raj.[15]

The emergence of Indira Gandhi as a powerful Prime Minister in the 1971 parliamentary elections through the use of the populist slogans of *Garibi Hatao* (Banish Poverty) and *Samajvad Lao* (Usher in Socialism) also adversely affected the panchayati raj system. She did not believe in the Nehruvian style of politicisation and decentralisation; instead she pursued the style of de-politicisation and centralisation for concentrating all the authority in her hands. This logically culminated in the decay of PRIs.[16] She abolished the Ministry of Panchayati Raj and shifted S. K. Dey to the Ministry of Coals. The department of panchayati raj was made a part of Ministry of Agriculture. These developments naturally proved injurious to the health of panchayati raj system and consequently it began to decay. The chief ministers who virtually became the subedars of empire during her tenure (1971-1977) gave fatal blows to PRIs. By way of illustration, Zila Parishads were abolished in Haryana by Bansi Lal, then chief minister of the state.[17] Elections of PRIs were never held in time. The extension officers of various line departments were also withdrawn from the panchayat samitis during his regime. The imposition of emergency on June 25, 1975 led to the establishment of a highly centralised authoritarian system at the national and the state levels. Consequently, the authority of the PRIs got further weakened.

After the Janata Party was voted to power at the centre in the 1977 general elections, a high powered committee on panchayati raj was set up under the leadership of Ashoka Mehta. It was done to fulfil the promise made by the Janata Party to revitalise the PRIs in its election manifesto. The Ashoka Mehta Committee suggested the creation of a two-tier structure comprising Zila Parishads and Mandal Panchayats for this purpose. It also suggested direct elections to the PRIs and advocated genuine devolution of powers to these bodies. It favoured consistent enhancement in their powers. However, the Ashoka Mehta Committee Report (1978) could not be implemented because the Morarji Desai-led Janata Party Government was ousted from power in 1979 due to a split in the Janata Party. And the Minority Government headed by Charan Singh and supported from outside by the Congress (I) had neither the time nor the desire, nor the strength to get its recommendations implemented.[18]

The Janata Party phase was notorious because of the political uncertainty caused at the centre as a result of factionalism in the Party. Indira Gandhi was able to restore her dominance in the 1980 parliamentary elections on the basis of the slogan, *Vote the Government that Works.* As earlier, she continued with her style of de-politicisation and centralisation, apart from adopting the path of confrontation while handling the Assam and Punjab problems. Consequently, the PRIs were again adversely affected. Instead of PRIs, her priority was the poverty alleviation programmes and employment generation programmes, which were subsequently combined into Integrated Rural Development Programme (IRDP). The rural development programmes of the Ministry of Rural Development, Government of India were taken out of the purview of the PRIs and handed over to a new entity, District Rural Development Authority (DRDA) which was headed by the Deputy Commissioner/District Collector. This proved to be the proverbial last straw on the camel's back for the PRIs which were reduced to weak civic bodies and ceased to be development mechanisms.[19]

Although the Ashoka Mehta Committee recommendations could not be implemented due to the adverse circumstances but the Janata-Kranti Ranga Government headed by R. K. Hegde in Karnataka, the Left Front Government led by Jyoti Basu in West Bengal and the Telegu Desham Party Government headed by N. T. Rama Rao in Andhra Pradesh, took the lead in creating the second generation of PRIs in their respective states. These PRIs were designed by customising the Ashoka Mehta Committee's recommendations in accordance with the specific conditions of these states. As a result of that the vibrant decentralised democracy was established in these states. The patterns of panchayati raj that had been adopted by them were, undoubtedly, an improvement on the paradigm suggested by the Balwant Rai Mehta Study Team and endorsed by Jawaharlal Nehru.[20] These were, indeed, bold initiatives which went a long way in strengthening decentralised rural governance in these states. They were certainly a marked improvement in the patterns that had been adopted in various states since 1959 on account of Nehru's persuasion. Besides, the West Bengal Model had an additional advantage. The Left Front Government introduced land reforms before introducing it. This brought about a qualitative change in the socio-economic structure of rural Bengal. That is why the local power structure got changed to a greater degree in West Bengal than in Karnataka and Andhra Pradesh which had not introduced land reforms. Be that as it may, the successful working of second generation of PRIs played an important role in motivating Rajiv Gandhi, then Prime Minister of India, to introduce the 64th Amendment Bill in Lok Sabha in 1989 regarding the strengthening of PRIs.

Rajiv Gandhi decided to follow the style of politicisation and decentralisation pursued by Nehru instead of adopting the style of de-politicisation and centralisation used by Indira Gandhi. By pursuing the Nehruvian strategy regarding the PRIs, he wanted to finish the power brokers at various levels of the power structure and to restore within party democracy in the Congress. Besides, he wanted to make PRIs inclusive for ensuring inclusive development. He realised that the bureaucratic mode of implementation of rural development programmes used by Indira Gandhi had proved inadequate for ensuring the benefit of those to the rural masses. He had also arrived at the conclusion that only 15 paise out of one rupee spent on these programmes, are able to reach the beneficiaries and the rest are pilfered on the way. Hence, he wanted to restore and strengthen Nehru's paradigm of panchayati raj system. Therefore, he wanted to accord constitutional status to PRIs. He also favoured direct elections to these bodies. Moreover, he wanted adequate reservation for women, Scheduled Castes and Scheduled Tribes in the PRIs. It can be argued that Rajiv Gandhi's paradigm of panchayati raj was based on that of Nehru. However, it was also a marked improvement on that because it was an attempt to genuinely democratise the institutions of grassroots democracy through direct elections, instead of indirect elections provided by Nehru's paradigm, but wanted to make them more inclusive than the earlier ones by giving due share to women and other weaker sections through adequate reservations. In order to achieve the aforesaid objective, the 64th Amendment Bill was passed by the Lok Sabha but failed to get the required (two-thirds) majority in the Rajya Sabha due to the concerted efforts of vested interests.[21]

Nehru's Paradigm of PRIs in the Era of Globalisation

The new Panchayati Raj System was created by the 73rd Constitutional Amendment Act of 1993. It is different from Nehru's paradigm of panchayati raj in several ways. First, it provides for a uniform three-tier structure of panchayati raj system in all the states instead of leaving every state free to have a pattern tailored to its specific conditions. Second, it introduces direct elections instead of indirect ones. Third, it provides one-third reservation to women and also reservation to the SCs & STs in proportion to their share in the population of the state at various levels, instead of the method of co-option which gave them only nominal or token representation. Fourth, it has added the 11th Schedule to the Indian Constitution which has identified 29 subjects wherein the states can give powers to PRIs, instead of leaving them entirely at the mercy of states. The PRIs can make and implement plans of economic development and social justice on those subjects that are devolved by the state legislature to them. Notwithstanding these changes in the format of panchayati raj system, it has been the continuation of Nehruvian strategy because the base for the 73rd Amendment had been created by Nehru's paradigm of panchayati raj. But it has to be recognised that it was a marked improvement.[22] At the operational level, it needs to be emphasised that the pattern of devolution to PRIs has been extremely uneven, with some states like Kerala, Karnataka and, recently, Maharashtra, in the lead, and other states like UP and Jharkhand as laggards.[23] An overview of panchayati raj over the last two decades indicates that panchayati raj is advancing everywhere and some laggards are leap-frogging over more advanced states to give remarkable returns.[24] Among all the states, Kerala came out with a "people's plan" through active participation of people at all the three tiers of Panchayats. The state devolved funds, functions, functionaries and prepared a campaign which is unparalleled in the country in terms of its scale and scope.[25] Reservation for women in PRIs has at least succeeded in bringing the women folk of rural India into the political forum. Representation of women in the formal structures of governance at the local level has recorded a steady increase.[26] With that, India is moving in the direction of being an inclusive democracy and it has begun to rise from below. The panchayati raj has begun to change the grammar of politics and has gone a long way to deepen democracy.[27] Notwithstanding these achievements, the PRIs are facing many problems including their struggle against the feudal and bureaucratic mindset. India does not only require inclusive democracy but also inclusive growth as both are interrelated but at the policy level there exists dichotomy. For instance one of the major objectives of Twelfth Five-Year Plan (2012-17) is to ensure inclusive growth but it does not delve in any significant measure into the question how the key requirements of inclusion are to be achieved. In the "twenty-five core indicators" listed by the Plan to "reflect the vision of rapid, sustainable and more inclusive growth,"[28] the PRIs find no place at all, notwithstanding the very comprehensive road map for Panchayati Raj (2011-2017), prepared by the Ministry of Panchayati Raj, Government of India coinciding virtually with the period of the Twelfth Plan.[29] In the recent report titled *Towards Holistic Panchayat Raj*, it is stressed that the panchayat raj must not deteriorate into sarpanch raj. In order to achieve this objective, the report urges that PRIs be structured legally and administratively to function as collegiate bodies, with elected members being involved in preparing programmes.[30]

The moot question needs to be answered here is how far Nehru's paradigm of panchayati raj accompanied by centralised planning and mixed economy as strategy of economic growth and development, is relevant after the adoption of New Economic Policy (NEP) by India in 1991. The NEP has been unfolded in the form of Liberalisation, Privatisation and Globalisation (LPG) reforms. In view of the changed scenario, one may be tempted to reach a hasty conclusion that Nehru's paradigm of panchayati raj as well as its improved version in the form of 73rd Constitutional Amendment has become obsolete and irrelevant. But the fact of the matter is that the strengthening of the scheme of democratic decentralisation or panchayati raj system has become all the more necessary in the present era for saving the rural sector in general and rural poor in particular from the negative fallout of the LPG. In fact, India has entered an era of glocalisation in which, on the one hand, people are being pushed upwards by the forces of globalisation, and on the other, they are being pulled downwards by the forces of localism.[31] In the given context, this improved version of Nehru's paradigm of panchayati raj requires further strengthening. According to the report on *Towards Holistic Panchayat Raj 2013*, the Central Government is already improving the design of the programmes of Centrally Sponsored Schemes (CSS) of public goods and services that might best be done by shifting their delivery from line departments and parallel bodies to the PRIs. In the fundamental shift to making CSS panchayat-driven and people-oriented, the principal onus is placed on the Central Government, not State government,[32] in keeping with Prime Minister Manmohan Singh's injunction that "before we set this right at the centre we cannot be asking the states to do so."[33] The expert committee has underlined that the effective holistic panchayati raj being a constitutional duty and obligation, is binding on the Central government as much as it is on the States.[34]

Moreover, the PRIs also need to be strengthened as a multi-pronged strategy for inclusive democracy and inclusive growth apart from fighting the forces of secessionism, terrorism and naxalism, which, in addition to other factors, may be attributed to the centralisation of power and persistent denial of autonomy to various ethnic groups. One of the main reasons for the emergence of the problem of left-wing extremism is the tribal areas wherein the model of development being pursued by India has led to deprivation and displacement. Sixty-five years after independence, almost every Indian feels alienated from the political and administrative process, the sense of alienation being the greater the lower down the economic scale and social hierarchy that a person finds himself or herself in, and also the more distanced he or she is geographically from imposing Bhawans where his or her future is decided.[35] This alienation is manifest in the form of political violence in different parts of the country. The strengthening of decentralised democracy at various levels is likely to prove more useful than the use of army or paramilitary forces, and the PRIs can be an effective vehicle for that provided they are empowered in the real sense of the term, instead of making them dependent upon the state governments. But this requires a radical change in the mindset of the ruling elite and bureaucracy at various levels apart from the capacity building of elected representatives of PRIs by providing them training and making them aware of their roles and responsibilities. These changes may happen at a slow pace but they are bound to happen in the days to come.

Notes and References

1. For details, see S. C. Jain, *Community Development and Panchayati Raj* (Bombay: Allied Publishers, 1967).
2. Ranbir Singh, "Nehru's Model of Nation Building," Suneera Kapoor (ed.), *Thought and Vision of Jawaharlal Nehru* (New Delhi: Anamika Publishers, 2005), pp. 45-46.
3. These observations are based on the discussion of the Principal Author of the paper with Prof. Paul Wallace of Columbia University, Missouri (USA) in 1972.
4. For details, see S. Bhatnagar, *Panchayati Raj in Kangra* (New Delhi: Orient Longman, 1967).
5. For details, see Nikhil Kolpe, *Power to the People from Gram Sabha*, ANSSIRD, Mysore, 2005.
6. For illustration, Kamla Nehru Panchayat Siksha Kendra was set up at Beeswan Meel (Sonipat) and Orientation Training Centre at Nilokheri (Karnal) in Punjab. Now these places are a part of Haryana.
7. The NIRD has set up SIRDs (State Institute of Rural Development) and Extension Training Centres in all the States.
8. For illustration, Punjab Panchayat Samitis and Zila Parishads Act provided for the election of two representatives of the Cooperative Societies as the Primary Members of the Panchayat Samitis.
9. The Indian Institute of Public Administration, New Delhi had been set up by Pandit Jawaharlal Nehru as the apex Institute in the discipline at Delhi. Its branches had been set up in all the States.
10. For illustration, Diwakar Committee had been set up to study the institution of Gram Sabha.
11. While the Maharashtra model has provided for a strong Zila Parishad, the Rajasthan model gave the key role to Panchayat Samiti.
12. Shiv Raj Singh, "Jawaharlal Nehru and Public Administration," Suneera Kapoor (ed.), *Thought and Vision of Jawaharlal Nehru* (New Delhi: Anamika Publishers, 2005), pp. 111-20.
13. Ranbir Singh, "Panchayati Raj System in Haryana," G. Ram Reddy (ed.), *Patterns of Panchayati Raj in India* (New Delhi: Macmillan, 1976).
14. S. R. Mehrotra, "Jawaharlal Nehru: A Reassessment," Suneera Kapoor (ed.), *Thought and Vision of Jawaharlal Nehru* (New Delhi: Anamika Publishers, 2005), p. 26.
15. Saroj Malik and Shamim Qureshi, "The Evolution of the Concept of Panchayati Raj from Democratic Decentralisation to Good Governance," Ranbir Singh and Surat Singh (eds.), *Local Democracy & Good Governance, Five Decades of Panchayati Raj* (New Delhi: Deep & Deep Publications, 2011), p. 171.
16. The attempt to reverse the System in India came a decade after Nehru's death, and it came from his own daughter. S. R. Mehrotra, n. 14.
17. Maru Singh Committee appointed by Bansi Lal Government had recommended that Zila Parishads be strengthened. Bansi Lal preferred to dissolve it.
18. Saroj Malik and Shamim Qureshi, n. 15, pp. 171-72.
19. Ibid.
20. Ibid.

21. D. Sunder Ram, "Democratic Decentralisation and Good Governance in India: Promises and Perils," Ranbir Singh and Surat Singh, eds., *Local Democracy & Good Governance, Five Decades of Panchayati Raj*, New Delhi: Deep & Deep Publications, 2011, pp. 122-23.
22. Saroj Malik and Shamim Qureshi, n. 15, pp. 172-73.
23. Mani Shankar Aiyar, "Towards Holistic Panchayat Raj," *Yojana*, vol. 57, August 2013, p. 7.
24. Ibid.
25. Pradip Kumar Parida, "Locating Space for Citizens in Contemporary Governance: The Challenges of Global vs. Local," *World Politics*, vol. 34, no. 11, November 2013, p. 39.
26. Anupam Hazra, "The Women Reservation Bill: Can We Hope For Gender Equality," *Kurukshetra*, vol. 58, no. 8, June 2010, p. 9.
27. Ash Narain Roy, "People's Movement, a Quest for Inclusive Democracy?" *Yojana*, vol. 57, August 2013, p. 34.
28. Planning Commission (Government of India), *Twelfth Five-Year Plan (2012-2017), Faster, More Inclusive and Sustainable Growth, Volume 1* (New Delhi: Sage Publications, 2013), pp. 35-36.
29. "Road Map for Panchayati Raj (2011-17): An All-India Perspective," see www.panchayat.gov.in.
30. Government of India, *Towards Holistic Panchayat Raj, Twentieth Anniversary Report of the Expert Committee on Leveraging Panchayats for Efficient Delivery of Public Goods and Services, Volume 1 (Policy Issues)*, New Delhi, April 2013.
31. Ranbir Singh, "Changing Contours of Indian Federalism," Arshi Khan and Kushal Pal (eds.), *Federalism, Democracy and Conflict Resolution* (Macmillan Publishers, New Delhi, 2012), pp. 34-41.
32. Government of India, *Towards Holistic Panchayat Raj*, n. 30, p. 9.
33. Prime Minister, Manmohan Singh reiterated this point at the National Convention to commemorate the 50th Anniversary of Panchayati Raj on Gandhi Jayanti, October 2, 2009. Cited in n. 30, p. 9.
34. Government of India, *Towards Holistic Panchayat Raj*, n. 30, p. 75.
35. Mani Shankar Aiyar, n. 23, p. 4.

7

Jawaharlal Nehru, Neo-Liberalism and Social Democracy: Mapping the Shifting Trajectories of Developmental State in India

Ronki Ram

This paper intends to critically evaluate the impact of neo-liberal market-economy on caste and various caste-related social ameliorative measures of the Indian developmental state precisely meant for the inclusion of socially excluded sections of Indian society. It further explores the complex relationship between caste/poverty/inequality and neo-liberal market-economy in globalising India and its impact on the nature of the Indian developmental state. Though scholarly literature abounds on economic liberalisation, globalisation, inequalities, caste, poverty and democracy, the complex question of how economic liberalisation affects the interrelationship between caste and market on the one hand, and its impact developmental state in contemporary globalising India on the other, has not been addressed adequately so far. This paper is a modest attempt to fill such gaps in the scholarly literature while anchoring the neo-liberal discourse in the larger Nehruvian perspective based as it was on mixed economy, community development programme and welfare state. In other words, this study draws heavily on the Nehruvian vision for critically examining the possible implications of neo-liberal economic reforms[1] for the survival of social democracy in India and their direct impact on the socially excluded sections of society popularly known as Dalits.[2]

The paper is divided into three parts. The first problematises the phenomenon of social democracy in India in contradiction to its counterpart in Europe. In the process, it also engages the Nehruvian mixed economy model in highlighting the significance of the institutions of social democracy for the deepening of liberal democracy[3] in India. The second part delves deeply into the neo-liberal challenge to social democracy and its consequences for the overall health of democracy in the country. It builds on the premise that since liberal (electoral) democracy was planted in India during the British Raj, it needs tender nurturing, as envisioned by Jawaharlal Nehru, to spread its branches into the hitherto highly stratified social sphere in the country. Relationships between caste, democracy and market are delineated critically in the third part.

I

Social Democracy in India with a Difference

Social democracy calls upon the state to play a positive role for the protection as well as promotion of the interests of the downtrodden, minorities and the other weaker sections of society. It expects that state need not be confined solely to law and order system. The state is rather expected to play the role of a harbinger of social and economic justice as well. It is in this context that the extended contractarian tradition of the welfare state comes into head-on-collision with the forces of neo-liberal market-economy. Social democracy aims at removing social inequalities by bridging the gulf between "formal validity" of rights and their actual realisation in the real-world living conditions, what Meyer and Hinchman called "real-world efficacy of universal basic rights."[4] As long as a gap remains between the formal validity of rights and their efficacy in a plural society like India, the functioning of democratic institution "remains wedded to a purely formal, procedural notion of decision-making."[5] For a democracy to rise above the façade of formal institutional mechanisms of rule-based decision-making, it must ensure that all the members of a society have acquired equal social status to contribute effectively in the democratic processes of the country. A democratic set-up relies much on the actual and meaningful participation of citizens. Any sort of social and economic disability would not only deprive its victims of equal opportunities, but also precludes the natural growth of democracy in a given society in the true sense of the term. It is in this context that social democracy helps liberal democracy become both "social and effective."[6] It emphasises the realisation of social and economic rights in addition to civil and political rights, and guarantees social inclusiveness. "Social democracy, as a general type," argue Meyer and Hinchman, "features a democratically controlled and proactive state that pursues equitable and broad-based development within a largely market economy."[7]

Social democracy owes its origins to Europe. It transforms "delegative democracy" and "passive citizenship" into democracy with active participation and social citizenship.[8] Though theoretical thinking about social democracy in Europe goes back to the early twentieth century,[9] but practically it was first introduced in Europe during the turbulent interwar years in the form of state welfare, compromise between labour and capital, and employment security measures.[10] The world economic depression of 1929 and the subsequent World War II has led to the realisation among the policymakers in the capitals of Europe that if the world had to be saved from similar future turbulence within and among the sovereign states, developmental as well as welfare state must be given a respectable chance to strengthen those social conditions that help deepening democratic structures and their legitimacy.[11] In other words, liberal democratic regimes based on political freedom and unrestrained capital accumulation had to accommodate the interests of those peoples who were pushed towards the margins while helping them come into the mainstream under the welfare tutelage of the state. It was such a thinking of state welfare accompanied by the fear of violent overthrow of the capitalistic system of democratic governance that gave rise to the growth of social democracy in Europe in the aftermath of World War II. In Latin America, too, social democracy was experimented with in the wake of democratic response to the neo-liberal market driven economic crisis.

Domestic Origins of Social Democracy

The story of the emergence of social democracy in India, however, is different from that of Europe. Unlike Europe and Latin America, social democracy in India did not emerge as a response to rabid capitalism and severe economic depression. Instead, it started taking shape in colonial India, as aptly argued by Manmohan Singh, the then Prime Minister of India, "to liberate ourselves from centuries of misrule, from the scourge of poverty, ignorance and disease, from tyranny and bigotry, from caste prejudice and communal divisions."[12] The founding fathers of independent India were well aware that if free India had to mature into a full-fledged democracy, its social sphere needs to be thoroughly overhauled.[13] On the completion of the Draft Constitution (November 25, 1949), B. R. Ambedkar, Chairman of the Drafting Committee of the Constitution, sounded a grave warning in his famous address in the Constituent Assembly:

> On the 26th of January 1950, we are going to enter into a life of contradictions. In politics we will have equality and in social and economic life we will have inequality. In politics we will be recognising the principle of one man one vote and one vote one value. In our social and economic life, we shall, by reason of our social and economic structure, continue to deny the principle of one man one value. How long shall we continue to live this life of contradictions? How long shall we continue to deny equality in our social and economic life? If we continue to deny it for long, we will do so only by putting our political democracy in peril. We must remove this contradiction at the earliest possible or else those who suffer from inequality will blow up the structure of political democracy which this Assembly has so laboriously built up.[14]

The social democratic vision of independent India as nurtured during the freedom struggle and also during the drafting of the Constitution got further reflected in the Resolution of the Government of India adopted for the creation of the Planning Commission in March 1950.[15] The Resolution clearly defined the scope of the work of the Planning Commission in the following terms:

> The Constitution of India has guaranteed certain Fundamental Rights to the citizens of India and enunciated certain Directive Principles of State Policy, in particular, that the State shall strive to promote the welfare of the people by securing and protecting as effectively as it may a social order in which justice, social, economic and political, shall inform all the institutions of the national life, and shall direct its policy towards securing, among other things—that the citizens, men and women equally, have the right to an adequate means of livelihood; that the ownership and control of the material resources of the community are so distributed as best to subserve the common good; and that the operation of the economic system does not result in the concentration of wealth and means of production to the common detriment.[16]

Thus an all-inclusive vision of development and an egalitarian social order underlined the basic spirit of the Constitution as well as the ambitious Five-Year Planning projects of the Planning Commission of India. To translate the ideals of the founding fathers for the establishment of an egalitarian social order, a number of special provisions were incorporated in the Constitution of independent India as well as in the resolution adopted for the creation of the Planning Commission. Amongst them state affirmative action is the most prominent. It aimed at overcoming historic caste-based social exclusion and oppression. Along with reservations in education, employment and legislature, rural development programme, Public Distribution System (PDS), public health programmes, cooperatives, the Right to Information Act, the Right to Education Act, mid-day meals programme, Mahatma Gandhi National Rural Employment Guarantee Act, the Food Security Act, the Sarva Shiksha Abhiyan, and the Sampoorna Grameen Rozgar Yojana are a few more significant state initiatives aimed at the creation of social democracy in India.

Yet another important measure towards the formation of social democracy has been a series of attempts, under the Directive Principles of State Policy, to democratise and decentralise governance and the devolution of authority from the centre to the grass-roots Panchayati Raj Institutions (PRIs). Thus the Constitution of India, as aptly argued by Manmohan Singh, the then Prime Minister of India, is "a unique social charter—the boldest statement ever of social democracy."[17] Whether these varied measures have been able to facilitate the growth of social democracy in India or not, is a matter of contention.[18] But the incorporation of such measures in the Constitution is vindication enough that the founding fathers of independent India wanted to deepen the roots of liberal democracy while placing it on the strong footing of social democracy. Social democracy is broadly defined as:

> … a way of life which recognises liberty, equality and fraternity as the principles of life. These principles … are not to be treated as separate items in a trinity. They form a union of trinity in the sense that to divorce one from the other is to defeat the very purpose of democracy.[19]

Frozen in the centuries-old stratified structure of the Hindu social order, the principles of equality and fraternity are yet to find a clear expression and a significant space in the liberal democracy of independent India. Social life in India is still governed by the birth-based principle of graded inequality that tends to elevate some (upper castes) and degrades many (Dalits). Even after six decades of India's independence and despite the widespread reach of various anti-untouchability laws,[20] the Dalits continue to be subjected to social exclusion and all sorts of humiliation. They have continuously been deprived of education, basic human rights, equal social status, and equal opportunities in the fields of art, culture, science and technology.[21] It is against such deep-rooted asymmetrical social structures of Indian society that the institutions of social democracy become highly significant for the survival of liberal democracy.

Social democracy in India, thus, emerged as a response to deep-rooted caste-based social disabilities as against the fiscal crisis of 1929 and the upheaval generated by World War II in Europe. The central focus of social democracy in Europe was on economic equality.[22] Whereas in India the main focus of social democracy has been on deepening democracy while empowering the downtrodden to come forward to democratically struggle for their long-denied human rights as enshrined in the Constitution. In other words, it is the "social" as against the "economic" that provided impetus to the rise of social democracy in India. It is in this regard that the role of state affirmative action is noteworthy, which aims at distributive justice that helps the downtrodden make an equal contribution towards strengthening the base of liberal democracy. It intends to empower them in such a way that they reap the fruits of hard-earned freedom, at par with the privileged twice born. In other words, state affirmative action aims at rescuing Indian society from the clutches of the centuries old institution of caste and the all-pervasive social exclusion and discrimination embedded in it.[23] It is in this context that the neo-liberal market-economy and the institution of social democracy come face-to-face in a mutually antagonistic posture with serious implications for the sustainability of the growing sapling of liberal democracy in India.

Main argument here is that social democracy in India is different from its counterpart in Europe. In India, it aims at building an indigenous base for the restoration of an egalitarian social order that in turn facilitates the internalisation of the democratic values of equality, freedom and fraternity as incorporated in the Constitution. It underscores the urgent need for demolition of the discriminatory social structures. Since democracy thrives on numbers in a closely contested sphere of electoral politics, the burden of tradition becomes too difficult to be avoided. Given the typical communal character of almost all the electoral constituencies in India, caste has come to acquire a leading role in the arithmetic of electoral politics, thus blocking the ongoing processes of deepening of democracy in the country. There is a general impression that instead of blunting the fangs of caste, the institution of liberal democracy has further sharpened them. How to overcome caste and other similar socially stagnating forces, is really an uphill task for the policymakers in India. It is in this context that social democracy aims at deepening the roots of liberal democracy in India—established on the pattern of British parliamentary set-up—while facilitating ethnically divergent and socially fragmented vast majority of rural poor to become active participants in the political processes at the grass roots. In fact, the inherent contradiction between the indigenous institution of caste and the transplanted institution of democracy is what acted as a stumbling block in the way of deepening the roots of democracy in India. This contradiction subsequently assumed the form of a tug of war between tradition and modernity.[24]

Yet another key argument that I want to raise in this paper is that the entry of neo-liberal market-economy in India in the 1990s has further compounded the ongoing tug of war between tradition and modernity to the disadvantage of the latter by entrenching, albeit indirectly, the oppressive caste structures in the country. Neo-liberalism reiterates that the social and material interests of the citizens would be better served if they were left free to flourish in the market "prompted by the profit motive to supply essential services." It laid emphasis on the merit of unrestrained individualistic economic endeavours, independent of any sort of state interference. It does not tolerate any interference whatsoever by the institution of the state.[25] It aims at deregulating national economies, liberalising international trade, and creating a single global market.[26] The neo-liberal market-economy primarily focuses on economic growth and profit.[27] Given its exclusive concern for economic growth and profit, and insensitivities towards the rabid discriminatory social structures, will it be feasible for economic liberalisation to plough through the arid land of caste hierarchies and rampant social exclusion in India? Or would it further deepen inequalities, caste hierarchies and social exclusion by tightening caste-rope around the neck of the nascent institutions of social democracy? Would it also not delay, if not preclude, the often talked about trickle-down impact of the economic liberalisation on the lives of the multitudes of the Indian poor with a majority of them historically pushed to the margins? It is against this backdrop that the model of neo-liberal market-economy needs to be evaluated rather critically vis-à-vis the implications of the shrinking space of social democracy for the ongoing process of deepening of democracy in India.

In the tug of war between tradition and modernity, the forces of neo-liberalism quite interestingly seem to toe the line of the primordial and ascriptive institution of caste. They discriminate against the poor and the marginalised sections of the society. Neo-liberalism, thus, poses a serious challenge to the formation of social democracy in India. Neo-liberalism is often paraded as a custodian of enormous "opportunities," but what such "opportunities" are and whom they benefit is a question that directly concerns the Dalits. In an existential asymmetrical world, where we actually live, such opportunities, no doubt, open many doors to the *haves*. But it shuts door for the *have-nots*, a large majority of whom happen to be low castes, socially excluded, tribals, women, and other vulnerable sections of the society. The have-nots are the worst victims of the much-hyped regime of neo-liberal economic reforms.[28] Taking side with the lower caste victims of the "economics of market," which are mercilessly excluded from the business domain, social democracy compensates them in ensuring a respectable space in the "politics of democracy."[29] In other words, social democracy aims at overcoming the primordial and ascriptive hurdles in the way of arduous but steady march of liberal democracy. It is in this very context that Nehruvian perspective of social democracy in India becomes the most interesting and promising option.

Nehru: Beyond "isms"—a Prelude to Social Democracy

In the formative years of independent India, Jawaharlal Nehru effectively grappled with a queer dilemma of a tug of war between the protagonists of public and the private sectors.[30] Given the specific Indian social context, he preferred, however, a middle path between the two given models of economic development. Nehru was of the firm opinion that neither a purely public sector based economy nor an entirely private sector oriented model of development could help independent India get rid of its chronic poverty and entrenched inequalities. For him the real challenge was not only of distribution but also of growth which in turn is further hinged on particularly highly segmented social structures in the country. The opening lines of the First Five-Year Plan (1951-56), published by the Planning Commission under the chairmanship of Jawaharlal Nehru, emphasised that:

> ... the economic condition of a country at any given time is a product of the broader social environment, and economic planning has to be viewed as an integral part of a wider process aiming not merely at the development of resources in a narrow technical sense, but at the development of human faculties and the building up of an institutional framework adequate to the needs and aspirations of the people.[31]

Nehru was well aware of the need of creating an egalitarian society for the survival of liberal democracy in India. But at the same time he was equally fully convinced that in the absence of sufficient growth, the dream of an egalitarian society based on distributive justice was impossible to realise. He was of the firm view that in order to distribute equally amongst all, India must have enough wealth in the first place. It is in this context that Nehru reiterated the fact that welfare state and socialistic pattern of economy are not synonymous. To quote him at some length:

> It is true that a socialistic economy must provide for a Welfare State but it does not necessarily follow that a Welfare State must also be based on a socialistic pattern of society. Therefore the two, although they overlap, are yet somewhat different, and we say that we want both. We cannot have a Welfare State in India with all the socialism or even communism in the world unless our national income goes up greatly. Socialism or communism might help you to divide your existing wealth, if you like, but in India, there is no existing wealth for you to divide; there is only poverty to divide. It is not a question of distributing the wealth of the few rich men here and there. That is not going to make any difference in our national income. We might adopt that course for the psychological good that might come out of it. But from the practical point of view, there is not much to divide in India because we are a poor country. We must produce wealth, and then divide it equitably. How can we have a Welfare State without wealth? Wealth need not mean gold and silver but wealth in goods and services. Until very recently economic policies have often been based on scarcity. But the economics of scarcity has no meaning in the world of today.[32]

Thinking about the economically poor and socially stratified Indian society, Nehru was of the firm opinion that the choice was not between capitalism and socialism. It was not an either-or situation. He was well aware of the fact that the problems India was grappling with could not be tackled efficiently either by capitalism or socialism alone. The simultaneous challenge of achieving economic growth and an egalitarian social set-up made the choice rather problematic. Relying on both a rationalistic and scientific approach and an innovative way of mixed economy, Nehru was able to sail through the troubled waters rather smoothly. He was thoroughly convinced, as aptly argued by Appadorai:

> ... that any method which "delivered the goods" and gives satisfaction to the masses could be used to raise their living standard, and that method need not necessarily be an extreme method belonging to the school of capitalism or of socialism.[33]

The following quotation from Jawaharlal Nehru's Letters to Chief Ministers dated March 3, 1953 vindicates his preference for a mixed economy model:

> Indeed, I am inclined to think that in a democratic society, a so-called mixed economy is inevitable, though the public sector may grow and be the dominant partner. The private sector however will continue to have an important place, but the major industries would tend to be in the public sector. We have laid down that in a planned economy the private sector has to conform to the national plan and therefore has to be controlled to some extent. That appears to be obvious if we are to have any planning.[34]

Nehru knew well that Indian society was basically an unequal society based on the hierarchical principles of caste and deep-rooted social discrimination. For a democracy to survive in such a fragmented society, it has to reach its economic and social realms simultaneously. He argues that:

> The proper way is to have full democracy of not only political democracy but economic democracy. It should give an opportunity to large numbers of people to profit by the democratic method and to have more or less equal chances to progress. Political democracy should inevitably lead up to economic democracy. Even in countries which are supposed to be highly capitalistic the tendency to economic democracy is obvious. The tendency, in other words, is towards some form of socialism.[35]

As far as specific Indian social context is concerned, Nehru was of the opinion that:

> In the context of society today, the caste system and much that goes with it are wholly incompatible, reactionary, restrictive, and barriers to progress. There can be no equality in status and opportunity within its framework, nor can be political democracy and much

> less economic democracy. Between these two conceptions conflict is inherent and only one of them can survive.[36]

Thus for tackling the problem of a poor and caste-ridden society like India, the model that Jawaharlal Nehru chose for its overall development was based on a socialistic pattern of society with some tolerance towards the private sector. To quote him again at some length:

> The pattern of society that we look forward to is a socialist pattern of society which is classless, casteless. So far as the Congress is concerned, for a long time past, it has laid down its objectives as a casteless, classless society, which, obviously, can be attained only in a socialistic pattern. But I would beg of you not to imagine that because socialism conceives of nationalised industry, therefore you must have all industry nationalised. ... In regard to the public and the private sector, it is obvious that with the limited resources we have in the hands of the State, we cannot do all that we want to do at the present moment. We shall, of course, try to do as much as we can. But some people suggest that we must prevent the private sector from functioning in the field of industries. I do not understand this attitude. I want a socialist society in India. I want to get out of this framework of an acquisitive society, but I am not going to get it by merely passing resolutions and raising slogans. I want India to move in that direction, carrying a large number of people with it.[37]

The Nehruvian mixed economy model with an emphasis on the public sector received further legitimacy under the regime of Indira Gandhi.[38] As coherently argued by Steger and Roy, Indira Gandhi in fact:

> ... expanded her father's economic model by nationalising the largest banks and insurance companies as well as some energy industries. Deeply suspicious of free-market philosophies, she

> went on to nationalise a number of Indian subsidiaries of powerful multinational corporations such as Coca-Cola, in the process thwarting foreign direct investment for many years to come.[39]

It was during this fairly long socialist era (1947-84) in independent India that the institution of social democracy evolved to an extent that strengthened in turn what Nehru called the delicate plant of parliamentary democracy in the country.[40] However, since 1984 the mixed economy model started losing ground to what economist Arvind Panagariya has described as "liberalisation by stealth—1984-91"; and economist Jagdish Bhagwati as "reform by storm—1991 to the present."[41]

Thus it was in 1991 that eventually the Nehruvian mixed economy model came to be replaced by what is popularly known as the neo-liberal market-economy under the aegis of globalisation. It is in this context that the ambitious project of neo-liberal market-economy, based as it is on the rolling back of the state, not only obfuscates the mixed economy model of Jawaharlal Nehru but also inhibits the flow of state affirmative action to the direct detriment of social democracy in general and the multitude of Dalits in particular.[42] It entered India through "stealth" in the form of "statement" as against "resolution."[43] It focused primarily on delicensing, removal of import quotas, cutting down tariff levels, liberalisation of the inflow of foreign capital, capital goods, imported inputs, capital markets, industrial liberalisation, removal of MRTP constraints, opening of yet newer areas hitherto reserved for the public sector, tax concessions, voluntary retirement scheme, hidden closing of non-viable units, widespread use of contracted/casual labour, sub-contracting work to the small-scale sector, taming labour, etc.[44]

II

Nehru and the Dilemma of Social Democracy

Against the above discussed Nehruvian vision of social democracy and justice, the post-1990 period of neo-liberal economic reforms tends to side with the dominant and oppressive social structures of the historic caste system.[45] It blocks, albeit indirectly, the state affirmative action by squeezing the space occupied by the public sector under the mixed economy regime. As mentioned earlier, the neo-liberal market-economy model has been introduced primarily to end the fiscal crisis as well as to get rid of chronic poverty.[46] Whether the most sought after economic liberalisation project would be able to tackle the all-pervasive problem of poverty, in conjunction with the handling of fiscal crisis, without minimising the surging menace of caste, is indeed a serious challenge that India faces today. Another equally formidable challenge is whether it would be possible for social democracy, as it evolved within the Nehruvian model of mixed economy, to survive in the wake of an overall economic transformation on the patterns of neo-liberal market-economy. Economic liberalisation, caste and social democracy, thus become the most prominent challenges that contemporary India faces.

Among the above-mentioned core challenges that contemporary India faces, the challenge of economic liberalisation seems to be the latest, while that of the caste certainly remains the oldest. Social democracy, the third crucial challenge, figures in-between these two prominent challenges. However, it remained peripheral to the critical thinking of the builders of modern India. Although during the Indian freedom struggle a sharp division between the moderates and the extremists brought into focus the "social" aspect of colonial India, the "political," however, took precedence over the former after India won freedom. Ultimately, the form of democracy that India has come to acquire is a parliamentary (electoral) democracy that in fact was also implanted on Indian soil during the British rule. It did not evolve under natural conditions from within.[47] The social institution of caste happened to be very much alive even after the introduction of electoral democracy in the country.

Caste enjoys the dubious distinction of being the most perennial and complex phenomenon in the country. As an exclusionary social phenomenon, it has eclipsed the Indian (read Hindu) society for ages and continues to affect its social set-up, economy and polity even today.[48] Over the years, it has proved to be a stumbling block in the way of substantive democratisation from within. Both during the long spell of Muslim rule and the subsequent British Raj, the scourge of caste has expanded beyond imagination. In the post-colonial India, it assumed a new potent identity against its traditional hierarchised stance.[49] Articulating on the Indian social structure Jawaharlal Nehru wrote that caste system in India did not only survive "… the powerful impact of Buddhism and many centuries of Afghan and Mughal rule and the spread of Islam, but also the strenuous efforts of innumerable Hindu reformers who raised their voices against it."[50] Ironically, the constitution-based state affirmative action is often criticised on the grounds that it has further aided the institutionalisation of caste as a socio-political identity.[51] Given the widespread presence of the institution of caste, it is often said that the institutionalisation of periodic electoral processes on the one hand, and state affirmative action on the other, have further entrenched social stratification in the country. Thus, in the 1990s, when India allowed the private sector to flourish in a relatively unrestrained way to accelerate economic growth and to bridle widespread poverty, the chronic but ever present forces of caste-based social exclusion and inequalities once again resurfaced with rather a vengeance. It is often forgotten that the rolling back of the state accompanied by an unrestrained flow of global capital would not only widen the existing inequalities, but also subvert the incipient regimes of social democracy with serious implications for the ongoing processes of the deepening of democracy in a country like India.

Mixed Economy and the Deepening of Democracy

To sustain the transplanted sapling of democracy in India, Nehru adopted, as discussed above, mixed economy model of economic development. The mixed economy model provided space both to the public and private sectors. Nehru was of the firm opinion that for economic restructuring of a beleaguered post-colonial country like India, marked by various social disabilities, a solid economic foundation is a prerequisite for the sustainability of its hard earned freedom. He was equally aware of the need for a private sector under such hostile circumstances.

> The work of laying this solid foundation does not generally attract private industry because it does not pay for years to come. I am not talking about individuals. I am talking about the private industrialist in general. He would like a return on his capital within a year or two. In a country like India, the burden of development therefore falls on the Government. Of course, we welcome private capital and private enterprise, but, the responsibility for development, as I said, falls on Government. In a highly developed country like America, conditions are different. But in India it has become inevitable that if we have to build on solid foundations and go up, government must be party to it. The public sector thus becomes very important.[52]

Thus as far as economic planning was concerned, Nehru was pragmatic and rationalistic in his approach. He knew well that neither a tightly centralised nor a totally free market economy model would be suitable for the kind of development that independent India wanted to achieve in order to survive as a free, secular and democratic country. As argued by Guha:

> Nehru's economic philosophy was more complex than is sometimes supposed—for instance, he saw planning as necessary not merely to augment productivity, but also to overcome the sectarian affiliations of caste, language and religion.[53]

For Nehru any progress that does not include the millions of poor in the country is not progress at all. For him:

> [p]rogress does not ultimately consist of merely industrial enterprise. That is only a symbol of it. Progress ultimately has to be measured by the quality of human beings—how they are

> improving, how their lot is improving, and how they are adapting themselves to modern ways and yet keep their feet firmly planted on their soil.[54]

And for realising such a vision, economic development has to focus on social equality and distributive justice in a country like India beset with varied social maladies and chronic poverty. While deliberating on the Hindu Code Bill, in one of his Letters to Chief Ministers dated October 4, 1951, Nehru observed that:

> For my part, I am convinced that progress in India must be on all fronts—political, economic and social. Unless this happens, we shall get held up. Some people think that we should keep the social aspect apart and concentrate on the political and economic. There can be no division. Our social organisation has shown both virtues and vices in the past. It has also displayed an amazing cohesion and continuity. It has also progressively weakened the political and economic set-up, apart from other consequences in the social domain. Whatever its virtues might have been in the past, it is clear that major changes are required in the present.[55]

It is in the context mentioned above that social democracy becomes a prerequisite for the survival of parliamentary democracy in India.

III

Bringing Nehru Back In: Rescuing Market from Caste

The new paradigm of neo-liberal market-economy fails to sustain the Nehruvian vision of all-round progress. On the contrary, it tends to strengthen the existing dominant structures of power in society by nurturing a close relationship with the institution of caste. Caste and market seem to reinforce each other. Markets thrive on capital and profit. Since capital has traditionally been accumulated largely by the upper castes, the free market-economy reinforces the hold of upper caste-business classes only.[56] It bestows upper castes with enormous opportunities and hefty profits. But it ignores the dalits who were historically denied access to capital. Earlier the dalits were denied all sorts of access to capital in the name of caste backed with sacred scriptures. Now they are denied access in the corridors of the free market-economy in the name of capital and technical know-how. It is in this context that the dialectics of inverse relationship between democracy and untouchability and the complementarity between market and caste assumes critical importance for the understanding of the impact of neo-liberal market-economy on the day-to-day lives of the Dalits in general and the structures of social democracy in particular.

What I wanted to argue over here is that the neo-liberal market-economy model adopted by India in the beginning of the 1990s inclined to run in the opposite direction of what Jawaharlal Nehru cherished under his innovative model of mixed economy. In the fast recourse to economic reforms, the welfare ethos of the Indian state was allowed to be ignored. In the frantic search for a viable solution to the steeping fiscal crisis, the Indian ruling establishment seems to have adopted economic reforms without properly weighing their serious implications for the Nehruvian vision of mixed economy.[57]

The neo-liberal economic reforms thus complicated the existing contradictions between caste and democracy in contemporary India. What further complicates the process of deepening of democracy in India is the intermeshing of caste and poverty. The problem of chronic poverty in India does not seem to be merely an economic issue. It has equally been rooted in the asymmetrical social structures of ethnicity, caste and religion,[58] which in turn, "defy every norm of democratic justice."[59] It is against this backdrop that the status of Dalits who have been pushed to the bottom of the social hierarchy in Indian society needs to be examined rather more critically in the wake of the implementation of neo-liberal economic reforms. The bulk of Dalit population in India falls in the category of below poverty line. A majority of the Dalit population continues to live in:

> ... extreme poverty without land or opportunities for better employment or education. With the exception of a minority who have benefited from India's policy of quotas in education and government jobs, Dalits are relegated to the most menial of tasks, as manual scavengers, removers of human waste and dead animals, leather workers, street sweepers, and cobblers. Dalit children make up the majority of those sold into bondage to pay off debts to upper caste creditors. Dalit men, women, and children numbering in the tens of millions work as agricultural labourers for a few kilograms of rice or Rs. 15 to Rs. 35 (US $0.38 to $0.88) a day.[60]

The relationship between caste and poverty seems to be of symbiotic nature. They reinforce each other while posing a serious challenge to the nascent institution of social democracy in India. The inextricably intertwined phenomena of caste and poverty is so well entrenched that it has failed to recede even after the adoption of measures of economic reform in India in 1991. On the contrary, the latter has further been strengthening the anti-democracy nexus between caste and poverty in the country. The capital intensive and profit driven model of neo-liberal market-economy has, in fact, not only flared up the old, dormant caste contradictions in India, but also given rise to the new ones between Dalits and various "Backward and Other Backward Classes" that have mushroomed in the post-Mandal era. Though the neo-liberal market-economy has been promising to provide ample space to the socially excluded sections of society, by opening new and unrestrained opportunities for them in the fast emerging domain of free market-economy in India, the reality is the other way round. The neo-liberal free market-economy has failed to ward off the contagious effect of the hoary and exclusionary institution of caste in India. Untouchability and democracy are antithetical. Democracy is totally negated in the scheme of untouchability. Democracy is premised on the liberal principles of freedom, equality and fraternity. On the contrary, untouchability thrives amidst inequality and denial of human rights. It promotes social segregation and denies freedom to the socially excluded sections of society. It rests on asymmetrical social structures of difference and domination that preclude impulses and assertions of democracy. It is at this crucial juncture of vendetta between democracy and untouchability that the institution of free market-economy enters into the whirlpool of caste contradictions in the social set-up of the country.

In the tug of war between democracy and the constitutionally rendered illegal institution of untouchability, the forces of the free market-economy have sided with the latter. They strengthen the hands of the capital rich upper castes by making it almost impossible for the capital-starved dalits to participate in the glamorous domain of finance capital. Since capital lies mostly with the upper castes, it is only they who matter the most in the multiplexes/malls of the new market-economy. It is only the most affluent whom the market has been pushing into billionaires.[61] There is hardly anyone from the ex-untouchables communities in India who has joined the elite club of billionaires. Thus market does not only favour the upper castes, it also accentuates the gulf between the rich and the poor. Since poor and lower castes are co-terminus, market further marginalises the lower castes by preventing them from entering into business operations.

If the practice of untouchability debarred the dalits from the public sphere, the free market-economy has discouraged them from entering into the domain of business. If the former had restricted the spheres of "public" or the "social" to the upper-caste privileged few, the latter seems to have mortgaged the entire economic domain of the country to the upper castes only. Market has elevated a few upper castes and degraded many socially excluded lower castes. Quite interestingly, untouchability and free market-economy join together in favouring the upper castes with immense wealth/privileges as against the lower castes who, in spite of working hard, have to live a life of abject poverty and severe deprivations. This in turn deprives them (lower castes) substantially of the periodic opportunities to compete for power berth in the electoral bogies of political democracy in the country. Elections over the years, in fact, have become very costly affairs. They are beyond the reach of the poor and socially excluded sections of society. Thus social exclusion and poverty deprive the lower castes of the opportunity to compete on an equal footing with their rich and upper-caste rivals in the exorbitantly costly and limited electoral arena of political democracy in India.

It is in this overarching context of social democracy that the responsibility and the task of safeguarding the developmental character of the Indian state, especially with regard to the empowerment of Dalits, becomes very crucial. Jawaharlal Nehru articulated, much in advance, the serious implications of the lopsided development for the growth of social democracy in a caste-ridden country like India. He therefore underlined the inclusion of the downtrodden into the governmental set-up of the country by adopting a mixed economy model of development. He warned against the incompetence of the private sector in steering the ship of the economic development of the country on its own. Instead Nehru laid emphasis on the public sector while keeping the private sector well within the control of the government.[62] In other words, a balance needs to be created between the forces of market and the principles of social justice. It is in this context that Jawaharlal Nehru's concern for "full-fledged, full-blooded democracy with adult suffrage" becomes highly important. To quote him:

> When you have political democracy of that type, you are inevitably pushed to what might be called economic democracy. There is no escape from it. Full-fledged political democracy means, progressively, what might broadly be called economic democracy.[63]

Economic liberalisation regimes in India can no longer ignore the stark realities of unequal and discriminatory patterns of social life and chronic poverty. Any attempt to work out the economy in isolation of the hard-core social realities would have serious and far-reaching implications not only for polity and society but also for the economy in the long run. It is in this context that the project of economic liberalisation needs to be understood, in consonance with the complex "social" and "political" context of the Indian economy. To get rid of centuries-old caste-based social discriminations, exclusion and chronic poverty of millions of downtrodden in India, the ambitious project of economic liberalisation, perhaps, needs to be clubbed together with another equally ambitious project aiming at total transformation of the entire gamut of Hindu social order; thoroughly cleaning its long accumulated muck of caste and social exclusion. Can economic liberalisation alone help generate new avenues for rapid economic growth and equal opportunities ("growth with redistribution" or "capitalism with a human face") for all in a society like India marked by rampant social hierarchies and inequalities? This is an urgent and critical issue that needs serious attention. And it is in this context that the economic and political philosophy of Jawaharlal Nehru still appears relevant. Nehru's middle path for economic growth along with social equality might have failed to achieve not even one-third of the economic growth that we have witnessed in the post-1991 era. But the emphasis placed by Nehru on achieving economic growth with social equality becomes more relevant today. Failure to engage with the Nehruvian vision of all-round development in the era of neo-liberalism is likely to result in further perpetuation of chronic poverty and inequalities leading to social unrest and political violence, with the downtrodden and the marginalised becoming the worst victims.

Notes

1. For divergent accounts of the controversial issue of the beginning of economic reforms in India, see De Long, 2003; Hatekar and Dingre, 2005; Nagaraj, 2000; Nayar, 2006; Rodrik and Subramanian, 2004; Panagariya, 2004; Virmani, 2004; McCartney, 2009.
2. The term "Dalit" is used in this paper as a social category that incorporates the Scheduled Castes (SCs), the Scheduled Tribes (STs), and the Other Backward Castes (OBCs)—constitutional categories referring to socially excluded and economically backward sections of Indian society. However, in the current political discourse, the term Dalit is mainly confined to the SCs only. To be more precise, it covers only those SCs who are classified as Hindus, Sikhs and Buddhists but excludes Muslim and Christian Dalits. A majority of the Dalits belonged to the poorest people's category in India (Thorat, 2010).
3. Democracy in India is conceptualised as variedly as political democracy, liberal

democracy, parliamentary democracy, constitutional democracy, formal/ institutional democracy, procedural democracy, etc. In the present essay, however, Indian democracy is referred to as liberal democracy. Meyer and Hinchman define liberal democracy as "a pluralistic regime that respects human rights and abides by the rule of law" (Meyer and Hinchman, 2007: 2).

4. Thomas Meyer and Lewis P. Henchman (2007), *The Theory of Social Democracy* (Cambridge: Polity Press, 2007), p. 2. For detailed accounts of social democracy, see Callaghan, 2002; Callaghan, 2000; Gray, 1996; Hicks, 2001; Hirst, 1996; Huber and Stephens, 1998; Lipset, 1959; Lipset, 1994; Merkel, 2002; Milner, 1989; Pontusson, 1992; Przeworski, 1992; Rothstein, 1996; Rothstein, 2002; Thomson, 2002; Vanderbroucke, 1998; Vivekanandan, 2000.
5. Ibid.
6. Ibid., p. 229.
7. Ibid., p. 234.
8. Ibid., p. 1.
9. Edward Bernstein, *Evolutionary Socialism: A Criticism and Affirmation* (originally published in German in 1899 and first published in English in 1909. Reprint, New York: Schocken Books, 1961. See also, Sheri Berman, "The Roots and Rationale of Social Democracy," *Social Philosophy and Policy*, vol. 20, no. 1, 2003, pp. 113-44.
10. John Callaghan, "Social Democracy and Globalisation: The Limits of Social Democracy in Historical Perspective," *British Journal of Politics and International Relations*, vol. 4, no. 3, October 2002, pp. 432-36; and Richard Sandbrook et al., *Social Democracy in the Global Periphery: Origins, Challenges, Prospects* (Cambridge: Cambridge University Press, 2007), p. 12, and also see Donald Sassoon, *One Hundred Years of Socialism: The West European Left in the Twentieth Century* (London: Fontana, 1997), p. 42.
11. Seymour M. Lipset, "Some Social Requisites of Democracy: Economic Development and Political Legitimacy," *American Political Science Review* 53 (1), 1959, pp. 69-105 and Seymour M. Lipset, "The Social Requisites of Democracy Revisited," *American Sociological Review* 59, 1994, pp. 1-22.
12. Manmohan Singh, "Relevance of the Global Experience of Social Democracy for India," November 20, 2010, p. 1. http://indiacurrentaffairs.org/relevance-of-the-global-experience-of-social-democracy-for-in, accessed January 2, 2011.
13. Jawaharlal Nehru, *Letters to Chief Ministers 1947-1964*, vol. 2: 1950-1952, G. Parthasarhi, General Editor (Delhi: Oxford University Press, 1986), p. 502.
14. "Three Historical Addresses of Babasaheb Ambedkar in the Constituent Assembly: In Search of Remedies for Current Instability of Polity" (New Delhi: B. R. Ambedkar Foundation Research Cell, 1999), pp. 53-54.
15. Sukhamoy Chakravarty, "Nehru and Indian Planning," *South Asia Research*, vol. 9, no. 2, November, 1989, pp. 95-101.
16. The First Five-Year Plan, Planning Commission: Government of India, 1952, p. 1.
17. Manmohan Singh, n. 12, p. 1.
18. Meghnad Desai, "Equality or Inclusion: The Dilemma of India's Democracy," Chandan Sengupta and Stuart Corbridge (eds.), *Democracy, Development and Decentralisation in India* (New Delhi: Routledge, 2010), p. 10.

19. "Three Historical Addresses of Babasaheb Ambedkar ..." n. 14, p. 53.
20. The Protection of Civil Rights (Anti-Untouchability) Act of 1955 and later on under the Scheduled Castes/Scheduled Tribes (Prevention of Atrocities) Act of 1989.
21. Ghanshyam Shah, et al., *Untouchability in Rural India*, New Delhi, 2006.
22. Meghnad Desai, n. 18, p. 9.
23. K. S. Jacob, "Caste and Inequalities in Health," *The Hindu*, August 22, 2009.
24. S. Gurumurthy, "Is Caste an Economic Development Vehicle?" *The Hindu*, January 1, 2009.
25. Manfred B. Steger and Ravi K. Roy, *Neoliberalism: A Very Short Introduction* (Oxford: Oxford University Press, 2010).
26. Ibid., p. x.
27. Economic liberalisation is primarily concerned with the problems of economic domain. It is not concerned with what transpires within the political sphere of democratic regimes. For a detailed account, see Dreze and Sen, 1995; Bhaduri and Nayyar, 1996; and Nayyar, 2007: pp. 388-89.
28. S. R. Ahlawat (ed.), *Economic Reforms and Social Transformation* (New Delhi: Rawat Publications), 2008.
29. For "economics of market" and "politics of democracy" phrases, I am indebted to Deepak Nayyar (Nayyar 2007: pp. 362-69).
30. *Jawaharlal Nehru's Speeches*, vol. III (New Delhi, Government of India: The Publications Division, Ministry of Information and Broadcasting, 1958), pp. 12-18, 62; and S. Gopal and Uma Iyengar (eds.), *The Essential Writings of Jawaharlal Nehru* (New Delhi: Oxford University Press, 2003), pp. 170-71
31. The First Five-Year Plan, n. 16, p. 7.
32. *Jawaharlal Nehru's Speeches*, n. 30, pp. 17-18.
33. A. Appadorai, *Essays in Politics and International Relations* (New Delhi: Asia Publishing House, 1969), p. 38.
34. Ramachandra Guha (ed.), *Makers of Modern India* (New Delhi: Penguin, 2010), p. 339.
35. *Jawaharlal Nehru's Speeches*, vol. IV (New Delhi, Government of India: The Publications Division, Ministry of Information and Broadcasting, 1966), pp. 150-52.
36. Jawaharlal Nehru, *The Discovery of India* (Calcutta, Signet Press, 1946), p. 270.
37. *Jawaharlal Nehru's Speeches*, n. 30, pp. 12-13.
38. Rahul Mukherji, "Introduction: The State and Private Initiative in India," in Rahul Mukherji (ed.), *India's Economic Transition: The Politics of Reforms* (New Delhi: Oxford University Press, 2007), p. 9; and Atul Kohli, "Politics of Economic Growth in India, 1980-2005, Part II: The 1990s and Beyond," *Economic and Political Weekly*, April 8, 2006, pp. 1361-70.
39. Manfred B. Steger and Ravi K. Roy, n. 25, p. 92.
40. *Jawaharlal Nehru's Speeches*, n. 30, p. 157 and John P. Lewis, *India's Political Economy: Governance and Reform* (New Delhi: Oxford University Press, 1997), pp. 73-78.
41. Manfred B. Steger and Ravi K. Roy, n. 25, p. 91; see also, Lewis 1997: Chapters II-IV.
42. Amit Bhaduri, "A Failed World View," *Economic and Political Weekly*, January

31, 2009, pp. 35-39; and Amit Bhaduri and Deepak Nayyar, *The Intelligent Person's Guide to Liberalization* (New Delhi: Penguin Books, 1996); Sukhadeo Thorat and Nidhi Sadana, "Caste and Ownership of Private Enterprises," *Economic and Political Weekly*, vol. 44, no. 23, June 6, 2009, pp. 13-16; K. S. Chalam, "Caste and Economic Reforms," Seminar 471, November 1998, pp. 33-37.

43. Atul Kohli, "Politics of Economic Growth in India, 1980-2005, Part II: The 1990s and Beyond," *Economic and Political Weekly*, April 8, 2006, p. 1363 and Rob Jenkins, *Democratic Politics and Economic Reforms in India* (Cambridge: Cambridge University Press, 1999).
44. Matthew MacCartney, "'Episodes' or 'Evolution': The Genesis of Liberalisation in India," *Journal of South Asian Development*, vol. 4, no. 2, 2009, pp. 212-13; Atul Kohli, n. 43, pp. 1361-1363.
45. Before the Indian economy could actually open its gates to the surging tides of world market-economy, the study of economic liberalisation had already deepened its roots in the domain of social sciences in the country. However, in terms of content and scope, neo-liberalism is yet to enter mainstream political sociology with a vast body of pertinent literature confined to the discipline of economics (cf. Bardhan, 2007: 397). It rarely focuses on the intricate but often neglected relationship between caste and economy as well as contradictions between the emerging structures of neo-liberal market-economy and the nascent institutions of social democracy (see also Basu, 2010: xvi; Thorat and Newman, 2010: 7).
46. Montek S. Ahluwalia, "Economic Reforms in India Since 1991: Has Gradualism Worked?" *Journal of Economic Perspectives*, vol. 16, no. 3, 2002, pp. 67-88.
47. Ashutosh Varshney, "India's Democratic Challenge," *Foreign affairs*, vol. 86. no. 2, 2007, pp. 93-94.
48. Barbara Harriss-White, *India's Market Society: Three Essays in Political Economy* (New Delhi: Three Essays Collective, 2005), pp. 67-149.
49. Clarinda Still, "From Militant Rejection to Pragmatic Consensus: Caste among Madigas in Andhra Pradesh," *Journal of South Asian Development* 4:1, 2009, pp. 7-23.
50. Jawaharlal Nehru, n. 36, pp. 258-59.
51. Atul Kohli, "Introduction," in Atul Kohli (ed.), *The Success of India's Democracy* (New Delhi: Foundation Books, 2002), p. 17.
52. *Jawaharlal Nehru's Speeches*, n. 30, p. 62.
53. Ramachandra Guha, n. 34, p. 335.
54. Jawaharlal Nehru as quoted in Stephen Hay, edited and revised, *Sources of Indian Tradition: Vol. II—Modern India and Pakistan*, 2/e (New Delhi: Penguin, 1991), p. 351.
55. Jawaharlal Nehru, n. 13, p. 502.
56. Aseem Parkash, "Caste and Capitalism," *Seminar* 633, May 2012, pp. 68-71.
57. Amit Bhaduri, "A Failed World View," *Economic and Political Weekly*, January 31, 2009, pp. 38-39.
58. George Akerlof, "The Economics of Caste, the Rat Race and Other Woeful Tales," *Quarterly Journal of Economics*, vol. XC, no. 4, 1976, pp. 599-617; B. R. Ambedkar, *Annihilation of Caste, Jalandhar: Bheem Patrika*, 1995 (first published in 1936); Deepak Lal, *Hindu Equilibrium*, vol. I, *Cultural Stability*

and Economic Stagnation (Oxford: Clarendon Press, 1988); James G. L. Scoville, "Towards a Model of Caste Economy," in James G. L. Scoville (ed.), *Status Influences in Third World Labour Markets: Caste, Gender and Custom* (New York: Walter de Gruyter, 1991), pp. 386-93; Amit Thorat, "Ethnicity, Caste and Religion: Implications for Poverty Outcomes, *Economic and Political Weekly*, vol. 45, no. 51, December 18-24, 2010. Sukhadeo Thorat and Katherine S. Newman (eds.), *Blocked by Caste: Economic Discrimination in Modern India* (New Delhi: Oxford University Press, 2010).

59. Javeed Alam, *Who Wants Democracy?* (Hyderabad: Orient Longman, 2004), p. xvii.
60. Human Rights Watch 1999. *Broken People: Caste Violence against India's Untouchables* (New York, 1999), p. 2; Sukhadeo Thorat, "How Socially Inclusive Has Growth Been? Growth, Inequality and Poverty during 1983/2005—Implications for Inclusive Policy," *Presidential Address at 93rd Annual Conference of the Indian Economic Association*, December 27-29 (Chandigarh: Panjab University, 2010), pp. 3-53.
61. Harish Damodaran, *India's New Capitalists: Caste, Business, and Industry in a Modern India* (Ranikhet: Permanent Black, 2008), pp. 13-16; Suneet Chopra, "Neo-Liberalism and Social Justice," *People's Democracy*, vol. 32, no. 6, July 6, 2008, p. 3. http://pd.cpim.org/2008/0706_pd/07062008_15.htm, accessed on January 14, 2011.
62. S. Gopal and Uma Iyengar (eds.), *The Essential Writings of Jawaharlal Nehru* (New Delhi: Oxford University Press, 2003), pp. 170-71.
63. *Jawaharlal Nehru's Speeches*, n. 30, p. 60.

8

Nation-Building, Natural Resources and Regional Development in India: Revisiting the Nehruvian Vision

Ambrish Dhaka

The first Prime Minister of India, Jawaharlal Nehru, in his maiden speech on the eve of Indian independence pledged that every Indian should think of giving himself to the service of the country. What he meant by service was to serve the millions of Indians who bore suffering in the process of securing freedom. This freedom, most importantly, also meant the end of poverty, ignorance, disease and inequality of opportunity. Another most important objective which Nehru kept reminding the people was the need for the right kind of environment in the country that would offer opportunity for increasing the production. It not only hurt each one's freedom but also was the big hurdle in ameliorating the economic problems of the masses. Nehru underlined that freedom and power bring responsibility, and it is up to this sovereign body, the Constituent Assembly, that proves itself worthy of taking up the challenge.[1] The vision of Nehru could be termed as philanthropist when he said about Mahatma Gandhi that his ambition was to wipe every tear from every eye, and let this be our enduring objective in order to build this country. He dreamt of India, but also of the extended mankind. He believed that all nations and peoples are closely knit and that one cannot remain unaffected by the good and the bad that happens to us or others. He moved the pledge in the Assembly with the sense of dedication that would let attain India her rightful place in world, and with the duty to the promotion of the welfare of mankind.[2] The initiative taken for building India was itself an act that revealed his experience and ability to do so. He had strong faith in what one should see clearly through the objectives that one wishes to attain and also the methods one should employ to achieve them. Any mismatch is one of the elemental failures that are often lost sight of. The agonies of partition and the assassination of Gandhi took a heavy toll in his mind and trust, but he did not relent and, in fact, even broadened his commitment to the cause of rebuilding. His focus was on how to bring about conditions for development by establishing peace and harmony in society. He believed that no development can be ensured unless the there is trust and stability in the production process, which could only be guaranteed by an assured environment. Communal violence not only downgraded these capabilities, but also created difficulties in altering the antiquated tenure system and bringing industrialisation to the countryside. One of the important delineations he made was the vicious circle of poverty, communalism and its expression in numerous conflict situations. He stated that "communalism threatened to crush the free spirit in us, the communalism of the Muslim, of the Hindu and of the Sikh."[3] In like manner, the feeling of provincialism hurt the larger unity of India. The sole rectitude that could come through this quagmire was from the traditions of democracy. The essence of democracy is tolerance, he asked for tolerance not only amongst those who agreed, but even from those who did not agree. Therefore, he advocated the sustained practice of self-discipline, hard work and the spirited attitude towards freedom for all. He viewed global peace as the ultimate goal of all international relations; this he sought as well with the neighbours in the region. The only war he wished to fight was the war against poverty.

Nehru defined a twofold strategy to attain economic change by addressing the natural resource utilisation in a major way that would bring huge economies of scale and enable the surpluses to be invested for greater economic wealth. Secondly, he was also particular about the vast mankind which hardly had any training that could be utilised for this cause. No doubt nation-building amidst these challenges was a herculean task, and the leader knew that empty speeches would not do all. The nation needed material growth so as to include every section of society that could be assuaged in terms of share of the larger Indian pie. With his vision and deeds in mind, this paper attempts to analyse the situation India is facing today. Second phase of nation-building, whether one calls it Bharat Nirman or the "shining" India, one is reminded of the analogy of challenges that present-day intellectuals of the country face. There are even greater challenges of communalism and provincialism, which are in cocktail with terrorism and economic corruption of a very large order. An important area of debate lies within the realm of nation-building and the reason why Nehru chose to direct it. Dichotomy is often seen in terms of the Nehruvian versus Gandhian approaches to "post-colonial" India. The Nehruvian approach is defined with the focus on heavy industrialisation and capital-intensive development. The Gandhian approach is characterised by rural based, decentralised and small-scale labour-intensive development. The second aspect of the dichotomy is seen as Nehru's aim at addressing the international community of nations whereas Gandhi's vision is linked to internal, introspective grass-roots societal change. The dichotomy lies in the inevitability of both the objectives. The requirement of resources was needed at both the ends but how to go about it has been the subject of the debate.[4]

There was an element of unity amongst the two and both cherished the idea of *Swadeshi* and indigenisation of development. The extra emphasis that Nehru laid was on the nationalist perspective of development. He said, "I have no doubt that we do not raise the people's level of existence without the development of major industries in the country. In fact I will go further and say that we cannot even remain a free country without them. Certain things like adequate defence are essential to freedom and these cannot be had unless we develop industry in a major way."[5] Nehru had embraced the ideals of John Stuart Mill which said that "no great improvements in the lot of mankind are possible unless a great change takes place in the fundamental constitution of their modes of thought."[6] Nehru also believed that "for a hungry man or a hungry woman, truth has little meaning. He wants food. And India is a hungry, starving country and to talk of truth and good and even of many of the fine things of life to the millions who are starving is a mockery. We have to find food for them, clothing, housing, education, health and so on—all the absolute necessities of life that every man should possess ... so science must think in terms of the 400 million persons of India."[7]

The third vital dimension of Nehru's vision was his ideological disposition towards the harmonising blend of socialism and capitalism. A mixed economy was one of the key precepts of Nehru's idea of developing India. According to him, the "free enterprise will never appeal to the masses of our people. It will lead to the use of our resources often for purposes that are not of primary importance. It will mean the exploitation of the profit in which the individual may be interested but not society as a whole."[8] He put forth in the parliamentary debate on the Second Five-Year Plan argued in March 1956 that in "an unplanned free enterprise approach ... progress will be lopsided. We can put up factories here and there, but it will result only in riches here and greater poverty there."[9]

Nehru's Ideas about Resources and Development

The ideas needed implementation and Nehru knew what is the most needed. The planning process was the most urgent need in order to gallop into the array of high developing societies. He believed that through planning he could attain multiple objectives nailing the myriad challenges simultaneously. The poverty stricken masses could not generate enough savings to invest and upgrade their lifestyles, therefore planning would help create mass public goods that would enhance their capabilities. The rich class, which is profit-minded, if provided with infrastructure, would be willing to share a part of it to enhance the potential of state and society building. Thus, state intervention would help in addressing the overall growth of the economy and address the problem of distributive justice. He stated that one needs "to avoid large concentration of wealth in individual hands. Such a concentration is bad for society even though that wealth may sometimes be used for good purposes ... absence of state control means cut-throat competition, chaos and disaster."[10] This fear of getting out of communal chaos and soon landing into capitalist chaos was very much in the mind of Nehru, therefore he suitably softened his policies by introducing socialist pattern of production with assimilation of private capital. A mixed economy most suited a country like India which had a vibrant and globally conscious middle class and nationalist entrepreneurial class. The task of allocation of resources between the rich and the poor, and between the individual and the community was to be a very judicious one. Nehru knew that the socio-economic scenario of the country at the time of independence needed an urgent solution to this. The allocation of resources through planning process seemed to him the only way out.

The role of natural resources in national growth was envisaged by Nehru as he attached greater importance to river valley projects. He believed if the vast hydel potential of the Himalayas could be optimally harnessed then the economic transform that is desired could be achieved. Hence, energy as a fundamental requisite for accelerated economic growth is essential. Minerals are equally important for the extension of industrial activity. All these required careful thinking which could only be realised through planning process. Thus, Planning Advisory Board and the

Five-Year Plans (FYP) became the bedrock of the nation-building process through which proper harnessing of natural resources was made possible. The Planning Commission was set up in March 1950 as a part of the Directive Principles of State Policy. One of the principal goals of the Commission was to formulate the Plan for the most effective and balanced utilisation of the country's resources.

Nehru's vision got ample focus in the First Five-Year Plan. The plan elucidates, "the rivers have had a powerful influence on national and local life."[11] It goes on to say that "an integrated development of the land and water resources of India is of fundamental importance to the country's economy."[12] The First FYP also delineated that there is need to have a countrywide hydrographic survey. The Central Water Commission was established for the purpose in 1945. The Ministry of Irrigation and Power was created as early as in 1951 under the name of the Ministry of National Resources and Scientific Research. Later, a separate Ministry of Irrigation and Power was set up in August 1952 to look after the subject of irrigation as well as power. In 1969, an Irrigation Commission was set up to look into the scope for future irrigation development programmes in the country in a comprehensive manner. Institutions such as the Central Water Commission (CWC) are one of the earliest efforts to optimise riverine development in terms of regional planning and economic growth. The underpinning idea of the designing organisations is that one needs rapid growth to provide the basis for expanding incomes and employment and also to provide the resources needed to finance programmes for social uplift. This is further addressed by the issue of distribution so that its benefits in terms of income and employment are adequately shared by the poor and weaker sections of our society, especially the Scheduled Castes (SCs) and Scheduled Tribes (STs), Other Backward Classes (OBCs) and minorities.[13]

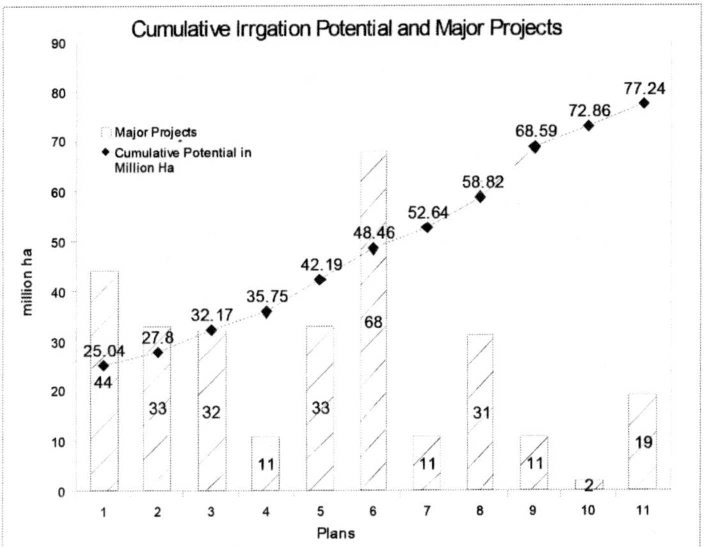

Source: Planning Commission, Government of India, 12th Five-Year Plan, Vol. 1, Chapter 5. (Accessed from http://planningcommission.nic.in.plans/planrel/fiveyr/12thplan/pdf/12fyp.vol.pdf. pp.144-90).

The second aspect of river water resources has been the generation of hydroelectricity through turbines. In fact, the share of hydroelectricity had been quite significant in the initial years of development. The Nehruvian vision was apparent in the forward thinking that was seen in terms of future potential. The First FYP mentions the potential use of vegetation derived fuels that can be used "until atomic power and solar energy come into the field." The first ever estimation survey was done in 1919 for hydel power potential, which indicated 3.5 million kW as the realisable potential. The idea of expansion of electricity to rural areas gained popularity as it would be possible to quickly increase agricultural output. Creation of river valley planning that could be the basis of agrarian planning was the key spirit of the First FYP. This was undoubtedly Nehru's idea. Nehru believed that hydroelectric power would be the big push to India's dream of development. He said, "this Himalayan range, with its rivers, minerals and other resources ... could transform the whole of India with exceeding rapidity."[14] He attached more importance to big river valley schemes, dams, reservoirs, hydro and thermal electric power for the necessary drive. The tale of the Indian hydropower has not been all that glorious. Only around 17 per cent of the total potential has been harnessed till 2002. The hydroelectric potential of the country is estimated at 600 billion kWh. The long gestation period in the erection of structure and environmental clearance, rehabilitation and resettlement issues have often restrained its speedy implementation.

Planning for the Future

India is endowed with the latest technological advances that have been ongoing as a perennial process of river valley development, which Nehru had envisioned as a programme for constant pursuit and monitor. The Department of Science and Technology (DST) now has taken the lead in providing a new kind of technological input that has revolutionised the planning of river valley projects, namely, Remote Sensing and Geographic Information Systems. Today no country can visualise its regional planning and balanced growth without it. One can gaze at the salient features of these novel approaches and how we have progressed in the overall approach to river valley development, an idea which was so dear to Jawaharlal Nehru. The second generation of resource appraisal came with the Indian Space Research Organisation's (ISRO) success in cost-efficient remote sensing techniques that provided all the national wealth in a plotted format that could be estimated with great accuracy. Remote sensing is actually one of the front-end techniques that are used in early warning generation systems, prognostic modelling, resources mapping, geographic information systems and all such appraisal of natural resources that are vital to our national growth.

Satellite data are of several types and are valued according to their resolution and sensing techniques. The Indian remote sensing programme began with the launch of the IRS series of satellites since March 1988, with the launch of IRS-1A. Later on the IRS-1 series came to end with 1D being launched in September 1997. The P series is on the run now, with IRS-P5 and P6 being launched for high-resolution images. The resolution is as high as 2.5 metres in case of IRS-P5. The National Remote Sensing Centre (NRSC), Hyderabad is engaged in the application of IRS data "for a diverse range of applications such as crop acreage and production estimation of major crops, drought monitoring and assessment based on vegetation condition, flood risk zone mapping and flood damage assessment, hydro-geomorphological maps for locating underground water resources, irrigation command area status monitoring, snow melt run-off estimation, land use and land cover mapping, urban planning, biodiversity characterisation, forest survey, wetland mapping, environmental impact analysis, mineral prospecting, coastal studies, integrated surveys for developing sustainable action plans and so on."[15]

The challenges in the realm of energy security are no less in terms of resource optimisation. The growth of import bill due to fluctuating crude oil prices and the increasing demand for natural gas in various sectors of the economy have raised the dependency on the global oil and gas market. India's energy is from non-commercial sources such as, agricultural waste, cattle dung and fuelwood as much as 60 per cent in 1960-61, which has not reduced much in the 1980s with roughly 40 per cent still being derived from it. The planning process initiated by Nehru had taken ample consideration in this regard and India's peaceful nuclear energy programme was his brainchild which he wished to see grow. The vast thorium deposits have been quite suitable for the generation of electricity. The technology denial by the West prompted him to set up the National Physical Laboratories (NPLs) which were aimed at rapidly catching up with the scientific progress made by others in vital areas of societal contribution. The seeds Nehru sowed during his time are now paying India rich dividends, and one finds that his timely thought out priorities have enabled India to survive several challenges during the post-independence and post-Nehruvian periods.

Conclusion

Nehru spoke of the importance of all these ideas in his speech on new economic policy delivered at the Constituent Assembly. It was a historic speech outlining the developmental vision of India. In fact, the resolution moved by Kazi Syed Karimuddin said that "this country shall be a socialist economy based on the principle of nationalisation of key industries and cooperative and collective farming and socialisation of the material resources of the country."[16] The nationalisation of banks and key industries was just another side of the coin, which maintained national ownership of natural resources through giant schemes. The river valley projects actually meant to collectivise agricultural production in terms of equal opportunity to produce more and thereby ameliorate the precarious food security situation at the time of independence. This was the time when projects like Bhakra-Nangal Dam in 1959—the highest gravity dam in the world—and Hirakud Dam in 1956—the longest in the world—got completed. The Colombo Plan was initiated for supplying manpower for the completion of the Damodar Valley Project catering to the needs of Bihar and Bengal. The First FYP undertook the building of four big dams, namely, Tilaiya, Konar, Maithon and Panchet Hill, and a barrage at Durgapur. The Damodar Valley Corporation, modelled after the Tennessee Valley Authority (TVA), and the Tungabhadra project in South India are two epochal events reflecting his vision and its eternity in successive times.

However, the vision of Jawaharlal Nehru also had been under the wider influence of global events of change. He was highly impressed with the Soviet approach to transforming the social relations of production and wanted a similar thing to happen for agrarian India. But his own ideological disposition had made him aware of the limitations of such action in the Indian socio-political environment. Nehru understood the conflict between labour and capitalists as one of the foremost challenges to the initiation of the production process in India. He wished somehow to bring down this level of confrontation to a harmonious level. The alternative for him lay in addressing the agenda of change in rural India with the help of river valley planning that would create numerous smaller and newer opportunities for growth, and include more participation of the common man. The difficult task before this was the need of the basic infrastructure industries, which were capital intensive. India had inherited some recluse form of development from British India, but its spirit was mauled by the socio-political price that was paid at the time of independence. The vision of India's first Prime Minister Jawaharlal Nehru is a testimony to the great leadership that India had at that time that laid a strong foundation for the growth and progress that India can take pride in by judging the firm steps of development taken so far and those in the future ahead.

Notes

1. Jawaharlal Nehru, "A Tryst with Destiny," Speech delivered at the Constituent Assembly, New Delhi on August 14, 1947, in *Independence and After: A Collection of Speeches, 1946-1949 by Jawaharlal Nehru* (New York: The John Day Company, 1971), pp. 3-4.
2. Ibid.
3. Jawaharlal Nehru, "Free India is One Year Old," A talk broadcast from New Delhi on August 15, 1948 in *Independence and After...*, p. 13.
4. R. Radhakrishnan, "Postcoloniality and the Boundaries of Identity," *Callaloo*, 16 (4), 1993, pp. 750-51.
5. O. P. Misra, *Economic Thought of Gandhi & Nehru: A Comparative Analysis* (New Delhi: MDP, 1995), p. 101.
6. Ibid., p. 114.
7. Ibid., p. 116.
8. S. R. Singh and M. P. Srivastava, *Socio-Economic Ideas of Nehru and Globalisation* (New Delhi: Anmol Publications, 2004), p. 19.
9. Ibid., p. 20.
10. Ibid.
11. First Five-Year Plan, Chapter 26: Irrigation and Power, Planning Commission, Government of India, New Delhi, http://planningcommission.nic.in/plans/planrel/fiveyr/welcome.html, accessed on February 8, 2009.
12. Ibid.
13. Central Water Commission, Ministry of Water Resources, Government of India, New Delhi, www.cwc.nic.in, accessed on April 12, 2014.
14. Jawaharlal Nehru, "Production, the First Essential," Speech delivered at the Industries Conference, New Delhi, December 18, 1947 in *Independence and After...*, p. 155.
15. National Remote Sensing Centre, Government of India, Indian Remote Sensing Satellites, http://www.nrsc.gov.in/satellites.html, accessed on October 10, 2009.
16. Jawaharlal Nehru, "Our Economic Policy," Speech delivered at the Constituent Assembly, New Delhi on February 17, 1948, in *Independence and After...*, p. 163.

9

Foreign Policy in India's Development Since Nehru Era

Baljit Singh

This paper examines four hypotheses. First, the foreign policy and economic development of a country are closely related with each other and Jawaharlal Nehru used foreign policy as a tool to promote economic development at home. Second, Nehru and his successors used foreign policy as an instrument to change international economic relations and international economic order for the benefit of developing countries as they believed that economic change at home is closely connected with international economic structures. Third, the LPG reforms have not only brought a change from inward to outward strategy of economic development but also changed the thrust of India's foreign policy from non-alignment to neo-liberalism and from third world solidarity to an emerging power. Fourth, the globalisation driven economic crisis across the world including US, has set the process of its retreat in motion and thereby significantly altered the external milieu of India's foreign policy in which again the issue of reforms in the Bretton Woods institutions and change in international economic order are gaining momentum.

I

The foreign policy and economic development of a country are closely related and shaped by and with each other. The former is deeply embedded in the domestic and external environment of a country. The economy is the part of the domestic environment and international economic structures are the part of the external environment, and thereby work as effective determinants of a country's foreign policy. If a country has a strong economy, it makes it confident from within to have an independent foreign policy and to exercise freedom of action and influence, while reacting to various issues confronting the international community. An independent foreign policy depends upon the sound economic health of a country, and the requirements of economic development of a country have always determined the nature of a country's foreign policy, ranging from independent to dependent. To have a proper understanding about the chemistry of their relationship, it is necessary to put their relationship in a perspective. The relationship between India's foreign policy and economic development started taking shape immediately after its independence. Nehru recognised the significance of economic factors in the determination of the foreign policy of a country, when he articulated that:

> ... foreign policy [of a country] is the outcome of economic policy and until India has properly evolved her economic policy her foreign policy will be rather vague, rather inchoate and will be groping.[1]

Generally, it is argued that the non-aligned policy of India was the product of Cold War politics because the world was divided into two power blocs and India was not interested to align with either—as alignment could have adversely affected its freedom of action in foreign affairs. Nobody denies this rationale for non-aligned policy posture of India but India opted for non-alignment due to various economic reasons. First, Nehru articulated that non-alignment policy was an absolute economic necessity for newly emerging and underdeveloped countries as their core national interest was to maintain political stability at home through economic development which required technical and financial assistance from varied sources. In order to obtain assistance from diverse sources, India made a conscious choice to remain non-aligned in a highly aligned world. Second, for developing countries, relatively heavy dependence on foreign aid became inevitable. It was the natural function of the foreign policy to ensure the availability and maximisation of the quantum of such aid. It was also the function of foreign policy to avoid political pressure from the aid giving states. These politico-economic objectives of foreign aid could be achieved only through a policy of non-alignment since such a policy alone could ensure the diversification of the sources of aid as well as prevent the exercise of political pressure by one of the two superpowers. Nehru perceived this logical connection between non-alignment and foreign aid when he said: "even in accepting economic help ... it is not a wise policy to put all our eggs in one basket."[2] Third, Nehru believed that alliances, "involve military obligations that divert scarce resources from the urgent necessities of economic development."[3] He was a firm believer that the security of a country cannot be ensured through alliances but through economic development. Fourth, according to Nehru, the maintenance of universal peace was an economic as well as political necessity for these countries.[4] Peace was thus related intimately to the economic well-being of the country and it is because of this relationship that it so eagerly sought maintenance of peace. It was the policy of non-alignment that was best suited to the maintenance of world peace.[5] If India became aligned with any bloc, it would lose that tremendous vantage ground which we have of using such influence as we possess in the cause of world peace.[6] Peace is the prerequisite for development because military preparation will consume the meagre resources of developing countries and war or conflict will adversely affect the foreign trade and thereby upset the process of their economic development. Therefore, it was in India's economic interest to avoid its entanglement in the conflict situation prevailing at the global level. Fifth, Nehru was able to see that economic change in India was bound up with India's economic cooperation with the other nations of the world.[7] To draw attention to Nehru's role in conceiving the idea of economic cooperation, and adopting it to meet the needs and urges for social and economic progress, not only of India, but also of all the emerging nations of the world. Nehru thus helped to start and carry through a process of change in international economic relationship, not merely for the benefit of India, or of the emerging nations, but of the world as a whole.[8] The Non-Aligned Movement (NAM) was conceived as a platform not only to promote cooperation amongst the developing countries from Asia, Africa and Latin America but also to negotiate critical economic issues pertaining to the international economic order with developed countries.

II

Indo-Soviet Treaty of Peace and Friendship of 1971 was considered a departure from the non-aligned policy of India. Apart from this, India along with other developing countries, questioned the international economic order from the platform of Non-Aligned Movement (NAM), which was not suitable to their economic requirements. NAM countries asked for the New International Economic Order (NIEO), which should take care of the genuine economic concerns of the developing countries. Soviet Union supported the developing countries' demand for NIEO. Both the developments were considered as pro-Soviet and anti-West. Regarding the first development, two arguments are given. First, the statist position was that the policy of non-alignment is very much alive and the agreement, an outcome of the changing regional security scenario of India, did not amount to an alliance partnership with the Soviet Union. Due to the Sino-Indian war of 1962, the rise of China as a nuclear state in 1962 and the emerging nexus between US, China and Pakistan in 1971 in the South Asian region, India had to reach an understanding with the Soviet Union to improve its regional security scenario. That does not mean that India has joined an alliance, it is a bilateral agreement signed with the Soviet Union to serve India's national security interest. Second, the argument given to defend this position was that in the 1950s, the Soviet Union was critical of India's non-aligned policy, like the USA, but in the 1960s, it started appreciating the policy. Besides this, the planned process of economic development which was certainly a socialist device qualifies India for the Soviet economic, technology and military support, not alliance partnership. Regarding NIEO, India clarified that the NIEO is essential to project its and developing countries' economic national interests abroad. Instead of subscribing to the Existing International Economic Order (EIEO) advocated by Bretton Woods institutions, India asked for NIEO and collaborated with the developing countries and used the platforms of Non-Aligned Movement and the United Nations General Assembly (UNGA) to bring about the desirable change in international economic structures which were not suitable for the economic interests of developing countries. Besides this, these institutions/structures are the outcome of Bretton Woods system (1944), which the developing countries were not part of because at that time most of them were colonies, not independent countries.

India along with other members of NAM advocated the cause of NIEO in the United Nations not at the behest of the Soviet Union but of its own accord, and on behalf of developing countries. India was sure that the NIEO would bring a meaningful change in the external economic scenario of developing countries, which would facilitate the economic growth of developing societies. Hence, the non-aligned credentials of India's foreign policy are beyond question. Rather, India made an effective use of NAM to put across the viewpoint of developing countries and convinced the UNGA to take suitable steps in this regard. The increasing strength of developing countries in UNGA had proved a blessing in disguise and UNGA passed two resolutions in its Sixth Special Session held in 1974. G-77, the diplomatic arm of NAM in the UN, began to play a significant role by dictating terms on a whole range of issues. Developed countries did not take the idea of NIEO positively; on the contrary, they not only defended EIEO but also adopted a hostile attitude towards developing countries which culminated in the North-South controversy. The North and South were led by the developed and developing countries respectively. The US hit back with a vengeance at the NAM majority in the UN by squeezing its funding of the world body, refusing to accept the declarations being issued by the majority in the General Assembly and walking out of the UNESCO.[9]

III

Globalisation brought a change in the content of international relations in which economic interest figures prominently vis-à-vis political and strategic interest within national interests. It has further reflected a change in the pattern of international interactions and bilateral relations amongst the nation-states. The absence of economic interdependence between the major rivals, like the USA and the USSR, not only resulted in conflict but also in the primacy of political and strategic interests in the national interest vis-à-vis the economic interests. Lack of economic interdependence among the nation-states and the major rivals led to the supremacy of high politics vis-à-vis low politics in their national interests and foreign policy agenda. Globalisation altered this equation between high politics and low politics in the national interests of major rivals by making them economically interdependent regardless of the clash of their political and strategic interests and their respective national interests. Increasing economic interdependence has resulted in a visible change in the foreign policy behaviour of twenty-first century arch rivals, the USA and China, in which they have been exercising a great deal of restraint when bilateral political and strategic friction occurs. A realist view emphasising the high politics while downplaying the low politics does not match with the contemporary reality of international politics in which the arch rivals have become economically interdependent, apart from the increasing economic dependence of poor nations on the rich nations. Dependence resulted in the primacy of economic interest vis-à-vis political and strategic interest in the national interest of dependent nations. It also culminated in the subordination of their foreign policy behaviour to their donor states, thereby losing the freedom or autonomy in their foreign relations, apart from shaping the agenda of development contrary to the aspirations and requirements of their people. India could not remain immune from this change, which has been set in motion since the last 30 years and accelerated after the Soviet demise.

Nehru was again proved correct in globalised India when he said that foreign policy is the outcome of economic policy. This argument was substantiated when a change in India's economic policy in 1991 brought a change in its foreign policy. Since then India's foreign policy has witnessed a major shift in terms of ideology by acquiring neo-liberal overtones in which it started subscribing to the agenda of Bretton Woods institutions. It was contrary to the position India held from 1947 to 1990 regarding these institutions in which it not only questioned their system of voting but also the international economic order constructed on the edifice of the institutions and the regime created by the Bretton Woods system. The shift was reflected in its economy from inward to outward oriented model of development. Due to this economic change, India's foreign policy acquired neo-liberal overtones in which it subscribed to the neo-liberal policy advocated by the IMF and IBRD, and thereby to the EIEO, apart from abandoning the cause of NIEO, which was one of its foreign policy objectives till 1990. Dumping the cause of NIEO and being the part of the process (Globalisation), which has been consolidating the EIEO by introducing the LPG reforms in its economy, clearly reflected an ideological shift in its foreign policy from non-alignment to neo-liberalism—that was reflected in the Washington Consensus, a consensus between the IMF, the World Bank, and the US Treasury about the right policies for the developing countries—that signalled a radically different approach to economic development and stabilisation.[10]

Apart from a visible change in its economic paradigm from inward to outward process of economic development and an ideological shift in its foreign policy, these reforms have made economic diplomacy a prominent instrument of its foreign policy. India's Look East Policy (LEP) towards South-East Asian (SEA) region is a classic case in point. The main objective of LEP has been to increase India's economic cooperation and integration with the SEA states, whose economies grew at a high growth rate as they had embraced globalisation before India. The ASEAN region was a role model for the economic success story of globalisation, notwithstanding the economic crisis these countries faced in the late 1990s. Their economic success due to globalisation became an attraction for India, when it introduced LPG reform in its economy. Since then, India has been working actively to engage ASEAN countries through regional and subregional economic cooperation. In the last decade, India's keen interest in the formation of subregional cooperation forums like Bay of Bengal Initiative for Muti-Sectoral Technical and Economic Cooperation (BIMSTEC) and the Mekong Ganga Cooperation (MGC) is clearly discernible. Establishment of various regional initiatives has marked the beginning of a new era of political and economic cooperation amongst neighbours in South Asia and South-East Asia, in which India is not only a participant but an active initiator.[11]

Due to its proximity to SEA markets, India's North-Eastern Region (NER) enjoys a locational advantage as it provides continental thrust to India's LEP. The LEP has now focused on the economic development of the NER of India and its gradual economic integration with Myanmar, and to prevent the use of Myanmarese territory as a safe heaven for anti-Indian elements. India's moves, such as the development of infrastructure in the states of NER and in Myanmar, and the military assistance to the junta, have all been designed to make the India-Myanmar border an area of peace and tranquillity in collaboration with Myanmar.[12] Realisation of one of the major goals of LEP, namely, NER's economic integration with Myanmar and SEA demands the development of NER's connectivity to the outside world in general and to Myanmar in particular which links NER with the outside world.[13] The proposal to develop India's NER through economic diplomacy, which has been the defining code of its LEP, has further substantiated the argument that foreign policy and economic development are related to each other. Because of neo-liberal trend and the increasing importance of economic interest in India's national interest, and thereby the growing significance of economic diplomacy to achieve its national interest, there has been a noticeable change in the power equation amongst the ministries involved in foreign policy formulation in India. Foreign policy formulation, while taking the help of the other ministries, is no more the sole prerogative of South Block. Developing greater coordination between commerce and foreign ministries and giving trade a strategic dimension remains an important challenge for India's policymakers.[14]

To understand the aforesaid change in India's foreign policy in the post-Soviet and globalised world, there are two schools of thought. The first school argued that economic and social changes in the advanced countries in the 1980s greatly strengthened capital at the expense of labour, with the increasing role of finance in the world economy being both cause and consequence. Consequently, the dominant forms of economic thought shifted from Keynesian economics towards the ideological ascendancy of the mono-economics of neo-liberalism, the most right-wing and conservative form of neoclassical economics. But the view that Indian foreign policy changes after 1991 have been determined essentially by changed external circumstances, thereby altering the national interest, is simply the conceit of a realist way of thinking.[15] Economic nationalism, at the core of India's national interests during the Nehru and post-Nehru period, became insignificant in globalised India. Import substitution and inward oriented strategy of economic development and the policy of non-alignment were used as tools to consolidate economic nationalism. The outward driven strategy of economic development advocated by neo-liberalism/globalisation has undermined the economic nationalism, which happened to be at the core of India's national interests throughout the Cold War. Neo-liberalism has not only shaped the economic policy of India but also de-centred India's philosophy of economic nationalism. It has been connecting Indian economy with the global economy in order to ensure its growth and economic development, which is a setback to the philosophy of economic nationalism. Advocators of globalism argued that Nehru was also a strong supporter of internationalism and used international cooperation as a tool to promote economic development in India and developing countries. Nehru was for internationalism but not at the cost of economic nationalism, and wanted to institutionalise and promote internationalism through nation-states, which happened to be almost sole actors in the arena of international politics. He never wanted to demolish nationalism at the cost of internationalism because the nationalism was the core of nation-states, which were instrumental in the promotion of internationalism. Contrary to that, neo-liberalism promoted globalism at the cost of economic nationalism and thereby undermined the authority of state actors, as it glorified the role of non-state actors like IMF, IBRD, WTO, WEF, G-7, G-20 and Multi-National Corporations (MNCs). Globalism promotes economic development, while undermining the ideology of economic nationalism and thereby reducing the base of state actors including the Indian State. Hence, globalism was exactly contrary to Nehru's concept of internationalism and nation-state's philosophy of economic nationalism.

Since the last twenty years, the key geo-economic principle guiding Indian foreign policy, regardless of which party or coalition has been in power, is the extension and consolidation of neo-liberal globalisation. The key geopolitical principle has been the effort to establish, consolidate and deepen the strategic relationship between India and the US, which means acquiescing and participating in the US project of establishing its informal global hegemony.[16] Developing countries could not genuinely make use of the United Nations to bring a desirable change in the EIEO or to replace it with NIEO, in spite of this fact that they have been in majority in the UNGA because the global power equation was not favourable to them. When the developing countries asserted their numbers in the world body, the developed countries stopped taking interest, and they were told to shift the headquarters of the United Nations from New York to any other place of their choice. But, in the 1990s, the UN became more of an instrumentality of the foreign policy objectives of the five permanent members of the United Nations Security Council (UNSC), and particularly that of the United States.[17] The US revived its interest in the UN in the 1990s, more so during the Democratic Administration of President Bill Clinton (1992-2000), but it did so by shifting the focus away from the General Assembly to the Security Council, and used it to stamp American military policies in Somalia, Rwanda, Haiti and the Balkans.[18] The focus was shifted from the UNGA to UNSC because, in the former, the developing countries are in a majority, whereas in the latter the developed countries have a privileged position. Whatever friction there was in UNSC during the Cold War period was moderated to a great extent due to the demise of the Soviet Union.

The second school is of the view that the imperatives of corporate globalisation and reconstruction of India's foreign policy in the post-Soviet world compelled India to articulate a new foreign policy agenda without making a formal departure from non-alignment and the NAM. The Group of 77 (G-77), consisting of developing countries, ceased being a vehicle for the promotion of India's economic interests at the global level, therefore India began to look at a forum like the Group of 15 (G-15)—a group within developing countries—to project its interest in a more articulated and focused manner at the global level. According to C. Raja Mohan, the excessive emphasis on normative principles that guided India's foreign policy and the insular economic philosophy for a couple of decades, severely limited India's manoeuvrability in the international system.[19] Since India started facing problems in the early 1980s, the then Prime Ministers, Indira Gandhi and Rajiv Gandhi, attempted to moderate the ideological accents that had begun to distort Indian diplomacy. Rajiv Gandhi, in particular, tried to loosen the diplomatic straitjacket that was limiting India's external options. By reaching out to the West and trying to change the internal economic orientation, he prepared the ground for a fundamental re-evaluation of foreign policy. In the 1990s India initiated a root-and-branch overhaul of its economy to facilitate globalisation, and the imperatives of India's foreign policy dramatically changed.[20] The biggest change in the

India's foreign policy in the 1990s has been shedding of the dirigiste anti-western orientation that was popular among the generations of the Indian elite after independence.[21] From preparing for and conducting nuclear tests to forcing the international system to deal with the sources of terrorism in Pakistan, India had initiated a self-confident, outward-looking and proactive diplomacy during the 1990s.[22] Building issue-based coalitions and approaching problems in a functional rather than ideological manner has become far more important to India's approach to global issues from trade to management of environment. The voice of an economically strong India will be heard with more respect than that which pretends to lead a non-existent Third World trade union.[23] Economic reforms enabled India not only to overcome economic crises, but increased the economic growth rate of globalised India significantly as compared to the pre-globalisation period. Improvement in the rate of growth of its economy has strengthened India's claim to cross the threshold of the Third World. Now India's claim to be an emerging power is based on its economic strength apart from its strength of being the largest democracy and a strategic power from the developing world. Ideological climate within India and abroad had changed and therefore there was no scope for Third World solidarity.

IV

Change in global economic scenario in the wake of the Tequila crisis of Mexico (1994-95), Asian crisis (1997) and the collapse of Argentina's economy (2001) did not only initiate debate on globalisation but also culminated in the articulation of Post-Washington Consensus (PWC) apart from the formation of World Social Forum (WSF) as a critique of neo-liberal philosophy. Emergence of World Social Forum (WSF) from Latin American continent in general and Brazil in particular at Porto Alegre in 2001 articulated counterpunch to the discourse of globalisation. The WSF countered the argument of World Economic Forum (WEF) that there is no other alternative (TINA) of development except globalisation. The WSF argued that there are so many alternatives (TAMA) of development. The Fourth

WSF was held in India in Mumbai 2004 but much before that some sort of contestation of globalisation was set in motion when India started collaborating with like-minded countries in the ministerial meets of World Trade Organisation (WTO). Hosting of the WSF global meet in India in 2004 is a great opportunity and challenge to people's movements and to all civil and political organisations across the world especially the people of Asia and Africa. The WSF 2004 offered a platform for all those opposed to imperialist and neo-liberal globalisation, war and sectarian violence, and have a commitment to democratic values, plurality, dignity and peace.[24]

Although the NAM was disarticulated but the large-sized developing economies have successfully tried to respond to their common predicament in international economy by exploring scope for mutual cooperation. Within the WTO ministerial meets, the developed countries have been advocating the cause of free trade whereas the developing countries are asking for fair trade, consequently the WTO has failed to take off. The developed countries are more organised as compared to the developing countries. Developing countries also established G-20 on August 20, 2003 to argue their case in the WTO. It is an issue-specific coalition of developing countries, which have joined hands to push for greater liberalisation in agricultural trade by pressuring the G-7 countries to reduce their massive subsidies on agriculture. It was India, Brazil and South Africa who had catalysed and facilitated its formation and have managed it since then.[25] The Group was formed in the backdrop of the Seattle fiasco and ahead of the WTO meeting at Cancun. Although the G-20 has evolved essentially around the issue of agricultural trade, it has broader political implications in the sense that the very formation of G-20 has introduced North-South divide in the WTO.[26] The political economy of G-20 is that it constitutes 60% of world population, 70% of its farmers, and 26% of the world's agricultural exports to increase the agricultural export.

Apart from G-20, India is also a part of the IBSA Forum which is not only contesting neo-liberal philosophy of globalisation but is also a forum to project India's economic interests abroad. IBSA Forum is a strategic partnership between three geostrategically located and economically emerging powers to make globalisation a positive force for development in developing countries, apart from their quest for greater autonomy in global economic affairs and for a better deal in the international trading system.[27] It is also known as New Non-Alignment which aims to maintain the autonomy of its members in their international affairs apart from shaping the international political and economic processes. The Brasilia Declaration issued by the IBSA Forum also highlights the need to reform the international financial system so as to meet the developmental needs and prevent the recurrence of national and regional financial crisis. The Fourth IBSA Forum Summit was held at Brasilia in Brazil on April 15, 2010. The leaders of the three countries stressed the need to reform the Bretton Woods institutions in order to increase their effectiveness and enhance their accountability and legitimacy, apart from reforms in the UN in general and the UNSC in particular. They stressed the need for increasing the role of developing countries in IMF and IBRD. IBSA Forum appreciated the outcome of the UN Conference on South-South Cooperation, held in Nairobi in December 2009, wherein the leaders of three emerging countries concurred that South-South cooperation is a particular and essential instrument for development. Developing countries tend to share common views on national development strategies and priorities when faced with similar development challenges.

Another grouping of emerging economies consisting of Brazil, Russia, India and China (BRIC) came into being on the margins of the UNGA in September 2006, and when South Africa joined it in 2011, it became BRICS. The report of BRICS was released in its recently held summit in New Delhi (2012), which focuses on the synergies between the economies, highlighting their role as growth driver of the world economy. The global financial crisis inflicted significant loss in output in all the BRICS economies. However, real GDP growth in India and China remained impressive even though they also witnessed some moderation due to weakening of global demand. The crisis also exposed the structural weakness of the global financial and real sectors.[28]

Notwithstanding the criticism of NAM at home and the USA's pressure from abroad not to participate in the NAM Summit, India made it a point to attend the 16th Summit of NAM held at Tehran in Iran in August 2012. Criticism at home was driven by the argument that NAM had lost its relevance in the neo-liberal world, and could not make a mark at the international level even before. The USA was putting pressure on India not to attend the Tehran NAM Summit because the USA is not sailing well with Iran, and its national interest demanded that India being a strategic partner of the US should not attend the NAM Summit. But both the strategic and economic interests of India demanded that it should participate in the Tehran NAM Summit, and India did participate. The Indian delegation in the recently held NAM Summit at Tehran was led by none else than the then Prime Minister of India. India's participation in the NAM Summit in the backdrop of US pressure provided a boost to its international prestige, reassuring the world that it is not yet a client state, and reflected its commitment to the NAM.[29] It further validates its claim that India is an emerging power and does not buzz to the pressure of the US. While addressing the NAM Summit at Tehran, the then Prime Minister Manmohan Singh underlined the necessity of improvement in global governance apart from the need of restoring a just and fair economic and financial order.

India has been using the multilateral forums and tactical coalitions like NAM, G-20, IBSA and BRICS to raise issues like reforms in international financial, trading and political institutions such as IMF, IBRD, WTO and the United Nations to establish a just and fair global economic financial order apart from a fair international trading system. Through its foreign policy, India is actively pursuing these critical issues not only to serve its and developing countries' economic interests abroad but also to accelerate the speed of economic growth. The retreat of globalisation set in motion after the international financial and economic crisis which had been taking shape since the late 1990s, and which erupted in February 2008 in the USA, created a congenial environment for India's economic diplomacy to bring meaningful change in global financial and trading institutions apart from rethinking about strategy of economic development at the national level. Joseph E. Stiglitz in his book *Freefall: Free Markets and the Sinking of the Global Economy* argued that the financial and economic crisis of the US was set in motion much before 2008, however, the Bush Administration acknowledged it only when Lehman Brothers faced bankruptcy in September 2008, which invited the US State to rescue not only the bankers but also the various business houses facing the crisis situation. The collapse of Lehman Brothers was the consequence of the economic meltdown, not its cause; it accelerated a process that was well on its way.[30] A new period of state intervention, regulation, and creeping protectionism has begun. Indeed, globalisation itself is revising. The logic that everyone wins in a single market, has been undermined. Global trade, capital flows, and immigration are declining. It also has not gone unnoticed that nations with insulated financial systems, such as China and India, have suffered the least economic damage.[31] The role of the state is expanding again, together with a regulation of markets. This is evident in the US, where Obama has moved towards more activist and bigger government. The quasi-nationalisation of the banking and automotive industries, as well as the pending reform of the financial system, makes this clear. Recently, the French President, Nicolas Sarkozy, celebrated "the return of the state" and "the end of the ideology of public powerlessness."[32]

V

To sum up, it can be articulated that foreign policy and development have remained two sides of the same coin in India from Nehru to contemporary period. India's foreign policy has always reflected its developmental needs abroad and thereby facilitated the process of economic development at home. India's non-aligned policy posture was driven by its developmental need during the Nehru period. Subsequently, by its policy to harp on Third World solidarity throughout the 1970s, through NAM with a purpose to achieve its economic national interest in particular and that of developing countries in general by raising the issue of NIEO at the international level. Globalisation did not only bring change in strategy of economic development but also changed the philosophy of Indian state from liberal to neo-liberal and its foreign policy thereof from non-alignment to neo-liberalism. This changed the content of international relations and thereby prioritised the economic interest vis-à-vis political and strategic interest within the broader framework of national interests of nation-states including India. Under the influence of neo-liberal philosophy of globalisation, India abandoned the cause of NIEO throughout the 1990s on the one hand, and made economic diplomacy as a major instrument of India's foreign policy on the other. India's LEP towards the SEA region is a classic case in point apart from its being a part of G-20, IBSA Forum, BRICS and of various other global, regional and subregional trading and economic organisations like WTO, IOR-ARC, BIMSTEC and MGC. The financial and economic crises confronting countries ranging from Asia to Latin America, Europe, North America including the USA from the late 1990s till date, have set the process of the retreat of globalisation in motion, in which India along with developing (G-20) and emerging economies (IBSA and BRICS), has been raising the issue of a fair international trading system apart from the international economic order based on justice as required for economic growth of the developing and emerging countries, including India.

References

1. *Constituent Assembly Debates*, Official Report, vol. 11, no. 5, December 4, 1947, pp. 12-16.
2. J. Bandyopadhaya, "Nehru and Non-Alignment," B. R. Nanda (ed.), *Indian Foreign Policy: The Nehru Years* (Delhi: Vikas Publishing House, 1976), p. 173.
3. Laurence W. Martin, *Neutralism and Non-alignment* (New York: F. A. Praeger, 1962), p. 95.
4. B. S. N. Murti, *Nehru's Foreign Policy* (New Delhi: The Becon Information and Publications, 1953), p. 31.
5. Nalini Kant Jha, "Domestic Foundations of Nehruvian Foreign Policy," Taufiq A. Nizami (ed.), *Nehru's World View Internationalism vs. Nationalism*, (Aligarh: Three Way Printer, 2002), p. 44.

6. Government of India, *India's Foreign Policy: Selected Speeches, September 1946-April 1961* (New Delhi, Publications Division, 1961), pp. 39-40.
7. K. B. Lall, "Nehru and International Economic Cooperation," B. R. Nanda (ed.), *Indian Foreign Policy: The Nehru Years* (Delhi: Vikas Publishing House, 1976), p. 186.
8. Ibid., pp. 186-87.
9. C. Raja Mohan, *Crossing the Rubicon: The Shaping of India's New Foreign Policy* (New Delhi: Viking, 2003), p. 44.
10. Joseph E. Stiglitz, *Globalization and Its Discontents* (New York: W.W. Norton & Company, 2002), p. 16.
11. Man Mohini Kaul, "Regional Groupings: An Overview of BIMSTEC and MGC," *South Asian Survey*, vol. 13, no. 2, 2006, p. 313.
12. A. Lakshmana Chetty, "India-Myanmar Relations: Growing Engagement," *World Focus*, vol. 31, no. 10, October 2010, p. 456.
13. Ibid., p. 455.
14. S. D. Muni and C. Raja Mohan, "Emerging Asia: India's Options," *International Studies*, vol. 41, no. 3, 2004, p. 332.
15. Achin Vanaik, "National Interest: A Flawed Notion—Explaining the Shift in Indian Foreign Policy in the Age of Neo-liberal Globalization and Its Implications for WANA Region," Anwar Alam (ed.), *India and West Asia in the Era of Globalization* (New Delhi: New Century Publications, 2008), p. 18.
16. Ibid., p. 19.
17. J. N. Dixit, *India's Foreign Policy 1947-2003* (New Delhi: Picus Books, 2003), p. 395.
18. Abdul Nafey, "IBSA Forum: The Rise of New Non-Alignment," *India Quarterly*, vol. 61, no.1, January-March 2005, pp. 4-5.
19. C. Raja Mohan, n. 9, p. 260.
20. Ibid., p.261.
21. Ibid., p.262.
22. Ibid., p.263.
23. Ibid., p. 270
24. Prakash Louis, "World Social Forum: Issues and Perspectives," *Social Action*, vol. 54, April-June 2004, p. 129.
25. Abdul Nafey, n. 18, p. 55.
26. Ibid.
27. Ibid., pp. 1-16
28. *The BRICS Report*, BRICS (New Delhi: Oxford University Press, 2012), see also www.bricsindia.in/brics- report.pdf, accessed on September 25, 2012, p. xiv.
29. Arun Mohanty, "NAM Summit: Course Correction at Tehran," *Mainstream*, vol. 50, no. 38, September 8, 2012, pp. 6-7.
30. Joseph E. Stiglitz, *Freefall: Free Markets and the Sinking of the Global Economy* (New York: Allen Lane, 2010), p. 29.
31. Roger C. Altman, "Globalization in Retreat: Further Geopolitical Consequences of the Financial Crisis," *Foreign Affairs*, vol. 88, no. 4, July-August 2009, p. 2.
32. Ibid., p. 5.

10

Asian Security Structure and Challenges for India: Efficacy of the Nehruvian Approach

Rajpal Budania

The Cold War structure of international politics has transformed. Major shifts in political, economic and strategic realms are taking shape and Asia has emerged as the epicentre of world politics. Contemporary Asia is a complex picture of cooperation and conflict. It consists of the world's major economies and military powers. Asia is redefining the international security order. It consists of acutely competitive security as witnessed between India and China, Pakistan and India, South Korea and North Korea, Israel and the Arab World, and China and the US. Asia has unleashed the second nuclear age and witnessed proliferation of nuclear weapons, which endangers peace and stability regionally and globally. Conflicts in West Asia, South Asia, North-East Asia and South China Sea make the region volatile. The dynamics of balance of power, asymmetrical warfare, extremism, terrorism, failing states, humanitarian crises, the clash of democratic and authoritarian values and systems are generating altogether new relationships and alignments. Asia also has the distinction for developing structures of cooperative security as happening through new regionalism. The Asian security is being shaped under the influence of both state and non-state entities. India has associated itself with major structures of political, strategic, economic, energy, and environmental security in Asia. The conflictual dynamics in

Asia's security architecture have influenced India's threat perception and policy responses. India has explored all the viable options for furthering its national interests and security. This article examines the Nehruvian approach to understand the present Asian security scenario and how Jawaharlal Nehru's vision of Asian solidarity and building relations on the basis of *Panchsheel* have guided India's policy formulations to challenges and opportunities emanating from the new Asian realities.

The Emerging Asian Security Structure

In the twenty-first century, Asia has emerged as the pivotal region in the realm of international security configuration. International power politics has shifted its sphere to Asia. Global powers are pitched in for strategic alignments and new geopolitical machinations are taking place in the context of power and influence in the Asian region. Asia has witnessed a complex trend of intensifying conflicts and at the time also the concerted efforts being made by the countries of the region for enhanced cooperation. Asia is still dominated by competitive security dynamics. The very existence of bilateral and multilateral conflicts in the region has put pressure on the states to evolve cooperative security mechanisms.

Asia has witnessed extreme form of Realism practised by states, particularly by the authoritarian state—China. Asian security has been deeply affected by China's aggressive policies. In fact, most of Asia's security problems are China-centric. First, China has had conflictual relations with most of its neighbours and also with other countries in the region. China has had a history of acrimonious relations with the former Soviet Union, India, Vietnam and also with South Korea, Japan and the countries of the ASEAN. Its strategic cooperation with Pakistan has been a critical factor in deteriorating security environment in South Asia. Secondly, China as the most powerful country in Asia has failed to make any sincere effort in resolving its bilateral conflicts and also in evolution of pan-Asian security structures for management and resolution of conflicts. In fact, its policies and role are always guided by extreme Realism, minimising chances of reconciliation and reciprocity required for evolution of cooperation security structures. Important countries in Asia are having problems and in some cases serious conflicts with neighbours. China is one country having serious differences with several countries like India, Japan, South Korea, Vietnam and others. In South Asia, India-Pakistan conflict is one of the oldest in the post-Cold War period. Pakistan is having problems with Afghanistan and even Iran. West Asia is conflict-ridden too. Israel is having historical conflict with several Arabian countries. So, all major subregions in Asia, such as North-East Asia, South Asia and West Asia are facing multi-pronged conflicts.

Asia has been the epicentre of nuclear proliferation. Countries like India, Pakistan, Iran, North Korea and Israel have overlooked nuclear arms control regimes and pursued their nuclear weapons programme. India, Pakistan and North Korea have actually carried out multiple nuclear tests discarding the will of the international community and even challenged the very efficacy of the nuclear non-proliferation treaty (NPT) in controlling nuclear proliferation. Paul Bracken has argued that the end of the Cold War has been succeeded by a new age called the "second nuclear age" which poses altogether new directions in nuclear proliferation and arms control mechanisms.[1] According to him several Asian regions, South Asia, the Middle East and East Asia, have witnessed proliferation upsurge and more and more states in these regions are basing their security policies on nuclear deterrence. There is clearly a multipolar world in the nuclear sense and this trend is irreversible. The second nuclear age as witnessed in Asia is very alarming as the weaponisation is sought on the basis of acute nationalism and in a clandestine manner. Moreover, the nuclear weaponisation in Asia is characterised by multi-pronged rivalries, command and control uncertainties, affordability factors, and pursuit of weaponisation by non-democratic and unstable regimes in Asia.[2] Again, as argued earlier, China is largely responsible for proliferation and helping in clandestine acquisition of nuclear weapons by Pakistan and even North Korea.

Several countries in the Asian region are affected by fundamentalism and terrorism. South Asia and West Asia have witnessed the rise of religious fundamentalism and terrorism. Nations are torn from within due to these twin challenges. Afghanistan, Pakistan, Iraq and several other countries are considered amongst the fast failing states. Their internal security is acutely fragile and their neighbours feel threatened due to their failure in controlling fundamentalism and terrorism. These states also happen to be lacking in viable democratic institutions.

Democracy, interdependence and cooperative structures contribute to resolution of conflicts and avoidance of war. Europe has witnessed the phenomenon of democracy, interdependence and institutional mechanisms for resolution of conflicts and establishing peace. However, Asia lacks in all the three factors.[3] Many countries remain undemocratic. Intra-regional or interregional cooperation and interdependence have not acquired as strong fundamentals as in Europe or North America. Institutional development has also been disappointing.

Security remains acutely contested and rivalled in Asia and the phenomenon of competitive security remains high on the security agenda of the Asian countries. Asia is witnessing acute kind of strategic rivalry. Even the United States perceives strategic challenges from Asia, particularly from non-democratic China, Pakistan, Iran, and North Korea. Strategic rivalry is both at bilateral and multilateral levels. Balance of power strategies are taking place between the main Asian rivals as between India and China, India and Pakistan, but at the same time we find that most of the democratic states of the region, along with the US and Australia, are developing common understanding and structures to balance China's hegemonic ambitions. Asian states in conflict are acquiring sophisticated weapons and systems. China and India are the two biggest importers of armaments in the world. Defence expenditure is rising rapidly and resembling the trend of the competition between the US and the Soviet Union during the Cold War. There are concerted efforts to modernise the armed forces and enhance their power projection capabilities.

Against this backdrop of competitive security, some effort has been made to develop institutional mechanism for increasing cooperation among the countries of the region. There is a general perception that cooperation must take place for addressing the security problems in the region. Though India and China are the most rivalled countries in the region, India's largest trade is taking place with China. China has become the largest trading partner to most of its neighbours. The Association of South-East Asian Nations (ASEAN) has set an example for the Asian community in the field of cooperation and interdependence. The Shanghai Cooperation Organisation (SCO) and the South Asian Association for Regional Cooperation (SAARC) are the other two examples of cooperation at the intra-regional level. The clamour for developing institutions for cooperation and management of conflicts in Asia is intensifying. In time to come, the region may witness cooperative processes acquiring roots and contributing to Asian peace and prosperity.

The emerging regional order in Asia is also a complex picture of competing states striving for power and influence in the region. China is clearly the most influential actor in the region and it wants to establish its influence and hegemony over the entire region. Since it has global ambitions it is natural for China to desire to control the region. India also wants to increase its role in Asia and wants to develop India-centric Asian order. India has all the potential to lead Asia. It has an advantage over China in terms of soft power. India's vibrant democracy, composite values and belief systems, strengths in the field of telecommunications, are the assets which China lacks. India-China rivalry has acquired the centre stage in Asian geopolitics. It is contended that realism is deep-rooted in the foreign and strategic policies of both India and China. One observer has stated:

> Asia's security dynamics are thus defined by old-fashioned realpolitik-based great power politics: two rising powers—China and India—and a reigning status quo superpower, the United States, trying to find common ground but moving toward potential

> long-term competition over their relative influence and status in the Asia-Pacific region. China's primary rival on the Asian continental landmass is India, another rising power with aspirations for an increased role and status in the international system. Relations between Asia's two giants have long been marked by competition, conflict, containment, mutual distrust, and rivalry.[4]

There is also a perception of ASEAN-led Asian order in the offing. In fact, ASEAN has unleashed new regionalism. Its success story has attracted all the major powers of not only the Asian region, but also the powerful countries outside the region, trying to be associated with the ASEAN. Undoubtedly, ASEAN has emerged as the core of the Asian security and stability. It has accommodated all the major powers of the Asia-Pacific region. It has truly promoted multilateral processes for Asia-Pacific security and development.

International politics of Asia has become very complex. Asia has many substantial powers, but no one is in a position to dominate the whole region. Barry Buzan has explained Asian security through his "regional security complex theory" (RSCT).[5] According to him, during the Cold War there were three "regional security complexes" (RSCs) in Asia, namely North-East Asian RSC, South-East Asian RSC, and South Asian RSC. There has been a transformation of the RSCs in Asia in the post-Cold War period. Now the boundaries between the North-East Asian and South-East Asian RSCs have blurred and the two have evolved into East Asian RSC. For Buzan, East Asia has three dominant actors: China, Japan and ASEAN. In contrast, South Asia is unipolar with India being the dominant actor. The Asian security super complex was heavily penetrated by the superpower rivalry during the Cold War. But in the post-Cold War period the external intervention has come down sharply. Still the US holds the key to the Asian balance of power. Asia has made weak efforts for having cooperative security regimes in place as in Europe. Buzan opines: "the main probability is for more of the same, with East Asian security staying within a fairly narrow band between mild conflict formation and a rather odd and weak sort of security regime in which an outside power, the US, plays the key role."[6]

Asia has become the most conflict-prone region in the world. The colonial legacies and unresolved disputes have endangered the regional security in a serious manner. Barry Buzan very aptly describes the Asian security scenario thus: "History has left numerous territorial disputes, status rivalries, fears and hatreds among the successor states and their peoples. It is hard to think of two adjacent countries within the region that do not have either or both of serious unresolved issues between them and active processes of securitisation. The region has no shared cultural legacy, few traditions of international cooperation and a worrying number of strong nationalisms."[7]

As already noted, Chinese hegemonism is a key factor in Asian security order. It has generated rivalries with the countries of the region and with the US outside the region. This has resulted in an informal formation of an anti-hegemonic alliance against China. India is the challenger to Chinese expansionism and hegemonic policies. To contain India, China has given strategic support to Pakistan. China's game plan for all the subregions in Asia is focused on increasing its influence and at the same time containing the influence of the US, India and Japan.

The emerging Asian security environment has created several security concerns for India's policymakers. India has been concerned over the tensions in North-East Asia over the issue of North Korea's nuclear weaponisation; over regime changes in West Asia; and China's support to Pakistan's weaponisation programme. Nuclear proliferation has added a challenge to India's strategic planning as India has not only perceived a threat from nuclear weapons with states but it is much more concerned over the possibility of extremist elements getting access to nuclear weapons. India cannot remain oblivious to China's expansionism in Asia in general, but in South Asia and South-East Asia in particular. Its increasing engagement with India's neighbouring countries with a view to countering India's influence is a key foreign policy challenge for India. India is equally concerned over the increasing threat of terrorism and extremism in the entire Asian region. India has been working on several options to deal with these threats and challenges. It is natural for India to increase its defence preparedness to meet with any eventuality. It is also cooperating with like-minded countries to deal with future challenges. Consequently, it has increased strategic cooperation with the US, Japan, Australia and the South-East Asian countries. One can easily see a balance of power dynamics being unleashed in Asia. But the scope of this paper is confined to Nehruvian approach and alternatives to these challenges.

Promoting India's Interests through Nehruvian Approach

P. N. Haksar rightly put it: "With the passage of time, Nehru will be of greater relevance, and not merely to my country, but to the world at large."[8] Jawaharlal Nehru was ahead of his time in having a foreign policy vision based on interdependence, economic integration and regional institutions of cooperation. No other leader in Asia even to this day has been able to conceive Asian security along these lines, let alone putting them into practice. Nehru was highly impressed by the European cooperation along these lines and vouched for South Asian confederation for similar cooperation. He said: "Confederation remains our ultimate goal. Look at Europe, at the Common Market. This is the urge everywhere. There are no two types of people anywhere nearer than those of India and Pakistan, though if we say it they are alarmed and think we want to swallow them."[9]

Until the 1962 fiasco, Nehru had unique confidence in believing that India could protect its national interests through idealistic strategies of peaceful coexistence, good neighbourly relations and non-alignment. India's responses were mostly reactive to regional challenges. Harish Kapur has observed: "it was not so much India did not see the problems at the micro-level; it was just that there appeared to exist a peculiar confidence in India's capacity to manage regional crises through, more or less, the same pattern of actions and initiatives that India was applying at the macro-level."[10]

There was convergence of Nehru's views on developing best of relations with China and also promoting the idea of Asian solidarity or "Asianism." Nehru had great praise for the Chinese civilisation. He believed China was an embodiment of "the same high degree of culture and civilisation continuing without any break. It absorbs and teaches even the barbarians who come to plunder."[11] Nehru could not wish away the necessity of India-China working and cooperating together to acquire a worthwhile place in global politics.

India-China relations are marked by several areas of divergence and mistrust. But both India and China are working together for better understanding and cooperation as envisaged by Jawaharlal Nehru. The political leadership of both countries has time and again emphasised the hard fact that cooperation between India and China on key issues in Asian security is a necessary condition for Asian peace and security. Without mutually beneficial and cooperative India-China relations, Asia cannot remain stable.

When India achieved independence from colonial rule in 1947, the entire Asia perceived India as a natural leader of resurgent Asia. Asian nationalists had special affinity for Jawaharlal Nehru and India. India's influence could be discerned from the enthusiasm shown by these countries in the First Asian Relations Conference, organised by Nehru in March 1947 in Delhi. The conference was aimed at Asian unity and developing understanding on issues related to the welfare of the Asian countries. The stated objectives of the conference were to bring together the leading personalities of Asia on a common platform "to study the problems of common concern to the people of the continent, to focus attention on social, economic and cultural problems of different countries of Asia, and to foster mutual contact and understanding."[12] Later in the Bandung Conference too, India carried great influence on the countries of Asia. Indian influence on Asia was unmistakable during the entire 1950s. In international politics in no region has optimal security been achieved without developing common perceptions of mutual and common security. It is a well-known fact that conflicts take place or remain unresolved primarily due to misperceptions and perceptions of hostility.

Nehru was of the view that Asian countries have remained isolated from one another because of European imperialism and they, therefore, are bound to come together once they achieve independence. At the 1st Asian Relations conference he stated:

> Much has happened during these years, but perhaps one of the notable consequences of the European domination of Asia has been the isolation of the countries of Asia from one another. India always had contacts and intercourse with her neighbour countries in the Northwest, the Northeast, the East and the Southeast. With the coming of British rule in India these contacts were broken off and India was almost completely isolated from the rest of Asia ... Today this isolation is breaking down because of many reasons, political and other. The old imperialisms are fading away. The land routes have revived and air travel suddenly brings us very near to each other. This Conference itself is significant as an expression of that deeper urge to the mind and spirit of Asia which has persisted in spite of the isolationism which grew up during the years of European domination. As that domination goes, the walls that surrounded us fall down and we look at each other again and meet as old friends long parted.[13]

Nehru's approach to interstate relations emphasised abhorrence to violent methods in settlement of conflicts. He said, "What we need is a passion for peace and for civilised behaviour in international affairs ... If we desire peace, we must develop the temper of peace and try to win even those who may be suspicious of us or who think they are against us ... We cannot seek peace in the language of war or of threats."[14] This observation remains at the core of India's foreign policy formulations even to this day. This observation entails the following principles:

- Peaceful management of interstate relations;
- Adversarial relations can be transformed into mutually beneficial relations by developing common perceptions;
- War cannot provide a durable solution to international conflicts; and

- Political approach is the most rational strategy to terminating or managing conflicts.

India's foreign policy is very much guided even to this day by these very principles. From the Korean conflict of 1950 till the recent Syrian conflict in Asia, India has consistently followed the Nehruvian approach to peacefully solving problems through dialogue rather than war.

Nehru believed that military approaches do not provide durable settlement of conflicts; rather that makes them more complex. P. N. Haksar has described:

> Nehru interpreted India's interests in a manner which did not conflict with the interest of maintaining world peace. And this idea of maintaining world peace was not a moral imperative. Nehru saw very clearly that in the world as it is constituted today, and as it emerged after the Second World War, war had ceased to be an instrument of policy; that the age of Baron von Clausewitz was over, that one could no longer talk of war being the continuation of politics by other means.[15]

Nehru was convinced that "entering into military alliances and establishing military bases in foreign territories accentuated discord and increased the possibility of a military conflict. There was no alternative to the peaceful approach, though it could not absolutely guarantee peace, since violence created more problems than it could solve. The only way to settle the differences was through negotiation, mutual concessions and accommodation."[16] Nehru's steadfast belief that the best way of achieving security was a positive policy of friendship with other countries has continued to guide India's foreign policy.[17] India's present foreign policy has taken several proactive measures to promote friendship with its immediate neighbours as well as other countries. In fact, the much talked of Gujral doctrine is an extension of Nehru's philosophy of peace and development-oriented foreign policies. The factor of non-reciprocity in its engagement with the smaller nations of South Asia is another example displaying Nehruvian thought of accommodation and mutual concessions.

India has consistently followed the Nehruvian policy of winning over friends and turning the adversary into a friend, or what Nehru called, "try to win even those who may be suspicious of us or who think they are against us." After independence, India wanted to develop equally cordial relations with both the superpowers of the day—the United States and the Soviet Union. It is a different matter altogether that it could not happen due to the prevailing Cold War geopolitics. India has consistently followed a policy of having the best of relations with neighbours and all the powers that matter in international politics. The Annual Report 2012-13 of the Ministry of External Affairs, Government of India, states:

> India aspires for a peaceful and secure periphery, expanding ties with its extended neighbourhood, cordial and balanced relations with major powers and mutually beneficial partnerships with developing countries.[18]

After the end of the Cold War, India has made concerted efforts to diversify its relations and develop cooperative relationships with the US and China, the two countries which remained hostile to India all through the Cold War. It is due to India's concerted efforts that today it has been able to forge a mutually cooperative relationship with the US and also China.

Overall, Nehru was in favour of a pragmatic foreign policy on the matter of promoting and defending India's national interests. In a speech to the Legislative Constituent Assembly on December 4, 1947, Nehru emphatically stated:

> Whatever policy we may lay down, the art of conducting the foreign affairs of a country lies in finding out what is most advantageous to the country. We may talk about international goodwill and mean

> what we say. We may talk about peace and freedom and earnestly mean what we say. But in the ultimate analysis, a government functions for the good of the country it governs and no government dare do anything which in the short or long run is manifestly to the disadvantage of that country.[19]

Nehru was conscious of the need for a pragmatic strategy to be adopted while pursuing India's national interests. He believed that "the problem of foreign policy for every country, including India, was to interpret its national interests so that it did not conflict with overall international interests ... the world of today insistently demands cooperation and not conflict."[20] He believed that basic interests of countries belonging to different social, economic and political systems need not be in clash with each other. Rather the countries must search for "ways of ensuring everyone's survival in the course of peaceful competition between the two systems. This is precisely what Jawaharlal Nehru had in mind when he spelt out the concept of 'one world' on the principle of peaceful coexistence."[21]

Nehru was far-sighted in wanting to establish a strong relationship with the countries of South-East Asia. It would not be an exaggeration to say that Nehru was a forerunner of India's "Look East Policy." Nehru knew where India's national interests lay in South-East Asia. One scholar has succinctly observed:

> The Asian Relations Conference was perhaps emblematic of that special relationship which India enjoyed with Southeast Asian states in the first decade following the end of the Second World War. One could perhaps see this as an early expression of an Indian "Look East" policy, with Nehru laying the foundation of an Asian community in which India would exercise an important influence. A united Asia, Nehru envisioned, would eventually replace the Atlantic community as the future nerve centre of the world.[22]

India has adopted a non-interventionist policy towards the countries of South-East Asia very much in accordance with

Nehruvian faith in *Panchsheel.* Its policy towards the region is based on shared goals, and like-minded objectives and principles. India has avoided being projected as a countervailing factor in the region's power equation. India has promoted cooperative relationship with China with a view to reinforcing its strategic interests in South-East Asia by promoting bilateral and multilateral processes. China has remained a significant factor in India's national interests and strategies. It was Jawaharlal Nehru's policy to develop common India-China perceptions on Asian security and cooperation. Under his regime, India believed that its engagement with the Asian region will be guided by India-China friendship. India's foreign policy was essentially based on liberal conceptualisation of international relations. P. N. Haksar explains:

> Jawaharlal Nehru had a deeper and subtler perception of the nature of the world emerging out of the Second World War. More than any other statesman or itinerant foreign minister, Nehru saw through the total inadequacy of the classical doctrines of the balance of power, and saw clearly that the national interest of each country needs to be defined in consonance and not in conflict with the overall interests of world peace ... Jawaharlal Nehru saw with a rare clarity of perception that the contemporary world could survive in the measure that the concept of cooperation could replace the concept of confrontation ... The actual experiences of the realities of contemporary international life are bringing in fresh evidence daily to bear upon the correctness of Nehru's understanding of the world.[23]

Conclusion

Against the backdrop of the competitive security and also the cooperative security processes taking place in Asia, India has developed its perceptions and policy options. Jawaharlal Nehru's vision of cooperative relations in Asia based on *Panchsheel* is still at the core of India's perceptions and policies with regard to Asian security. Undoubtedly, India has adopted a great degree of pragmatism in its assessment of challenges emanating from China and the emerging great power rivalry in the region. India's power capabilities have increased quite impressively after the end of the Cold War. It no more wants to be seen merely as a South Asian power. Its policy options include the perception that India has a key role to play in Asian political, economic and strategic order. Moreover, Asian region has become so volatile and conflict-prone that India cannot depend on one option or strategy to defend its vital interests. Consequently, India has deployed multiple options for preserving and defending its interests in the emerging Asian security conundrum. And these multiple options do not essentially negate the fundamentals of the Nehruvian vision of promoting India's national interests primarily through a political approach.

References

1. Paul Bracken, *The Second Nuclear Age: Strategy, Danger, and the New Power Politics* (New York: Times Books, 2012).
2. Paul Bracken, "The Structure of the Second Nuclear Age," *Orbis*, vol. 47, no. 3, Summer 2003, pp. 399-413.
3. See David A. Lake, "Powerful pacifists: democratic states and war," *American Political Science Review*, vol. 86, no. 1, 1992, pp. 24-37; Thomas U. Berger, "From sword to chrysanthemum: Japan's culture of anti-militarism," *International Security*, vol. 17, no. 4, 1993, pp. 119-50.
4. Mohan Malik, "India Balances China," *Asian Politics & Policy*, vol. 4, no. 3, 2012, pp. 346-47.
5. Bary Buzan, "Security architecture in Asia: the interplay of regional and global levels," *The Pacific Review*, vol. 16, no. 2, 2003, pp. 143-73.
6. Ibid., p. 143.
7. Ibid., p. 164.
8. P. N. Haksar, *Premonitions* (Bombay: Interpress, 1979), p. 30.
9. S. Gopal, *Jawaharlal Nehru: A Biography*, vol. III (New Delhi: Oxford University Press, 1975), p. 257.
10. Harish Kapur, *India's Foreign Policy, 1947-92: Shadows and Substance* (New Delhi: Sage Publications, 1994), p. 93.
11. Asian Relations Conference, http://icwadelhi.info/asianrelationsconference/index.php?option=com_content&view=article&id=51&Itemid=137.
12. Ibid.
13. Speech delivered at the 1st Asian Relations Conference by Jawaharlal Nehru at New Delhi on March 24, 1947, http://icwadelhi.info/asianrelationsconference/images/stories/jawaharlalnehru.pdf.
14. "Drift towards catastrophe: Broadcast from London, January 12, 1951," Jawaharlal Nehru, *India's Foreign Policy: Selected Speeches, September 1946-April*

1961 (New Delhi: The Publications Division, Ministry of Information and Broadcasting, Government of India, 1961), p. 184.
15. P. N. Haksar, n. 8, p. 27.
16. Miloslav Krasa (ed.), *Jawaharlal Nehru and the Foreign Policy of India* (Centenary Commemorative Volume) (Prague: Czechoslovak Society for International Relations and Oriental Institute of the Czechoslovak Academy of Sciences, 1990), p. 4.
17. Ibid., p. 5.
18. Ministry of External Affairs, Government of India, *Annual Report 2012-13*, p. i.
19. As quoted in V. K. Arora and A. Appadorai, *India in World Affairs, 1957-58* (New Delhi: Sterling Publishers, 1975), p. 1-2.
20. P. N. Haksar, n. 8, p. 27.
21. P. N. Haksar, *India's Foreign Policy and Its Problems* (New Delhi: Patriot Publishers, 1989), p. 40.
22. Tan Tai Yong and See Chak Mun, "The Evolution of India-ASEAN Relations," *India Review*, vol. 8, no. 1, January-March 2009, p. 21.
23. P. N. Haksar, n. 21, p. 98.

11

Nehru and India's China Policy

Baljit Singh

During the visit of India's Prime Minister to Beijing in October 2013, India and China signed nine agreements. Out of them, Border Defence Cooperation Agreement (BDCA) is considered as critical in the light of recent instances of Chinese military assertiveness along the Line of Actual Control (LAC). This development drives us to understand India's China policy from the Nehru era to the present, which can be broadly divided into three phases. The first phase deals with India's China policy from 1947 to 1962 in which it had witnessed a u-turn from friendship to military confrontation. The second phase from the post-1962 war to 1987 began with a stalemate and concluded with initiatives to revive and normalise relations with Beijing. The third phase educates us from 1988 to the present scenario in which New Delhi has been engaging, competing and cooperating with Beijing at bilateral, regional and global levels. The main thrust running across three phases is to understand India's changing perceptions about China which are always shaped by changing material reality and its policy responses thereof.

Friendship to Forward Policy

Right from the beginning, Nehru acknowledged the People's Republic of China (PRC) as a leading country in the Asian continent and perceived joint India-China leadership to achieve the goal of

Asian solidarity. There had been very little contact between the new leaders of India and China during the first half of the twentieth century but Nehru held a deep conviction that India-China friendship would be the basis of an Asian resurgence.[1] Nehru was also aware of the Chinese threat to India, however, generally, it is argued that Nehru could not anticipate the Chinese threat in time. His statements in parliament and outside parliament speak otherwise. Nehru was able to anticipate the Chinese threat to India at the initial stage. It is clear from the statement made by Nehru in Parliament on November 27, 1950. Nehru disclosed in the Parliament that:

> Ever since the Chinese revolution ... we naturally had to think of what the new China was likely to be. We realised that this revolution was going to be a very big factor in Asia, in the world and in regard to us ... Taken also with the fact of China's somewhat inherent tendency to be expansive when she is strong, we realised the danger to India. As the years have gone by, this fact has become more and more apparent and obvious. If any person imagines that we have followed our China policy without realising the consequences, he is mistaken.[2]

Briefing D. R. Mankekar before his visit to China in 1954, Nehru said:

> Some day or the other, these two Asian giants are bound to tread on each other and come into conflict and that would be a calamity for Asia. This is an eventually we should strive hard to avert.[3]

Further K. M. Panikkar, a close associate of Nehru, writing about his assignment in PRC as India's first Ambassador there, admitted that he "knew like everyone else, that with a Communist China, cordial and ultimate relations were out of question" but that he was optimistic working out an area of cooperation by eliminating causes of misunderstanding, rivalry, etc.[4] The policymakers were certainly not basking in the euphoria of *Hindi-Chini Bhai-Bhai* but were hoping that the threat posed by China could be prevented from materialising.[5] The trouble started brewing as early as 1950 and it was clearly perceived by India's policymakers. However, they were constrained by the inability of India to maintain a credible defence posture against both China and Pakistan simultaneously. Nehru, therefore, decided to launch a diplomatic offensive and tried to delay the potential conflict to the extent possible.[6] That is why he did not take a strong stand on Tibet in 1950 and pursued an active mediatory diplomacy to end the Korean War.[7] Tibet was a major factor which shaped India's China policy in the initial years. Although Nehru was eager to maintain Tibet as a buffer but he chose not to resist the PRC in Tibet strongly because he was more interested in pursuing Sino-Indian amity.[8] Nehru was also aware that to assist Tibet militarily in 1949 was beyond India's capabilities. Further, he was conscious of this fact that India's military help to Tibet would not improve its security scenario. Expanding Chinese military presence in Tibet emerged as security threat and exercised a critical impact on India's China policy. Responding to this altered national security situation became, and has remained, a fundamental determinant in India's China policy.[9] There was a debate on India's China policy between Nehru and Patel, though that debate could not last long because of the latter's death. Patel was more apprehensive about the implications for Indian security of China's military occupation of Tibet and construction of roads to forward frontier regions. Patel favoured vigorous moves—military modernisation, road construction and search for diplomatic patterns—to counter China's advances. He was also in favour of cooperation with the US to balance the new revolutionary China. However, his death in 1950 left Nehru's direction of China Policy virtually unchallenged till 1962.[10] China's experience in economic development has been a subject of intense interest to Indian policymakers. Prime Minister Nehru, during his first and only visit to China in 1954, visited heavy and basic industry complex in China's north-east before initiating development of a similar complex in India. A year later, he sent a delegation to study China's agriculture cooperatives as a means of increasing farm productivity.[11]

Nehru linked India's policy of non-alignment to his China policy. Non-alignment was considered essential for the fulfilment of India's economic revolution and for the avoidance of alienating the Soviet Union and China.[12] In 1954, as a manifestation of India's approach, India's Prime Minister Nehru and Chinese Premier Zhou Enlai signed *Panchsheel* Agreement, which embodied five principles of coexistence, namely, mutual respect for each other's territorial integrity and sovereignty; mutual non-aggression, mutual non-interference in each other's internal affairs; equality and mutual benefit; and peaceful existence.[13] In this agreement, India recognised without any qualification China's sovereignty over Tibet and conceded many of its rights and usages. In return, China allowed India to maintain certain trade and pilgrimage rights.[14] While discussing the issue of Tibet with Zhou Enlai during the latter's visit to New Delhi in December 1956, Nehru stated that:

> Our policy has been to deal with the Chinese Government about Tibet and the treaty on Tibet was also signed with the Chinese Government. We are naturally interested in what happens in Tibet as one of our neighbours but we do not want to interfere. Our main interest is from the point of view of pilgrimage—not only Buddhist pilgrims but Hindu pilgrims too for whom Kailash and Manasarovar are sacred places and abodes of God ... As Your Excellency has said, Tibet is a part of China but with full autonomous powers. Then I don't understand why there should be any trouble in Tibet at all.[15]

Nehru was of the opinion that India should extend whatever help it could to the Tibetan government. However, he drew a line between normal assistance and help that would challenge the suzerainty of PRC.[16] By accepting Tibet as a part of Chinese territory, India allowed China to be present at its border for the first time in history.[17] This resulted in debate on India's China policy. India seems to have lost the battle over Tibet to China, despite the fact that Tibet constitutes China's only truly fundamental vulnerability vis-à-vis India. India has failed to limit China's military use of Tibet despite its great implications for Indian security, even as Tibet has become a platform for the projection of Chinese military power.[18]

India's dilemma was that it wanted to help Tibetan resistance to Beijing but could not do it because of two reasons. First, as the US Central Intelligence Agency (CIA) decided to assist that resistance with training, arms and equipment to be parachuted into Tibet, India did not want to be identified with the US as it was pursuing a non-aligned policy and anti-imperialist policy. Second, India was well aware that it is beyond its military capability to assist the Tibetan uprising and thereby offending PRC. However, Nehru responded to an eruption of popular sympathy for the Tibetans, granted refuge in India for the Dalai Lama, Tibet's traditional leader, along with thousands of his followers. Tibetan refugees settled in the Indian side of the Himalayan mountains and became a base of support for the CIA supported anti-Chinese activities.[19] India's decision to provide asylum to Tibetan refugees gave Mao an opportunity to conclude that India was responsible for the uprising, its demand for Chinese evacuation of the Aksai Chin plateau was also a part of an Indian-American-Soviet design to erode Chinese control over Tibet.

Border

Apart from Tibet, another issue that clearly shaped India's China policy has been the boundary dispute, as China refused to acknowledge the McMahon line as a boundary between India and China as it was drawn by an imperial power. While talking about India's China policy, Nehru stated:

> We must realise fully that our policy in regard to China is one of friendliness and coexistence, allied with firmness in regard to any interference with our basic rights. Ultimately the basic right is the preservation of the frontier. There are some other rights and customs which are not very controversial. We shall not give up any basic right ... It is important today, and even more so in the long future, that India and China should have friendly relations and

> not have a dangerous frontier. The best way to ensure this on our side is to develop the border regions on this side not only in the sense of roads, etc., but in the sense of winning people there to the conception of India.[20]

However, the boundary issue was simmering since September 1957 when China announced the completion of a road across Aksai Chin but it clearly cropped up after the consolidation of China's control over Tibet. Nehru was shocked at China's refusal to recognise the McMahon line as a boundary between India and China (earlier Tibet) apart from the way the Chinese handled the Tibetan uprising in March 1959. It was a major setback to Nehru's China policy. Nehru's China policy became a subject of intense domestic criticism that pressurised him to provide asylum to Tibetan refugees including Dalai Lama in India and allowed them to carry out wider scope of activities, which was not liked by China. Further, Nehru attempted to demonstrate his toughness by ordering India's military to assert India's claim to contested territory by actually establishing control over that territory.[21] Mao read Nehru's call for forward deployment of Indian military patrols as evidence of aggressive rather than defensive intent. Nehru failed to understand China's verbal or written warning signals, conveyed over two years, and could not even conceive the possibility of a massive Chinese attack across the Himalayas.[22] In November 1961, Nehru ordered Indian forces to assert physical control over territory up to the line claimed by India, pushing out in the process any Chinese forces that might be in those areas.[23] While rejecting Beijing's proposal of a compromise settlement to the border involving Chinese acceptance of the watershed principle (that is, the McMahon line) in the east in exchange for India's relinquishing its claim to Aksai Chin in the west, and then ordering the forward policy, Nehru was in fact pursuing maximal and hard-line policies and military weakness was an invitation to disaster that came in October 1962.[24] Material reality for India's China policy changed in the late 1950s. China was a friend for India in the early 1950s, which turned out to be its enemy in the late 1950s. India's China policy changed accordingly. On November 2, 1961, the Indian Government issued a directive for the implementation of what it called "the forward policy," which was passed on by Army HQ to the area commanders concerned on December 5, 1961. It stated with regard to Ladakh that:

> We are to patrol as far forward as possible from our present positions towards the international border as recognised by us. This will be done with a view to establishing additional posts located to prevent the Chinese from advancing further and also to dominate any Chinese posts already established in our territory.[25]

While pursuing its forward policy, India made an incorrect assessment of its adversary because of which it proved counter-productive. India's assessment about China was that the Chinese would not react to establishing new posts by its troops but the reverse had happened. Therefore, neither India's policy of friendship nor its forward policy secured its national interest vis-à-vis China because the failure of the former resulted in the animosity of China, and the latter met with a humiliating defeat and loss of territory to its northern neighbour in the 1962 war. In this war, India's military forces were unprepared for the powerful Chinese military offensive, which continued for almost one month. During this phase India conceded many concessions to China ranging from Tibet to rejecting US invitations to contain China. Beijing had repaid Indian friendship first with hostility and then with outright invasion.[26]

Estrangement to Normalisation

India's defeat in 1962 resulted in a change in its China policy. Till 1962, it was based on the principle embodied in *Panchsheel* rather than based on calculations of power. Nehru's China policy failed, but it was not idealistic because he was aware of the Chinese threat and Indian limitations to handle it. By pursuing a policy of friendship with China, Nehru was just buying time to build Indian capabilities. After its defeat in 1962, India took various measures to build its military capabilities apart from making it clear that India-China relations cannot be normalised until the border issue was resolved. China was expecting that the 1962 war would force India to settle the boundary dispute to Chinese advantage but it did not happen. Further, this war changed India's regional security scenario, which brought it close to the Soviet Union as the Soviets were also having problems with China. Initially India looked towards the US for support against China but it did not come because for the US the enemy was the Soviet Union rather than China. China emerged as a common enemy for India and the Soviet Union. Meanwhile, the steady and rapid escalation of Soviet-China hostility during the 1960s made Moscow ever more ready to support India against China.[27] Nehru's aspiration of India-China cooperation for Asian resurgence was almost frozen for a generation. The India-China 1962 war was followed by China's demonstration of its weaponised nuclear capability in 1964. China's proximity with Pakistan and the emergence of US-Pakistan-China axis further affected India's regional security scenario to its disadvantage. These developments shaped India's policy towards China by bringing it closer to the Soviet Union apart from changing India's nuclear policy from single-track to dual-track. Nehru's successor, Lal Bahadur Shastri, was cautious about the growing domestic concern for China's nuclear threat. After China's nuclear test, he said that the Indian government did not favour emulating the Chinese example of developing and testing the nuclear bomb. He also asked the Indian people not to lose their faith in peace and peaceful methods.[28] Shastri approved a secret underground nuclear test project in 1965, but openly resisted the pressure from Indian National Congress Party about building nuclear capabilities for military use. Indira Gandhi proved to be a typical realist as she authorised the first nuclear test at Pokhran in May 1974.[29] Apart from that, Sikkim was annexed by the Indira Gandhi government in 1975 to bolster India's defence against China.[30] At the national level along with economic development, modernisation and expansion of the military had become priorities for India. Diplomatic relations between India and China remained snapped from October 1962 to June 1976. From July 1976 onwards, India again decided to engage China while restoring its diplomatic relations with the latter. India's Foreign Minister A. B. Vajpayee's visit to China in February 1979 resulted in the reopening for Indians of an ancient pilgrimage route to the sacred sites of Kailash and Manasarovar in south-western Tibet.[31] Following visits by Indian and Chinese Foreign Ministers to each other's capitals in 1979 and 1981 respectively, both sides agreed to find a mutually acceptable solution to the boundary dispute through negotiations. Eight rounds of talks were held between 1981 and 1987 but failed to find a solution.[32] Chinese transfer of nuclear and missile technology to Pakistan and China's protests over the elevation of Arunachal Pradesh to statehood, and Chinese intrusion in Sumdorong Chu Valley in Arunachal Pradesh in June 1986 continued to shape its policy towards China.

Engagement with Uneasiness

In this phase, there was again a change in India's China policy. India thought of engaging China notwithstanding the boundary dispute. Rajiv Gandhi as a Prime Minister of India paid a state visit to China in 1988. During his visit, India and China agreed to accelerate search for settlement of the boundary dispute, and Joint Working Group (JWG) was established to achieve that. Further, the two sides also agreed that pending solution of the border dispute, cooperation in other areas would be expanded.[33] This change in India's China policy was driven by the changing global geostrategic, political and economic reality. The Rajiv Gandhi government made a new beginning with China but the responsibility to carry it forward fell on P. V. Narasimha Rao. Under the leadership of Rao, India decided to respond positively to Beijing's desires for friendly ties with India. In September 1993, China and India signed an agreement "to maintain peace and tranquillity" along their disputed Himalayan border, which required both sides to respect the Line of Actual Control (LAC), till the final solution of the boundary dispute was found. It also required both sides to reduce their military forces along the border. This agreement was a major breakthrough and logical culmination of a series of developments since the late 1980s, especially the visit of India's Prime Minister to Beijing in 1988 and Chinese Premier to New Delhi in 1991; the Soviet collapse; and the consequent dramatic changes in global strategic environment.[34] Chinese President Jiang Zemin's visit to India in November 1996 resulted in an agreement on Confidence Building Measures (CBMs) in the military field along the LAC. It abjured the use of military force, led to some significant reduction of troops on either side, and spurred the process of clarifying the alignment of the LAC by adding technical experts to the JWG.[35] Although China changed its policy on Kashmir while not endorsing Pakistan's position on it, it kept bothering New Delhi, being Bangladesh's primary supplier of military equipment, apart from its increasingly close relationship with Kathmandu. Despite that proximity China could not replace India as Nepal's economic lifeline. Some experts asserted that China had essentially acquiesced to New Delhi's dominant role in South Asia,[36] and demanded India's acquiescence to Beijing's dominant role throughout Asia.[37] However, the objectives of China's South Asia policy, including *String of Pearls* policy, speak otherwise but the post-Cold War realism coupled with the focus on economic development dictated their common interests, which outweighed their differences for almost a decade. It resulted in warming of Sino-Indian relations wherein Beijing promised not to use the Pakistani card against India and offered flexibility on Sikkim,[38] apart from cautioning Islamabad against escalating the level of conflict during the Kargil war in 1999.

India continues to stress adequacy in defence along the border but at the same time, it has been careful not to provoke China militarily. The only exception to India's general policy of restraint occurred after Pokhran-II in May 1998, when New Delhi sought to justify the tests in terms of the Chinese threat.[39] A sense of China threat has been occupying Indian strategic thinking since the Chinese People's Liberation Army (PLA) entered Tibet in

1950, through the Sino-Indian war in 1962, the Chinese nuclear test in 1964 and the strategic ties with Pakistan since 1965, right up to India's nuclear tests in 1998, when Indian Defence Minister George Fernandes asserted that China was "potential threat number one."[40] While justifying India's nuclear tests, Indian Prime Minister Vajpayee wrote a letter to US President Bill Clinton in which he focused on the Chinese threat to India, even while avoiding specific identification of China. Consequently, for the next two years Beijing unfolded a series of measures designed to punish New Delhi for its anti-China stance. It was more concerned about India's China threat justification of nuclear weapons rather than India's nuclear weapons.[41] Notwithstanding India's justification for Pokhran-II, nuclear deterrence was seen as vital to secure India against China. India's justification for its nuclear tests not only irritated Beijing but was also instrumental in changing Washington's perception about New Delhi, which was reflected in the form of President Bill Clinton's visit to India in 2000. In this context, China ended its post-test campaign to punish India and quietly began making a series of concessions to New Delhi to keep India away from closer alignment with the US. Vajpayee visited China in June 2003 and signed a statement in which India recognises that the Tibet Autonomous Region is part of the PRC and reiterates that it does not allow Tibetans to engage in anti-China political activities in India.[42] China appreciated India's position on Tibet. In January 2005, China and India formalised their "strategic dialogue" apart from formally recognising Sikkim as a part of the Indian Union, thereby dropping a 30-year-long policy of non-recognition of India's annexation of that territory.[43]

India's understanding about China continues to sustain two parallel tendencies: one sees China as incorrigibly aggressive and expansionist, and the other perceives it as a benign neighbour.[44] India's perceptions on China can also be viewed through institutional lineages and legacies, in terms of views held by successive occupants in the Indian Ministries of Defence (MoD), External Affairs (MEA), Home Affairs (MHA) and more recently those working in the

Prime Minister's Office (PMO), which has lately centralised all policymaking. In recent years, the views of India's National Security Advisor have become increasingly open and emphatic.[45] The key players in India's decision-making about China are the PMO, the military and intelligence community, the MEA, MoD, political parties and business lobbies. Though officially India is committed to engaging China at multiple levels, there exist serious differences on how to deal with China.[46] To deal with China, India has articulated its policy responses at three different levels: bilateral, regional and global.

At the *bilateral level*, India has been engaging China on economic issues, border dispute and strategic domain. However, India's policy of rapprochement with China can be traced back to September 1968, when Indian leadership indicated that New Delhi kept its options open for seeking a negotiated settlement of all outstanding issues with Beijing, but it worked effectively only in the late 1980s. Establishment of JWG on the border dispute during Rajiv Gandhi's visit to Beijing in 1988 was the most significant outcome of the changed policy, which subsequently resulted in two agreements of September 1993 and November 1996. Apart from these, India has signed various agreements with China on the border question. The Agreement on Political Parameters and Guiding Principles for the Settlement of the India-China boundary Question, April 11, 2005; the Protocol of Modalities for the Implementation of Confidence Building Measures in the Military Field Along the Line of Actual Control in India-China Border Areas, April 1, 2005; the Agreement on Establishment of a Working Mechanism for Consultation and Coordination on India-China Border Affairs, January 17, 2012; and the Border Defence Cooperation Agreement, October 2013 are cases in point.

Another milestone of this changed policy was India-China bilateral trade. India-China trade has been overshooting the targets set by the respective political leaderships. China has already replaced the US as India's largest trading partner. Trade between the two countries has been expanding exceptionally fast since the late

1990s.[47] Indian investments in China have been welcomed; although India continues to restrict Chinese investment in a broad range of sectors deemed sensitive from a security perspective, investment flows, while still very modest, are increasing in both directions (Embassy of India in China). The growing economic connections, although not yet leading to meaningful interdependence, make future bilateral strains more likely to be "managed down" rather than escalated into full-blown rows.[48] China and India are ideally suited as trading partners given India's technology and services-oriented companies complementing China's manufacturing and infrastructure prowess.[49] Indian and Chinese investment links have been growing, with Indian companies such as Tata Consultancy Services (TCS) and Infosys setting up major global sourcing bases in China, and telecommunications giant Huawei setting up large R&D bases in India.[50] A number of Indian investors have established joint ventures, including Ranbaxy and Aurobindo Pharmaceuticals, while others have set up wholly owned ventures, including Infosys and Essel Packaging.[51]

Perhaps the biggest challenge to Sino-Indian rapprochement, but also a source of forward impetus, has come from the rapidly improving US-Indian relationship, particularly during the Bush Administration's second term in office between 2005 and 2009. During this time, India and the USA enlarged the scope and depth of their relationship, most notably in the form of 123 Nuclear Agreement, which legitimised India's nuclear weapons programme.[52] While a much improved relationship with the USA has helped India to counter the traditional pro-Pakistan tilt in US foreign policy, it has also made Sino-Indian rapprochement a greater priority for Beijing.[53] India prefers a US-led unipolar world to China-dominated Asia—but ultimately seeks a multipolar world with itself as a constituent pole.[54] While playing the US card, India also wants to avoid entrapment in the US-China rivalry. India also has ambitious, if slow moving, plans to build armed forces, including a serious three carrier blue-water navy, to back up its presence as the major local power in the Indian Ocean.[55]

Except justifying India's nuclear tests (1998) by quoting the Chinese threat, successive political dispensations in New Delhi avoided publically raising controversial issues with a view to maintaining cordiality in bilateral negotiations. The BJP-led NDA government was initially assertive when it cited the China threat for India going nuclear in 1998 but subsequently softened its stand on China and gradually moved towards cooperative relations with Beijing. But the NDA dispensation was clear that only a firm policy based on comprehensive strength, strategic alliances and proactive containment of China would force Beijing to abandon its hostility towards India.[56] Congress-led UPA-I and UPA-II dispensations have pursued the policy of engaging and balancing China. There are also sharp differences on China within the policy establishment because the elected political elite at the helm of affairs has always remained optimistic about normal relations with China, but the MEA oscillates between this optimism and a trust deficit with regard to Beijing. The MoD favours a hawkish policy vis-à-vis China, recognising that the PLA remains a bastion of anti-Indian sentiment in the PRC's ruling apparatus and the military establishment cautions against lowering its guard if India wants to avoid a repeat of a 1962-type defeat. The burden of history still weighs heavily on the policymakers elite in India.[57] According to Zhang Guihong, India's threat perception, mainly based on Beijing's capabilities instead of its intentions, reflects the burden of history and lack of self-confidence in New Delhi.[58] India's Foreign Minister described the rise of China as one of India's foremost security challenges.[59]

At the *regional level*, India has also been responding to China's regional policy initiatives. China has been cultivating South Asian States like Pakistan, Bangladesh, Sri Lanka and the Maldives through its *String of Pearls* policy with an objective to encircle India. Indian analysts fear a Chinese strategy of encirclement in Asia, which refers to China's numerous investments in building up port facilities in the Indian Ocean, such as at Bandar Abbas in Iran, Gwadar in Pakistan, Chittagong in Bangladesh and Hambantota in Sri Lanka.[60] China's support for Pakistan, as well as its encroachment into the Indian

Ocean, is viewed by some as part of a coherent strategy to encircle India and confine its influence to South Asia.[61] These concerns are accompanied by apprehension over the PLAN's ongoing expansion, which is viewed as a possible threat to India's strategic interests in the region.[62] However, Beijing never considered India a serious threat to its security until now because the political disputes between China and India are minor, thus reducing China's need to point a large number of missiles in India's direction.[63] Guihong articulated that China's interests and goals in South Asia and the Indian Ocean are mainly economic—more trade partners and secure oil transportation. But economic interests need to be ensured and protected by political relations and the security environment. China's military relationship with the South Asian countries is a part of this process, and is not necessary to be seen as targeting India.[64]

As China has been competing with India for influence in South Asia, likewise India has been competing with China for influence in South-East Asia (SEA) and East Asia (EA). India's *Look East Policy* (LEP) has been the main instrument for that which has enabled India not only to cultivate South-East Asia but also East Asia. With its help, India has already cultivated Myanmar, Vietnam, Singapore and Indonesia and many more states from SEA and EA. India has taken initiatives like Bangladesh, India, Myanmar, Sri Lanka and Thailand Economic Cooperation (BIMSTEC) and Mekong Ganga Cooperation (MGC) to promote cooperation at subregional level in the Bay of Bengal and South-East Asian region respectively. Although these subregional groupings are at the initial stages, India has consciously excluded China because India's growing linkages with countries of the Bay of Bengal region are to counter the increasing influence of China there.[65] Besides this, India is also a player in seabed resource extraction in the South China Sea (SCS) in areas that are contested between China and the other littoral states of that Sea.[66] There were clear signs of an emerging axis of democracies amongst India, the US, Japan and Australia in Asia by 2007, however India was conscious of the message it would have sent to Beijing. By playing its democracy card in the greater Asia region, India can associate itself with the US alliance system without accepting biding entanglements.[67] Continuing with Nehruvian tradition in its foreign policy, India does not want to be a part of any alliance system; however it has never hesitated to reach tactical understanding with the state that helped in serving India's national interests. India's tactical understanding with the Soviet Union during the Cold War period and with the US and Japan in the beginning of the twenty-first century, are classic cases in point. Despite repeated affirmations and clarifications, China takes a negative view of India's relations with the US and Japan. The *People's Daily*, a leading newspaper of China, claimed that the US and Japan had established a "ring around China" and that "China is seen in India as both potential threat and a competitor to surpass."[68]

India and China's competition for influence does not remain confined to South and South-East Asia. According to Zhang Guihong an emerging India does mean a strong competitor for China from South, West, South-East and Central Asia to the Indian and Pacific Oceans, where their interests and influences would clash.[69] India as an emerging power is expanding its areas of interests and influence in Asia and Indian Ocean, which are not and cannot be in alignment with China because of their competing strategic interests. India's extended neighbourhood cuts into China's own backyard in Central and South-East Asia, and both states seek to project their presence and power into the Indian Ocean.[70] Further India's involvement in East Asian countries' sea-lane security acts as a challenge to China's vested interests in the Indian Ocean region. India's engagement of East Asia is a response to China's strategy of encircling India with a ring of weapon-client states including Myanmar, Bangladesh, Sri Lanka and Pakistan, all of whom have been supplied with Chinese weapons.[71] Threatened by China's rise, India has expanded its naval presence from as far West as the Mozambique Channel to as far East as the South China Sea. It has been establishing naval staging posts and listening-stations on the Island nations of Madagascar, Mauritius, and the Seychelles, as well as military relationship with them, precisely to counter China's own very active military cooperation with these states.[72] In 2005 a Far Eastern Naval Command (FENC) was established at Port Blair in the Andaman Islands, which are located midway between the Bay of Bengal and the Strait of Malacca—a key choke point linking the Indian Ocean to the South China Sea.[73] Further to facilitate power projection into the Asia-Pacific, the Indian Navy is upgrading its base network. A second naval base on India's eastern shore is being constructed near Vizag, 30 miles south of the existing Eastern Naval Command Headquarters. However, India lacks capability to independently shape the regional order in Asia-Pacific but it has made its presence felt by integrating herself with the major democracies of the region and expanding its ties with China-wary nations. In pursuing strategic ties with nations that have traditionally had difficult relations with China—such as Vietnam, Indonesia, Japan and the United States—New Delhi lends its military and economic power to a regional security order that enhances stability in Asia by presenting Beijing with a series of structural constraints that may diffuse the negative aspects of China's rise and persuade it that attempts to dominate the region are unlikely to succeed.[74]

In addition to expanding naval infrastructure, India has been pursuing the proactive naval diplomacy to consolidate its position in the Indian Ocean. It has been conducting MALABAR naval exercise with the US since 1992, which got suspended after Pokhran-II in 1998 and resumed again in 2002. To further increase its reach in the Indian Ocean India has been hosting MILAN exercises with South-East Asian states since 1995, organised from India's Far Eastern Naval Command (FENC) at Port Blair in Andaman Islands. In 2008, apart from the ASEAN countries, the navies of Bangladesh, Sri Lanka, Australia and New Zealand were also invited to participate in the Milan exercises. China was not invited to participate in these naval exercises.[75] Within this denial setting, India's easterly and southerly projections into the extended neighbourhood of South-East Asia and the Indian Ocean have been more substantive.[76] The Indian Navy is also improving its maritime surveillance and operational capabilities by creating more naval infrastructure in Andaman & Nicobar,

Lakshadweep and Minicoy Islands, which constitute its strategic outposts. According to former Admiral Verma, they enhance India's forward operating capability in the Indian Ocean. It is no coincidence that Indian naval warships, aircrafts and helicopters operating from these bases can potentially cover all of China's energy routes from the Middle East to the Malacca Straits. That is what the Chinese calls the "Malacca Dilemma."[77]

New Delhi's perspective of Chinese policies that aim at strategic encirclement of India, as well as Beijing's outlook on India's attempt to limit China's influence in South and South-East Asia and its power projection into the Indian Ocean, has overridden their formulaic statements of shared interests as partners in strengthening a multipolar world.[78] The Indo-US nuclear deal, approved by Washington and New Delhi in 2008, carved out an exception for India from American law prohibiting commerce in civil nuclear energy with non-signatories of the Nuclear Non-Proliferation (NPT). The last-minute push of the Bush Administration to gain an unconditional exemption for nuclear commerce with India from Nuclear Suppliers Group (NSG) exacerbated China's suspicions that closer US-India friendship was aimed at containing China's rise. As China's growing strength creates uneasiness in the region, India's balancing role is welcome within ASEAN. Its naval presence facilitates comprehensive cooperation with other countries who have tense relations with China, most notably Japan. India's efforts to outflank China's encirclement were boosted after Beijing unexpectedly challenged US naval supremacy in the South China Sea and the Pacific Ocean. The Obama Administration reasserted the big picture strategic vision of US-India partnership first advanced by the nuclear deal. Rivalry between China and India in the Indian Ocean—now expanded to China and the United States in the Pacific—is solidifying an informal coalition of democracies in the vast Asia-Pacific region.[79]

According to Barry Buzan, India and China are clearly in sustained and conscious strategic interaction, which is still a lopsided one that favours China. China is stronger than India and feels less threatened by India than the other way round. China has a longer standing and deep-rooted position in South Asia than India has in East Asia. But India has the advantage of having the US as a friend, while China, for all its rising strength, has no great power friend.[80] As the South Asian states are not comfortable with India's emergence, similarly all the SEA states are hedging against the rise of China. Since the onset of the economic crisis in 2008, China has been more aggressive over asserting its position in a variety of territorial disputes in the South China Sea (SCS) as well as with Japan and India.[81]

The Indian Prime Minister has suggested that "China would like to have a foothold in South Asia and we have to reflect on this reality ... it's important to be prepared."[82] The Indian Defence Minister has argued that China's increasing assertiveness is a "serious threat"[83] and India's former National Security Advisor and Special Envoy to China, M. K. Narayanan, has openly accused Chinese hackers of attacking his website, as well as those of other Indian government departments.[84] However, the objectives of China's India policy are not clearly stated but Beijing's capability to pursue whatever goals it has in mind vis-à-vis New Delhi, is greater than at any time in the past. Keeping this in mind, India initiated a process of military consolidation and naval build-up apart from engaging the key states from SEA and EA in strategic partnerships. India has been responding to China's rise and its increasing assertiveness by cultivating Vietnam, Indonesia, South Korea, Malaysia, Myanmar and Japan. The China factor is a cementing force in evolving India's relations and partnership with these countries. With the rise of China in the recent past, Indo-Vietnam and Indo-Japan and Indo-US ties have become strategic in orientation. India and Vietnam have stakes in ensuring the security of sea lanes of communications and also share concerns about Chinese access to the Indian Ocean and South China Sea. At the July 2012 ASEAN Regional Forum in Phnom Penh, India made a strong case for freedom of navigation and access to resources in accordance with principles of international law.[85] New Delhi, which so often sits on the sidelines and avoids taking sides, seems to have recognised that it can no longer afford the luxury of inaction if it wants to preserve the credibility of a significant actor in East Asia and South-East Asia.[86]

At the *global level*, formally, New Delhi and Beijing repeatedly declare that neither country would view the other as a security threat. They characterise their relationship as "strategic and cooperative partnership" and professions of friendship and cooperation are regularly made in both capitals. They also cooperate to mutual advantage in international forums—especially when pitted against the developed world—on issues such as climate change, labour standards and trade.[87] India and China had signed their first-ever formal partnership agreement to strengthen bilateral cooperation on climate change in October 2009. According to the Chinese Ambassador:

> In international affairs, the two sides have maintained effective cooperation and coordination within the framework of the China-India-Russia Trilateral Mechanism, BRICS, the G-20, and other forums. China and India have been making joint efforts on major international issues, including climate change, the Doha Round talks, the global financial crisis, countering terrorism, energy and food security, etc., with a view to protecting the interests of our two countries and other developing countries, and promoting fair, just, and reasonable international system.[88]

On the issue of climate change at Copenhagen India banded together with China, Brazil and South Africa to voice the concerns of the developing world, while also displaying awareness of its own environmental vulnerability.[89]

A survey literature on India's China policy indicates that New Delhi has always desired to have cordial relations with Beijing since independence. Knowing well that the People's Republic of China was a potential threat to Indian security, Nehru still wanted peace with China because of various reasons. First, Nehru wanted to deal with this threat through diplomacy rather than through war because he was a strong advocate of world peace. Second, Nehru was conscious of the fact that India was not capable at that point of time to confront China militarily. While using diplomatic tools, he intended to buy time to build India's economic and technological capabilities and thereby to enhance its national power to ensure national security. Third Nehru did not want to divert whatever meagre resources India had from economic development to military build-up. Fourth, Nehru was of the opinion that India's friendly overtones to China on the issue of Tibet, the Korean War and its support for PRC's claim for a permanent seat in the United Nations Security Council would generate enough political capital to develop friendly relations with Beijing. Fifth, Nehru, being a champion of Asian nationalism and solidarity, thought that India-China friendship is an essential requirement for achieving it. India's policy of friendship with China suffered a major setback with the consolidation of Chinese position in Tibet in the late 1950s, which enabled Beijing to question the validity of the McMahon Line, which used to be the boundary line between India and Tibet. Apart from that, another issue which upset Nehru was the way China handled the Tibetan uprising in March 1959. China's assertiveness and incursions across the McMahon line forced Nehru to rethink India's China policy. Principles of *Panchsheel* could not moderate the latent conflict between India and China, and Nehru changed India's China policy from friendship to the policy of forward defence. Under this forward policy, Nehru ordered Indian troops in November 1961 to establish physical control over the territory up to the line India claims. Nehru underestimated China's probable response in addition to ignoring the fact that Indian armed forces were not modernised. However, forward policy was a defensive move on the part of India, which was interpreted by Mao as an offensive. Nehru's wrong assessment of India's adversary had proved counter-productive and India suffered a humiliating defeat in the October 1962 war.

Nehru's successors, including his daughter, Indira Gandhi, pursued the policy of estrangement and diplomatic relations were snapped with Beijing till 1976. The India-China war of 1962 and loss of territory to Beijing changed the regional security scenario for New Delhi, which not only brought it close to Moscow but also drove its nuclear policy from single-track to dual track, when Indira

Gandhi declared after Pokhran-I that India's nuclear policy is for peaceful purposes but if its security scenario demands, it can develop nuclear weapons as well. This was announced at the time when India demonstrated its technical nuclear capability on May 17, 1974. To further improve its defence vis-à-vis New Delhi initially made Sikkim an associate state of the Indian Union and subsequently its integral part. Notwithstanding these developments, India restored its diplomatic relations with Beijing in 1976 but the element of estrangement and indifference continued to define its China policy. New Delhi made it clear to Beijing that relations cannot be normalised until the border issue was resolved.

India's China policy has again witnessed change since the Rajiv Gandhi period when he visited China in 1988. The change that took place in New Delhi's China policy was that India agreed to normalise its ties with Beijing notwithstanding the boundary dispute. Both the countries also agreed to negotiate their boundary dispute and the JWG was constituted for that. Subsequent Indian leadership has also signed various agreements to engage China on various issues ranging from the border dispute to bilateral trade. Increasing volume of bilateral trade during the last couple of years indicates that India has been engaging China in spite of the fact that trade figures are favourable to Beijing and India has an unsustainable trade deficit vis-à-vis China. The various meetings of the JWG on the border dispute held since 1988 further substantiate the argument that India and China have been engaging each other; of course they have not been able to solve the boundary puzzle so far. Both countries are also cooperating with each other on various issues at the global level such as trade, climate change, a multipolar world, terrorism and religious fundamentalism. Their cooperation has been witnessed at various forums like WTO, BRICS and G-20. However, India's justification of the Chinese threat for going nuclear in 1998 halted the process of engagement for two years, but New Delhi's growing proximity with Washington forced Beijing to rethink its punitive action against New Delhi. Engagement has been the critical element of India's China policy but it does not explain it in its entirety.

Another element of India's China policy has been the ongoing competition between New Delhi and Beijing for influence and resources as both are aspiring to be major powers apart from sustaining their growth momentum. India and China have been competing with each other in South Asia, South-East Asia, Central Asia, East Asia, the Indian Ocean and Asia-Pacific. China's *string of pearls* policy has been its drive for influence in India's immediate neighbourhood and the Indian Ocean, which is critical for Beijing for its energy supply from West Asia. Some strategic thinkers in India are considering these moves of Beijing to encircle India. *Look East Policy* has been New Delhi's drive to increase its domain of influence in South-East Asia, East Asia and Asia-Pacific. Occasionally, the element of conflict has already manifested on the issue of border dispute in the form of incursions across the LAC. However, India does not want to engage China in confrontation in spite of the reported Chinese incursions across the LAC since the last couple of years. Rather, India has opted for the diplomatic route to address the occasional border incursions and has signed various agreements with Beijing for that, and recently the Border Defence Cooperation Agreement signed in October 2013. New Delhi is well aware that it will not be able to gain anything while engaging Beijing in confrontation because India has already suffered, while doing so in 1962. Although, India has improved its economic and military capabilities in comparison to the past but it still lags behind China. Beijing has tremendously improved its machinery of warfare and strategic infrastructure along the LAC and Tibet, whereas India's strategic infrastructure along the LAC is not at par with China, hence there exists a power asymmetry between them. In a nutshell, it can be articulated from the aforesaid analysis that there has been some continuity in India's China policy since the Nehru period. That has been to resolve disputed issues with China through diplomacy because there was, and there has been, a power differential between the two neighbours. Issues bothering Indian policymakers have been the unsettled border with China and China's increasing assertiveness along the LAC during the last few years, apart from Beijing's continuous support for Pakistan's nuclear and missile programme. India has been responding to that by engaging like-minded states from South-East Asia and East Asia and Asia-Pacific, including the US, in strategic partnership, or joint naval bilateral and multilateral naval exercises like MILAN and MALABAR. How long India will be able to manage or resolve the conflict on the boundary and other issues with China depends upon its diplomatic skills and hard power capability at its disposal, and Beijing's response thereof apart from the emerging power equations and changing geostrategic and geo-economic reality in Asia, Indian Ocean and Asia-Pacific in addition to the world at large.

References

1. Surjit Mansingh, "Rising China and Emergent India in Twenty-First Century: Friends or Rivals?"Kanti P. Bajpai and Harsh V. Pant (eds.), *India's Foreign Policy: A Reader* (New Delhi: Oxford University Press, 2013), p. 284.
2. Jawaharlal Nehru, *India's Foreign Policy: Select Speeches 1946-April 1961* (New Delhi: Government of India Publications Division, 1961), p. 369.
3. D. R. Mankekar, *The Guilty Men of 1962* (Bombay: Tulsi Publications, 1968), p. 110.
4. A. R. Rana, *The Imperatives of Non-alignment: A Conceptual Study of India's Foreign Policy Strategy in the Nehru Period* (New Delhi: Macmillan, 1971), p. 65.
5. Sita Gopalan, "India's China Policy," *Strategic Analysis*, March 1992, p. 1403, www.idsa.in/system/files/India's China Policy_SitaGopalan.pdf, accessed on December 28, 2013 at 7: 40 pm.
6. Ibid.
7. R. K. Jain, *India-South Asian Relations 1947-1980*, vol. 1 (New Delhi: Radiant Publishers, 1981), pp. 29-35.
8. Andrew Bingham Kennedy, *The International Ambitions of Mao and Nehru: National Efficacy Beliefs and the Making of Foreign Policy* (Cambridge: Cambridge University Press, 2012), p. 226.
9. John W. Garver, "Evolution of India's China Policy," Sumit Ganguly (ed.), *India's Foreign Policy: Retrospect and Prospect* (New Delhi: Oxford University Press, 2012), p. 84.
10. Ibid., p. 86.
11. S. K. Bhutani, "China and India: Competing Friends or Rivals," *India Quarterly*, vol. 65, no. 4, 2009, p. 384.
12. Michael Brecher, *Nehru: A Political Biography*, abridged edition (London: Oxford University Press, 1959), p. 213.
13. *Jawaharlal Nehru's Speeches, Volume III, March 1953-August 1957* (New Delhi: Government of India, Ministry of Information & Broadcasting, 1958), p. 262.
14. Gregory Clark, *In Fear of China* (London: Barrie & Rockliff the Cresset Press,

1968), p. 44.
15. Mushirul Hasan (ed.), *Selected Works of Jawaharlal Nehru, December 1, 1956-February 21, 1957* (Second Series), vol. 36 (New Delhi: Jawaharlal Nehru Memorial Fund, 2005), p. 601.
16. Sameer Suryakant Patil, "India's China Policy in the 1950s," *South Asian Survey*, vol. 14, no. 2, 2007, p. 287.
17. Ibid.
18. Harsh V. Pant, "India's China Policy: Devoid of a Strategic Framework," *South Asian Survey*, vol. 12, no. 2, 2005, p. 217.
19. John W. Garver, n. 9, p. 90.
20. S. Gopal, (ed.), *Selected Works of Jawaharlal Nehru October 1, 1953–January 31, 1954* (Second Series) vol. 24, New Delhi: Jawaharlal Nehru Memorial Fund, 1999, p. 597.
21. John W. Garver, n. 9, p. 91.
22. Surjit Mansingh, n. 1, pp. 284-85.
23. Steven A. Hoffmann, *India and the China Crisis* (Berkeley: University of California Press, 1998).
24. John W. Garver, n. 9, p. 92.
25. Neville Maxwell, *India's China War* (London: Cape, Bombay: Jaico, 1970), pp. 221-24.
26. Ibid.
27. John W. Garver, n. 9, p. 94.
28. Shyam Bhatia, *India's Nuclear Bomb* (Ghaziabad: Vikas Publishing House, 1979), p. 109.
29. Zhang Jiegen, "Contemporary Indian Strategic Culture and Its Nuclear Strategy," *International Review*, vol. 46, Spring 2007, p. 92.
30. Mohan Malik, *China and India: Great Power Rivals* (New Delhi: Viva Books, 2012), p. 38.
31. Surjit Mansingh, n. 1, p. 285.
32. Mohan Malik, n. 30, p. 39.
33. John W. Garver, n. 9, p. 96.
34. Mohan Malik, n. 30, p. 39.
35. Surjit Mansingh, n. 1, p. 288.
36. Waheguru Pal Singh Sidhu and Jing-dong Yuan, *China and India: Cooperation or Conflict* (Boulder: Lynne Rienner Publishers, 2003), p. 26.
37. John W. Garver, *Protracted Contest: Sino-Indian Rivalry in the Twentieth Century* (Seattle, WA: University of Washington Press, 2001).
38. Mohan Malik, n. 30, p. 41.
39. Kanti P. Bajpai, "Indian Strategic Culture," Kant P. Bajpai and Harsh V. Pant (eds.), *India's Foreign Policy: A Reader* (New Delhi: Oxford University Press, 2013), p. 114.
40. Guihong Zhang, "The Rise of China: India's Perceptions and Responses," *South Asian Survey*, vol. 13, no. 1, 2006, p. 98.
41. John W. Garver, n. 9, p. 100.
42. Surjit Mansingh, n. 1, p. 291.
43. John W. Garver, n. 9, p. 102.
44. C. V. Ranganathan and Vinod C. Khanna, *India and China: The Way Ahead After "Mao's India War"* New Delhi: Har Anand, 2000), p. 155.

45. Swaran Singh, "India-China Relations: Perception, Problem, Potential," *South Asian Survey*, vol. 15, no. 1, 2008, p. 86.
46. Mohan Malik, n. 30, p. 63.
47. Mehul Srivastava, "India-China Trade Tension Rise, *Bloomberg Businessweek*, February 11, 2009. www.businessweek.com/globalbiz/content/feb2009/gb20092011_202935.htm.
48. David M. Malone, *Does the Elephant Dance: Contemporary Indian Foreign Policy* (New Delhi: Oxford University Press, 2011), p. 94.
49. Sumit Ganguly, "The Rise of India in Asia," Devesh Shambaugh and Michael Yahuda (eds.), *International Relations of Asia* (Lanham, MD: Rowman and Littlefield Publishers, 2008), p. 158.
50. Nagesh Kumar, "India's Economic Engagement with East Asia: Trends and Prospects," K. Kesavpany et al. (eds.), *Rising India and Indian Communities in East Asia* (Singapore: ISEAS, 2008), p. 117.
51. Ji Ping, "China: Indians' New-Found Land," K. Kesavpany, A. Mani and P. Ramasamy et al. (eds.), *Rising India and Indian Communities in East Asia* (Singapore: ISEAS, 2008), p. 198.
52. David M. Malone, n. 48, p. 143.
53. C. Raja Mohan, *Crossing the Rubicon: The Shaping of India's New Foreign Policy* (New York: Palgrave Macmillan, 2004), p. 163.
54. Mohan Malik, n. 30, p. 63.
55. IISS, India Arms for the Future, *Strategic Comments*, vol. 15, no. 1, 2009 and Walter C. Ladwig III, "Delhi's Pacific Ambition: Naval Power, Look East and India's Emerging Influence in the Asia-Pacific," *Asian Security*, vol. 55, no. 2, 2009, pp.90-93.
56. Mohan Malik, n. 30, p. 49.
57. Ibid.
58. Guihong Zhang, n. 40, p. 99.
59. "Pranab Calls China a Challenge," *The Times of India*, November 5, 2008.
60. Vikram Sood, "India and Regional Security Interests," Alyssa Ayres and C. Raja Mohan (eds.), *Power Realignment in Asia: China, India and the United States* (New Delhi: Sage Publications, 2009), p. 260.
61. Brahma Chellaney, "Forestalling Strategic Conflict in Asia," *Far Eastern Review*, vol. 169, no. 9, November 2006, pp. 29-33.
62. Vijay Sakhuja, "Indian Navy: Keeping Pace with Emerging Challenges," Lawrence W. Prabhakar et al. (eds.), *The Evolving Maritime Balance of Power in Asia-Pacific* (Singapore: World Scientific, 2006), p. 191.
63. Bates Gill et al., "The Chinese Second Artillery Corps: Transition to Credible Deterrence," James C. Mulvenon and Andrew N. D. Yang (eds.), *The People's Liberation Army as Organization* (Santa Monica, CA: RAND, 2002), 510-87; Ashley Tellis, "The Changing Military-Political Environment: South Asia," Zalmay Khalilzad, et al. (eds.), *The United States and Asia: Towards a New US Strategy and Force Posture* (Santa Monica, CA: RAND, 2001), p. 208.
64. Guihong Zhang, n. 40, p. 99.
65. Shibashis Chatterjee, "Conceptions of Space in India's Look East Policy: Order, Cooperation or Community?" *South Asian Survey*, vol. 14, no. 1, 2007, p. 75.
66. Barry Buzan, "The South Asian Security Complex in a Decentring World

Order: Reconsidering Regions and Powers Ten Years On," *International Studies*, vol. 48, no. 1, 2011, p. 10.
67. Ibid.
68. S. K. Bhutani, n. 11, p. 389.
69. Guihong Zhang, "US-India Strategic Partnership: Implications for China," *International Studies*, vol. 42, nos. 3-4, 2005, p. 289.
70. David Scott, "India's 'Extended Neighbourhood' Concept: Power Projection for a Rising Power," Kant P. Bajpai and Harsh V. Pant (eds.), *India's Foreign Policy: A Reader* (New Delhi: Oxford University Press, 2013), pp. 355-56.
71. Shibashis Chatterjee, n. 65, p. 72.
72. Robert D. Kaplan, "Centre Stage for the Twenty-first Century: Power Plays in the Indian Ocean," *Foreign Affairs*, vol. 88, no. 2, March-April 2009, pp. 27-28.
73. Walter C. Ladwig III, "Delhi's Pacific Ambition: Naval Power, Look East and India's Emerging Influence in the Asia-Pacific," *Asian Security*, vol. 55, no. 2, 2009, p. 95.
74. Ibid., p. 109.
75. David Scott, n. 70, p. 357.
76. Ibid., p. 379.
77. Sandeep Unnithan, "China Threat, Indian Navy Unveils Forward Policy in Indian Ocean," *India Today*, indiatoday.intoday.in, accessed on December 27, 2013 at 1.30 pm.
78. Francine R. Frankel, "The Breakout of China-India Strategic Rivalry in Asia and the Indian Ocean," *Journal of International Affairs*, vol. 64, no. 2, Spring-Summer 2011.
79. Ibid.
80. Ibid., 12., Barry Buzan, n. 66, p. 11.
81. Ibid., p. 12.
82. "PM Warns on China's South Asia Foothold," *The Indian Express*, September 7, 2010.
83. Rajat Pandit, "Assertive China Worry, says Antony," *The Times of India*, September 14, 2010.
84. "Chinese Hacked PMO Computers, says Narayanan," *The Indian Express*, January 19, 2010.
85. Prak Chun Thal and Stuart Grudgings, "SE Asia Meeting in Disarray over Sea Dispute with China," Reuters, July 13, 2012.
86. Harsh V. Pant, "China Rises, India Ponders: India's Look East Policy Gathers Momentum," *Fearless Nadia*, vol. 1, Spring 2013.
87. Mohan Malik, n. 30, p. 44.
88. S. K. Bhutani, n. 11, p. 390.
89. David M. Malone, n. 48, p. 268.

12

Nuclear Technology and Nehru's Outlook

Suneel Kumar

> No country, no people, however powerful they might be, are safe from destruction if this competition in weapons of mass destruction ... continues.[1]
>
> —Jawaharlal Nehru, November 27, 1957

The advent of nuclear technology and, consequently, manufacturing of nuclear bombs transformed the nature of global security. Dropping of nuclear bombs on two Japanese cities, Hiroshima and Nagasaki, by the United States, on August 6 and 9, 1945 respectively, resulted in unconditional surrender of Japan and end of the Second World War. Although the use of nuclear weapons did bring an end to the most deadly conflict in human history, it failed to bring a world without war.[2] In the post-war period, bilateral and multilateral hostilities increased, leading to various local and regional wars. Nuclear arms race emerged among the great, medium and even small powers, which enhanced the global stockpiles of nuclear weapons. Parallel to the nuclear arms race, a general understanding emerged among academicians, journalists, politicians and statesmen, at the global level, to raise voice against nuclear armament. Eminent scholars like Albert Einstein, Alexander Haddow, Bertrand Russell, Eugene Rabinowitch, Joseph Rotblat, Otto Kahn and Max Born sought the abolition of nuclear weapons to avoid "the risk of universal death."[3]

Prominent social and religious figures like Archbishop Desmond Tutu, Claiborne Pell, the Dalai Lama, Edwin F. O'Brien, Notre Dame, Pope Benedict XVI, Pope John Paul II, Steve Allen, Ted Turner, and Theodore Hesburg called for the abolition of nuclear weapons. American statesmen such as Henry Kissinger, George P. Shultz, Sam Nunn and William J. Perry also advocated nuclear disarmament to lessen the probability of nuclear war.[4] Apart from this, on different occasions numerous nuclear disarmament groups/organisations including the Campaign for Nuclear Disarmament, Friends of the Earth International, Global Zero, Greenpeace, International Physicians for Prevention of Nuclear War, International Campaign to Abolish Nuclear Weapons, Mayors for Peace, Soka Gakkai, United Nations Office for Disarmament Affairs and World Union for Protection of Life raised the banner against nuclear weapons. These groups organised anti-nuclear debates, dialogues, demonstrations and protests at the global level while pleading for the creation of a nuclear weapons free world.[5]

In the context of nuclear technology and its civil and military use, Indian leadership, especially Mahatma Gandhi, C. Rajagopalachari, S. Radhakrishnan and Jawaharlal Nehru, also put their vision before the international community. By recognising the right to life, peace, progress and security of the individual, Nehru advocated the preservation of these rights by living peacefully together and also solving disputes through peaceful methods. He observed that human beings cannot convert each other by force or threat of force. And so, in spite of differences, only peaceful coexistence can ensure the survival of mankind.[6]

This paper is a modest attempt to analyse Jawaharlal Nehru's outlook on nuclear technology and its relevance in the contemporary world. In the light of public speeches and writings of Nehru, the first section of the article highlights different aspects of Nehru's outlook on nuclear technology in the context of the global community. The next section explains Nehru's viewpoint on nuclear technology in the Indian context. The last section examines the relevance of Nehru's ideas for global community in the Cold War and post-Cold War period. It also looks at how India has benefited from Nehru's vision for conducting the successful tests of atom and hydrogen bombs in May 1998, and developing Inter-Continental Ballistic Missile (ICBM) technology with capability of carrying multiple nuclear warheads, in April 2012.

Jawaharlal Nehru and Nuclear Technology

Nuclear technology is a "double-edged sword." It is hard to distinguish between the technology required for peaceful civilian purposes and the military application in manufacturing of nuclear weapons. Nuclear reactors require enriched uranium to function. If the enrichment plants producing the fuel for reactors are devoted to producing uranium with a high degree of enrichment, that product can be used for the development of weapons. Even if a reactor operates with a low degree of enrichment, as in case of most of the commercial nuclear reactors, plutonium produced in the fuel elements can be estranged chemically and used for weapons.[7] From this perspective, Nehru had observed the dreadful revolution brought by nuclear technology in military technology and also unlimited possibilities opened by its constructive application for human development.[8] Therefore, being associated with the idealist school of thought, he articulated a broader outlook on nuclear technology relating it to war, peace and development of the international community.

Brought up in the Gandhian tradition, Nehru carried the content of Gandhian philosophy in his thoughts and actions related to nuclear technology. He, along with Gandhi, had witnessed the death and destruction caused by the two world wars. Both had seen how military application of nuclear technology had wiped out Hiroshima and Nagasaki. After the dropping of nuclear bombs by the US on Japanese cities in August 1945, Gandhi had warned mankind how nuclear bombs could "spell certain suicide" for human beings. He argued that nuclear weapons cannot be curtailed through counter-nuclear weapons.[9] He also said that nuclear weapons can neither render non-violence obsolete nor have the capability of making peace. Despite the application of nuclear technology for military purposes by the United States, Gandhi saw the possibility of its utilisation for constructive purposes.[10] This notion of Gandhian philosophy left a deep impact on Nehru's psyche, which continued to shape and influence his outlook on diverse subjects, including nuclear technology.

Nehru had witnessed two world wars violating the right to life, peace, progress and security of human beings and, in addition, nuclear technology becoming a critical part of war and serious violator of human rights. He expressed a strong zeal for establishing a peaceful world order putting it high on the political agenda of India's foreign affairs. Pursuing the schema of a peaceful world order, Nehru rebuffed war as an instrument of foreign policy and denied its "biological necessity" for the survival of states.[11] Through war, countries refuse to understand and recognise the other's perspective, which, according to Nehru, discourages internationalism, produces reactions and leads to more wars.[12] For this reason, he urged every country to accept its responsibility to bring peace by eliminating war.[13]

Since Nehru was in favour of the elimination of war, he rejected the acquisition of both conventional and non-conventional instruments of war, including nuclear weapons. Considering weapons as the "enemy of humanity," Nehru saw the existence or procurement of any type of weapons as instigation of countries to act against each other. Amidst such antagonistic international atmosphere, countries indulge themselves in the arms race against hostile states or groups and design much more potent "engines of destruction."[14] Nehru witnessed a similar type of situation during the inter-war period (1919-1939) as well as the Cold War period, and thus he was against the arms race amongst nations. On March 24, 1951, Nehru termed nuclear technology as the symbol of the new age and viewed its use for military purposes as the main determinants of human behaviour.[15] Envisaging nuclear weapons as the "greatest threat" to human civilisation, he suggested that knowledge of nuclear technology along with chemical and biological technologies should not be used to forge weapons of mass destruction.[16] Countries like the US, the Soviet Union, Britain, France, and China had used this knowledge to construct nuclear weapons assuming their capacity for mass destruction to be a deterrent to war. And believing in this perspective some other countries had also started to think and act on these lines to develop nuclear weapons with similar objectives. Nehru disagreed with the different countries that were following this perspective. Reacting to this approach, he said that, in the short term, these weapons may act as a deterrent to war, but as peace cannot be built on the basis of terror, in the long term, such bombs cannot function as a deterrent against its use by the possessors. Besides this, some miscalculation, irrational decision, fear or even internal changes within a country can also trigger this force, after which it would be impossible to deter global conflict. For this reason, the post-world war thinking and behaviour of the states in world politics were dominated by the application of nuclear technology for military purposes and also set out to be regarded as an instrument of peace.[17] But Nehru did not see the procurement of nuclear weapons as a path to achieve peace or freedom. On April 2, 1954, he himself opines:

> … the way of atom bomb is not the way of peace or freedom. The only useful purpose it can serve is to put an end to the power-mad people in authority, to those who wish to dominate over others, to the race-proud who deny equality to others, to the men of privilege who rest on others' labour and suffering, to those who prosper when others starve and die.[18]

In other words, having this idea, Nehru never elevated nuclear weapons as "custodian," "gadget" or "agent" of peace.[19]

During the Cold War, a general perception, which prevails even today, was that nuclear weapons are a source of national security and, furthermore, that possession of such weapons promotes a sense of security among the nuclear powers. But Nehru did not consider nuclear weapons as a means of national security. He said that nuclear weapons are neither a means of national security nor contribute to the sense of security of any nation. In the Cold War era, even nuclear weapon states—as Nehru pointed out—had not been able to be fearless and ensure national security. Indeed, they had become more insecure and indulged in attaining more and more power through enhancement of stockpiles of weapons.[20] In that way, use of nuclear technology for military purposes had ultimately demoted the national security.

Alongside the demolition of national security, Nehru observed that military use of nuclear technology had eroded the existing balance of power among the countries. Prior to the manufacturing of nuclear weapons, the concept of balance of power had considerable weightage in international affairs. It was considered a guarantee of national security. Nonetheless, the addition of nuclear bombs in the great powers' armoury destroyed the viability and legitimacy of balance of power completely. Nuclear weapons erased differences between the capacity to impose punishment and of receiving it. Now, states that may employ such weapons were also not protected from the lethal effects of their own offence.[21] Under such circumstances, Nehru observed the balance of power turning into a menace instead of a means of national security.

The presence of nuclear technology forced Jawaharlal Nehru to emphasise the necessity of outlawing war, particularly nuclear war, to avoid co-destruction and encourage co-prosperity of the world. Along with this, he also lobbied for the legal prohibition on the application of nuclear technology for military purposes including the development of nuclear weapons. While calling for a ban on nuclear tests in 1954, Nehru became the first statesman in the world who took the first large-scale initiative to ban the use of nuclear technology for the manufacturing of weapons. He advised nations to enter into an agreement through common consent to abandon such weapons. While advocating the prohibition and elimination of nuclear, hydrogen, bacterial and other weapons of mass destruction on April 2, 1954 in the Lok Sabha, Nehru stressed some sort of "Standstill Agreement" among the concerned states on the discontinuance of production and stockpiling of these weapons.[22] He opined that during the Cold War, the presence of hatred, fear and animosity were the main reasons behind the nuclear arms race between the US and the Soviet Union. Observing that the elimination of these things was a must for the survival of mankind, Nehru appealed to the leadership of both countries to take some legal measures to reduce or dismantle their nuclear stockpiles.[23] Earlier, Nehru thought that there were little chances of the US and the Soviet Union to agree for any type of disarmament or dismantling atomic weapons, yet, through various communications, he continued to pursue them.[24] Responding to Nehru's suggestions, on May 10, 1954, the Soviet Union came up with a proposal for imposing a ban on nuclear tests as the initial step towards nuclear disarmament. Since the US did not agree to the Soviet proposal, again on July 12, 1956, Nehru placed another proposal for Cessation of All Explosions of Nuclear and Other Weapons of Mass Destruction before the UN Disarmament Commission.[25] After becoming the first to suggest to the international community the cessation of nuclear tests, he became the first foreign Prime Minister who visited Hiroshima in 1957. Visiting a place where nuclear technology had been applied, for the first time in human history, for destructive purposes, Nehru, himself, observed the capability of destructiveness of nuclear weapons. He said that use of nuclear weapons in war would be a "crime against humanity."[26] In the presence of nuclear weapons, he opined, any type of war is capable of certain destruction of human civilisation. It leads to dispersal of radioactivity even to distant regions which have nothing to do with the conflict. Besides, no one of the rival powers can think of defeating the other without being largely destroyed themselves.[27] Apart from the use of nuclear weapons in war, general nuclear experiments and explosions were also termed a "crime against humanity" by Nehru. He said that even without war, nuclear tests and nuclear explosions bring genetically adverse impact on existing and future generations and generate environmental hazards as these contaminate land, air and water directly. Continuing nuclear tests lead to armament race, enhance the possibility of accidents and increase the threat of war.[28] Thus, arguing to "outlaw" nuclear war, nuclear weapons and nuclear tests, Nehru opined that it is not the possession but outlawing of such weapons which can be a source of national security for different countries.[29]

Acting on this thought, on different occasions, Nehru urged the international community to impose universal nuclear disarmament. Prior to the advent of nuclear weapons, on August 25, 1940, in a note written at Wardha, he asked for "complete disarmament" of all countries in the context of conventional weapons.[30] But, after the development of nuclear weapons, in his speeches of February 2, 1955, November 27, 1957, October 3, 1960 and June 16, 1962, along with the progressive limitation on conventional weapons, Nehru asked the international community to include the prohibition of the manufacturing, storage and use of weapons of mass destruction in its agenda of disarmament.[31] In the Third Meeting of Commonwealth Prime Ministers' Conference on February 2, 1955, Nehru raised apprehensions about the proliferation of nuclear technology and opined that:

> As nuclear bombs became relatively easier and cheaper to make, the danger would increase that smaller countries might possess them, and we should then live in constant apprehension that some irresponsible country would be in a position to set fire to the world.[32]

Due to these trepidations, he termed disarmament as an "imperative" to the survival of mankind. He also suggested ending the nuclear tests and discontinuing the production of nuclear weapons.[33] Keeping in view that all the states should work towards universal nuclear disarmament, on November 27, 1957 in a press statement at New Delhi, Nehru appealed to the international leadership, including the United States and the Soviet Union, to stop nuclear tests and proceed for effective nuclear disarmament. Nehru said:

> I appeal to them (great leaders especially of America and Russia) to stop all nuclear test explosions and to show the world that they are

> determined to end this menace, and to proceed also to bring about effective disarmament.[34]

Besides the states, Nehru expected the United Nations (UN) to be associated with the efforts related to all type of disarmament. He considered disarmament the main duty of the UN and argued that if it fails in performing this duty, the UN fails in its main objective of preservation of peace at the global level.[35]

Apart from the legal prohibition, Nehru suggested to develop and mobilise a strong world public opinion against the probability of use and proliferation of nuclear weapons.[36] He stated that the UN along with those countries principally concerned in the production of nuclear weapons are required to disseminate the information regarding the destructive power of such weapons at the global level. People should be informed about the "known" effects of nuclear weapons, and enough indication of the probable "unknown" effects should also be communicated to the international community. This way, a strong world public opinion would be developed against nuclear bombs and other weapons of mass destruction. He thought that "informed world public opinion" was competent to prevent the progress of these weapons and the most effective factor in achieving the desired results.[37] As a result of Nehru's initial proposals, the community of nations achieved landmarks in the direction of nuclear disarmament in the form of various bilateral/multilateral agreements and treaties which sought to reduce or eliminate certain categories of nuclear weapons, to prevent the proliferation of such weapons and their delivery vehicles. Through bilateral agreements the US and the Soviet Union agreed to reduce or limit their nuclear stockpiles. Multilateral treaties like the Partial Test Ban Treaty (PTBT) of 1963, Nuclear Non-Proliferation Treaty (NPT) of 1967 and Comprehensive Test Ban Treaty (CTBT) of 1996 were held to facilitate the prevention of proliferation and development of nuclear weapons. Through diplomatic channels, Nehru had played a significant role in drawing up the PTBT which prohibited countries from nuclear testing in the atmosphere, outer space and under water, but not underground. India became the fourth signatory to the PTBT after the US, the Soviet Union and Britain, under the leadership of Jawaharlal Nehru. The CTBT banned nuclear tests everywhere on the planet including surface, atmosphere, underwater and underground. Various provisions of this treaty reflect Nehru's vision on nuclear technology.

Next to the outlawing of nuclear technology for weapon manufacturing and construction of world public opinion against such weapons, Nehru stressed the removal of basic sources of war and conflict to check the menace of nuclear bombs. On different occasions, he had termed political subjugation, racial inequality, economic inequality and wretchedness as the root causes of war. The existing unequal and exploitative arrangements always compel the sufferers to confront it which further creates every possibility of war.[38] Nehru had observed the presence of these negative elements in the existing international arrangements preparing the ground for unaccounted local, regional and global conflicts involving nuclear weapons. Thus, he emphasised the removal of basic causes of war, which, according to him, would facilitate in curbing the nuclear threat effectively.

Alongside other suggestions, to save mankind from the adverse effects of nuclear technology, Nehru proposed the establishment of atom-free areas around the world including areas of Asian, African and European continents. He suggested not using the designated areas for the military application of nuclear technology. Though Nehru was aware of the fact that "atom-free areas" could not be a solution to end the possibility of war and bring universal nuclear disarmament, but even then, he visualised the creation of such areas as a handy step to trim down the tensions among the rival countries.[39] The vision of creating nuclear-weapon-free zones in Asia, Africa and Europe was put forward by Nehru on June 16, 1962 and now this vision could be seen taking practical shape. Between 1962 and 2014, at least nine nuclear-weapon-free zones (NWFZs) have been created in different parts of the world, including five zones of Latin America and the Caribbean, South Pacific, South-East Asia,

Central Asia and Africa, one UN-recognised zone consisting of a single country, Mongolia, and three zones of Antarctica, the seabed, and outer space which are not part of any state. The Antarctic zone was created during the Nehruvian period but the other eight zones were created in post-Nehruvian era. Apart from the emergence of the NWFZs, some other countries like Austria (1999) have also outlawed nuclear weapons in their municipal law. The population, living in the NWFZs, is protected from the adverse affects of nuclear technology.[40]

Due to the use of nuclear technology for military purposes in Hiroshima and Nagasaki, the general thinking amongst the people had developed that nuclear know-how was only linked to the production of nuclear weapons and destruction of human beings. Most of the people were ignorant about its advantages for mankind. But, in case of Nehru, he was aware of the dual nature of nuclear technology from the time of its arrival on the global scene. He tried to disseminate information of the constructive part of the technology. He was optimistic that sooner or later mankind would forget the destructive part of nuclear technology. As Nehru speaks:

> .... probably, even the great destruction of that atomic bomb will be forgotten, while the use of atomic energy may in future powerfully influence the whole structure of the world.[41]

Though Nehru had no idea about when the use of nuclear technology would be perfected or brought into the life of the common man, he was optimistic that the rapid change and progress in the world would lead to enhancement of the positive part of the common man's life.

Understanding the duality, Nehru always highlighted both aspects of nuclear technology. He termed nuclear technology as a source of immeasurable pleasure and also unimaginable destruction. On the one hand, he sought to avoid the destructiveness of nuclear technology by outrightly rejecting its military application for the manufacturing of weapons, and on the other, stressed the peaceful and constructive utilisation.[42] In the context of peaceful use of nuclear technology, Nehru observed that it can be of immense advantage for both industrially developed countries as well as industrially backward countries. Moreover, on May 10, 1954, he had highlighted in the Lok Sabha that nuclear technology's use for peaceful purposes was much more important for the industrially backward countries of Asia and Africa rather than the industrially advanced countries. Industrially developed countries had already vast resources of energy other than nuclear power. The additional source of energy, in the form of nuclear power, is an advantage for these developed countries. But, having adequate power resources, developed countries can afford to restrain and restrict the use of nuclear technology. Conversely, industrially backward countries having less power resources and poor infrastructure cannot afford such restrictions. They cannot stop the utilisation of nuclear power for energy-related requirements. Any such restrictions would put the least developed countries of Asia and Africa in a disadvantageous position. Keeping such things in view, Nehru suggested the developed countries to cooperate with the least developed countries to fulfil their energy-related needs and not to put any restriction on these "power-hunger" countries for the use of nuclear technology to achieve peaceful objectives.[43] From Nehru's perspective, in this way backward countries can put themselves on the right path of development and also cooperate and coordinate with developed nations to achieve the larger objective of world peace.

Nuclear Technology, Nehru and India

Since Nehru had presented an integrated vision of nationalism and internationalism, he adopted the same approach regarding the nuclear weapons in formulating India's national policy on nuclear technology. Having a strong faith in the positive outcomes of science and technology, Nehru recognised the right of every country to devise and use the latest research for its development.[44] His approach on nuclear technology, in the Indian context, contained the element of duality. In a public speech at Bombay on June 26, 1946, on the one hand, he said that India would utilise nuclear technology for constructive purposes and, on the other hand, said that if India is threatened, it would attempt to defend itself by all means at its disposal.[45] Again, after independence of India, on April 6, 1948, before the Constituent Assembly of India, Nehru emphasised development of nuclear energy by India for peaceful purposes. But, on the same occasion, he also said that, "… if we are compelled as a nation to use it for other purposes, possibly no pious sentiments of any of us will stop the nation from using it that way."[46] Nehru did not favour the toleration of aggression made by one country against the other. He supported defensive strategies pursued by a country against the aggressor country or group of countries. Nehru had also emphasised that peace cannot be purchased by compromise with evil or by surrendering before such evil.[47] This reflects that one way or the other, he had accepted nuclear weapons as a means of national security in the context of India's security and, under compulsions, he was not averse to thinking about the nuclear option if required for India. In the global context and the Indian context, this was a paradox in Nehru's philosophy on nuclear technology.

Despite this paradoxical situation, Nehru did not illustrate India's intention to construct nuclear weapons. Contrary to this, Homi Jehangir Bhabha, the father of India's nuclear programme, was in favour of acquiring nuclear capability and the manufacturing of nuclear weapons. Bhabha had argued that India "must have" the capability. It should first prove itself through making nuclear weapons then talk of a world without nuclear weapons. Bhabha was of the view that, as a nuclear power, India would be able to attain more capability to convince international gatherings of nuclear disarmament.[48] While moving the Atomic Energy Bill in the Constituent Assembly on April 6, 1948, Nehru was optimistic that India's outlook in regard to nuclear energy would "… be a peaceful one for the development of human life … and not one of war and hatred."[49] Again on May 22, 1948 in a note for the Cabinet, Nehru linked nuclear technology with the social, economic and industrial development of India. He argued:

> It must always be remembered that atomic energy is not just meant for making bombs but is likely to be the basic form of energy used for us to keep in the forefront of this matter or otherwise our social, economic and industrial development will suffer.[50]

Even then, in a speech at a meeting of scientists in London on October 22, 1948, Nehru stated that "India is interested in atomic energy not with the object of making bombs but for peaceful purposes."[51] Again on March 23, 1949, while briefing the Constituent Assembly about India's atomic research programme, Nehru said that "We are not thinking in terms of atom bombs. We are thinking in terms of processing various minerals out of which atomic energy comes."[52] He made it clear even to India's scientists who were engaged in the nuclear research programme. In a communication to S. S. Bhatnagar on March 20, 1952, Nehru said:

> For us [India] the importance does not lie in the use of atomic energy for military and like purposes, but rather for the development of power for industrial and social use. It has already become apparent that such power can be developed and used ... If atomic energy can be used for these purposes, it can ultimately bring about almost a revolution in India.[53]

He also explained the economic significance of nuclear technology for India. He said that with new developments the cost of electricity generated from the nuclear technology would be cheaper than the conventional sources, like hydroelectric power. Moreover, power generated from the nuclear technology would be easily transportable from one part to another part of India.[54]

When Britain tested its first nuclear bomb named "Hurricane" on October 3, 1952, Nehru again showed India's disinterest in obtaining or developing nuclear weapons. Indeed, responding to the British nuclear test in a press conference at Madras on October 4, 1952, Nehru talked of the development of nuclear technology by India from the social and economic viewpoint. He said:

> We [India] are interested in atomic energy for peaceful purposes ... If this power can be utilised, as we use hydroelectric power, it would be a tremendous boon to mankind,...[55]

On July 24, 1957 in Lok Sabha, Nehru said that "... we are not interested in making atom bombs, even if we have the capacity to do so,..."[56] In 1959, the Government of India issued a statement claiming that its nuclear programme was at a stage "when we could, without external assistance, produce atomic weapons if we so wished."[57] Nehru made it clear to the international community that India is opposed to nuclear weapons. On September 17, 1961 again in a press conference at New Delhi, Nehru informed the international community about India's nuclear infrastructure and its capability to build nuclear weapons. Even then, he ruled out India's intention of military application of nuclear technology. On the one hand, he considered nuclear technology more important for the national development of India as compared to its national security and, on the other, made it clear that India would not give up the option to make nuclear weapons in future. That is why he had refused to support any mechanism which sought to limit India's potential and future decision-making on the nuclear bomb.[58]

After India's border conflict with China and its subsequent debacle in 1962, the nationalist parties like the Jana Sangh insisted that the Government of India to construct nuclear weapons so that in the long run, the national security of the country may be ensured against China.[59] The Jana Sangh spearheaded its demand in various public forums and even passed a formal resolution for the production of nuclear weapons. On March 23, 1963, in the Lok Sabha, Ramachandra Bade, a Jana Sangh member of parliament urged Jawaharlal Nehru, the Prime Minister to make the full use of scientific research in the field of nuclear energy and argued that that only those who want to see Russians or Chinese ruling India would be against the development of nuclear weapons.[60] Despite such demands, Nehru remained firmly against a military nuclear programme for India. Even a few days before his death on May 27, 1964, he said, "We are determined not to use nuclear weapons for war purposes. We do not make atomic bombs. I do not think we will."[61] Acting on these lines, Nehru created the entire required infrastructure, including nuclear power plants, for the utilisation of nuclear technology for civilian purposes, but did not go for development of nuclear weapons.

India's security scenario changed beyond its imagination after the death of Nehru. This happened largely due to China's nuclear test in October 1964. The Indian leadership sought security guarantees from the US, the Soviet Union and Britain to cope with a hostile nuclear China, but all the three countries rebuffed India. Then it attempted to develop a multilateral solution by calling for a non-proliferation treaty under which the existing nuclear powers would give up nuclear weapons and the others would not acquire them. The NPT came but did not serve India's purpose. India also decided for a subterranean nuclear project (SNEP) in 1965, but due to the death of Prime Minister Lal Bahadur Shastri and Homi Bhabha, this project was postponed in 1966. Under the leadership of Indira Gandhi, India demonstrated its nuclear capability by conducting its first nuclear test in May 1974. The test was termed "peaceful nuclear explosion" (PNE) but New Delhi refrained from declaring itself a nuclear power. Nevertheless, international assessment on India's nuclear test was different as the US started efforts to consolidate the global non-proliferation laws through debarring India from multilateral trade of sensitive technologies. In the 1990s, it became impossible to have any type of nuclear trade between India and international nuclear community. Thus, between 1974 and 1998, New Delhi developed nuclear material and expertise but restrained enough not to turn it into usable weapons. It lost a de facto but reliable political and military ally as the Soviet Union disintegrated in 1991. Besides this, in the 1980s and 1990s, China transferred nuclear and missile technology to Pakistan's clandestine nuclear programme and attempted to buttress strategic capabilities of Pakistan to balance India within the subcontinent.[62]

The post-Cold War era witnessed the rise of China and its recognition and treatment by the Western countries as a second global power. The treatment of China as global power not only hurt the self-esteem and pride of India, but made it pertinent for New Delhi to get out of the subcontinent box, regain the psychological parity with Beijing, and reassert its role in Asian balance of power through its nuclear policy.[63] This resulted in conducting nuclear tests in May 1998, which made India an overtly nuclear-armed state. Reacting to India's nuclear explosions, the US emerged as one of its most vociferous critics in G-8 and blocked its assistance from the financial institutions. In the UN Security Council, the US made it clear that even if India signs the NPT, it would not be recognised as a nuclear power. In spite of the hostile attitude of great power and placing of India in a category of a nuclear pariah, New Delhi did not stop making a nuclear bomb, it also successfully tested its first ICBM, named "Agni-V" capable of taking multiple nuclear warheads, in April 2012, and signalled its entry into an elite club of states with ICBM capabilities.[64] Hence, in the post-Nehru period, India applied nuclear technology for making nuclear bombs and missiles. The post-Nehruvian period witnessed a drastic shift in the outlook of the Indian leadership as ultimately it perceived nuclear and missiles technology a source of national security and also a deterrent to external invasion.

Contemporary Significance

In the Cold War era, when the international community was under the threat of a nuclear war, Nehru's outlook on nuclear technology received global attention. Accepting that war leads to armament and armament results in war, Nehru disliked both war as well as weapons. Therefore, showing integrity with an idealist school of thought, Nehru sought a peaceful world order for which he snubbed war in international affairs, stressed the constructive use of nuclear technology and lobbied for nuclear disarmament, including the prohibition of nuclear tests and production of nuclear weapons. He appealed to the great powers not to indulge in nuclear arms race so that destruction of mankind and environmental hazards could be avoided. He also urged the creation of nuclear weapon free zones to ensure a war-free world. With the passage of time, the international community not only witnessed the realisation of the Nehruvian vision in the signing of various bilateral/multilateral disarmament and non-proliferation agreements and treaties on nuclear technology and emergence of NWFZs to avoid the destructive aspects of nuclear energy, but also saw countries attempting to utilise it for constructive purposes. At present, the six land zones of NWFZs cover 60 per cent of the land area of the earth. At present, 39 per cent of the population of the world lives in NWFZs. Nine nuclear weapons states have 28 per cent of the world's land area and 46 per cent of the world population. The majority of non-Nuclear Weapon States, which are not the part of NWFZs, are located in Europe and North Pacific but these states have either the membership of the collective defence alliances with the nuclear weapon states or are surrounded by the same. Movement to declare areas such as the Arctic, Central Europe, Korean Peninsula, Middle East and South Asia as NWFZs is also taking shape, at various levels, for different reasons, which gives additional weightage to Nehru's viewpoint in the contemporary world.[65]

Nehru's advice to international community for prohibiting the military use of nuclear technology could also be seen becoming more relevant in the contemporary era. Although the Cold War disappeared, yet it has left a dangerous legacy in the form of thousands of nuclear weapons. In addition, nuclear testing has continued and more countries have acquired these weapons. Out of nine developing countries, which installed nuclear reactors to produce electricity, five countries—China, India, Pakistan, South Africa and North Korea—manufactured nuclear weapons. South Africa dismantled its nuclear weapons later. Argentina and Brazil embarked on programmes that could have led to nuclear weapons, but decided to abandon them. Black marketing of nuclear secrets and materials trade has also flourished. Terrorist organisations like *Al Qaeda*, having nefarious designs towards humanity, are making serious efforts to acquire nuclear technology for military purposes, creating a potential threat of nuclear terrorism. In the contemporary era, if the threat of nuclear world war has reduced, the risk of a nuclear attack has increased.[66] In the existing international security environment, the Nehruvian philosophy could be an answer to resolve the contemporary security crisis which is being faced by the global community.

Nuclear energy has now become a nucleus subject of debate for the developed countries as a result of their thrust on the global reduction in carbon emissions which is responsible for global warming. Furthermore, as the global community is facing an energy crisis now, supporters of nuclear technology say that it can contribute to the energy security particularly of developing countries. Since nuclear power does not release any harmful gas like carbon dioxide and methane, which are largely responsible for the greenhouse effect, it has the lowest adverse impact on the environment. Unlike conventional sources of energy, nuclear energy can be produced from nuclear power plants even in rough weather conditions. Production of nuclear energy requires a low amount of raw material. Although the set-up cost of nuclear power plants is relatively high, yet the running cost is low as the cost of uranium, which is used as a fuel to produce electricity, is quite low. Thus, it is not only environment friendly, but also an inexpensive long-term alternative to other energy sources. Since the stocks of coal, oil and natural gas are limited and expected to exhaust soon, nuclear technology can be the prime source of electricity due to its wide availability, accessibility, acceptability and affordability. Developing countries can meet the challenge of electricity demand and reduce the reliance on imported energy, at the same time decreasing carbon dioxide emissions by making nuclear power as a prime solution to energy security and economic development. Developing countries like Argentina, Brazil, China, India, Iran, Mexico, Pakistan, South Africa, and North Korea have installed nuclear reactors for electricity production. Several other developing countries, such as the United Arab Emirates, Turkey, Jordan and Vietnam are looking to build civilian nuclear reactors for the production of electricity.[67] Hence, constructive utilisation of nuclear technology, as per the Nehruvian viewpoint, can facilitate solving the energy crisis being faced internationally. This may also facilitate in controlling environmental hazards. Critics point out that though nuclear power directly does not emit greenhouse gases, but this occurs through the construction, operation and decommissioning of nuclear plants, and during the mining and milling of uranium. Adding to this, it is also difficult to dispose of highly radioactive material produced during nuclear power generation. Nuclear power plants are vulnerable to some unexpected, unavoidable and uncontrollable accidents like the SL-1 accident of 1961, K-27 accident of 1968, K-431 accident of 1985, the Three Mile Island (TMI) accident of 1979, the Chernobyl explosion of 1986 and the Fukushima disaster of 2011, which raise the security concerns about the nuclear power industry. The by-product of nuclear fission can be used as a weapon, and nuclear power plants can be the preferred target during a military clash between states.[68] Despite all these limitations of using nuclear power, it is less damaging as compared to the conventional energy industry. If proper safety measures are taken, one can overcome these drawbacks of nuclear power. If its legal prohibition and abandonment for military purposes can ensure the national, regional and global security, nuclear-generated electricity can contribute much to energy security and little to greenhouse gas emissions. Hence, to a large extent, Nehru's idea of nuclear disarmament, its non-proliferation and subsequent use for civilian purposes can be a panacea for global energy, environmental and security crises.

In the changing international security environment, even though India developed nuclear weapons, yet it continued to be a beneficiary of Nehru's thought and action on nuclear technology at the international level. First, today nuclear power is the fourth largest source of electricity production in India. In 2012, it has 20 nuclear reactors in operation in six nuclear power plants which are generating 4,780 megawatt (MW) electricity. Seven other under construction reactors are expected to generate an additional 5,300 MW electricity. Besides this, on October 11, 2012, the Nuclear Power Corporation

Limited (NPCIL) has disclosed India's plan to produce 63,000 MW electricity by 2032 through nuclear technology.[69] Thus, India is utilising nuclear technology to fulfil its ever increasing electricity demand in the industrial and domestic sectors due to the strong infrastructural facilities created by Jawaharlal Nehru. Second, India conducted nuclear tests at Pokhran in May 1974 and May 1998, again due to the strong infrastructural foundation laid down by Jawaharlal Nehru. Third, despite keeping away from the global nuclear game, which was largely devised, played and refereed by the United States, it succeeded in getting the right to civil nuclear trade and explicitly recognised as a "responsible nuclear state" in the global nuclear game. New Delhi neither signed the NPT nor agreed to any constraints on its nuclear weapons programme, but even then it offered civil nuclear trade and technology without any guarantee that its weapons programme would not indirectly benefit from such trade. This was an unprecedented legal exception which was granted to India outside the NPT and exceptional rules were formulated to accommodate it. Despite the resistance from China and Pakistan, Washington entered into a civil nuclear agreement with New Delhi and in September 2008, the Nuclear Suppliers Group granted India privileged international trading rights. Furthermore, when India tested its first ICBM in April 2012, capable of carrying multiple nuclear warheads, the international community did not raise any objection. Even the US made a "subdued" and "oblique" response to the launch of the ICBM by New Delhi and appreciated its solid non-proliferation record.[70] All this reflects that India has been able to receive tacit recognition of the US for its nuclear missile programme. All what has happened cannot be credited merely to the existing strategic environment or of India becoming strategically much more important for the US. The global nuclear disarmament activism of Nehru during the Cold War period had constructed a pro-peace image of New Delhi at the global level and, as a result, has earned India the recognition and respect of the international community as a responsible power. In the background, New Delhi succeeded in convincing the international community about its nuclear programme. Nowadays, the international community has raised apprehensions about the nuclear programme of different countries like Pakistan, Iran and North Korea in the context of its use, proliferation and security. In the eyes of the international community, these countries may not be responsible members of the community of nations as they may use nuclear weapons for aggressive activities against others. Likewise countries like Pakistan have failed to ensure the non-proliferation of nuclear technology. Moreover due to prevalent political instability, concerns have also been shown about the security of its nuclear weapons as various non-state actors are looking to procure these weapons. However, this has not happened in case of India. Despite the procurement of nuclear weapons by India, the international community keeps a strong faith that New Delhi would not use its military nuclear technology against any other country. The international community also respects New Delhi's nuclear non-proliferation record vis-à-vis the other non-nuclear states and non-state actors. Moreover, it has never ever raised any apprehension about the safety of India's nuclear weapons as has happened in case of Pakistan. Undoubtedly, in this context, India has benefited from the Nehruvian activism on the nuclear non-proliferation and disarmament.

Notes and References

1. Jawaharlal Nehru, "Ban Nuclear Tests," A Statement to Press at New Delhi, November 27, 1957 published in Sarvepalli Gopal (ed.), *Jawaharlal Nehru: An Anthology* (New Delhi: Oxford University Press, 1980), p. 428.
2. Thomas Donnelly, "Bearing the Burden," *Bulletin of the Atomic Scientists*, vol. 61, no. 4, 2005, p. 55.
3. Sandra Ionno Butcher, "The Origins of the Russell-Einstein Manifesto," *Pugwash History Series* (Virginia: Pugwash Conferences on Science and World Affairs, 2005), p. 18.
4. George P. Shultz, William J. Perry, Henry A. Kissinger and Sam Nunn, "A World Free of Nuclear Weapons," *Wall Street Journal*, January 4, 2007, p. A15; and Robert Marquand, "Nuclear Weapons: Is full Disarmament Possible?" *The Christian Science Monitor*, April 6, 2012 (online edition).
5. Other prominent organisations which indulged in the fight for global nuclear disarmament are European Nuclear Disarmament, Pax Christi International, Socialist International, World Information Service on Energy and World Disarmament Campaign.

6. Nehru, n. 1, pp. 428-29.
7. Jose Goldemberg, "Nuclear Energy in Developing Countries," *Daedalus*, vol. 138, no. 4, 2009, pp. 71-80.
8. Ministry of Information and Broadcasting (Govt. of India), *Jawaharlal Nehru's Speeches*, vol. I, September 1946-May1949 (New Delhi: Publications Division, 1949), pp. 24-25.
9. Mahatma Gandhi quoted in Mani Shankar Aiyar, "Towards a Nuclear-Weapons-Free and Non-Violent World Order," available at http://www.pnnd.org/pubs/AIYAR RajivGandhi.pdf, retrieved on July 15, 2013, p. 3.
10. Mahatma Gandhi, "Atom Bomb and Violence," *Harijan*, July 7, 1946 available at http://meaindia.nic.in/pmicd.geneva/?50031131, retrieved on May 14, 2013.
11. Jawaharlal Nehru, *The Discovery of India* (New Delhi: Penguin Books, 1946), pp. 628-29.
12. Ibid., p. 584.
13. Jawaharlal Nehru, "Problems of Peace," A Speech at the United Nations General Assembly, New York, October 3, 1960 available at http://www.indianembassy.org/policy/Disarmament/disarm4.htm, retrieved on June 15, 2013.
14. Ibid.
15. Jawaharlal Nehru, "The Shadow of the Bomb," An Address to the UNESCO India Commission, New Delhi, March 24, 1951 published in A. Appadorai (ed.), *Documents on Political Thought in Modern India*, vol. II (Bombay: Oxford University Press, 1976), p. 730.
16. Jawaharlal Nehru, "Standstill Agreement," A Statement in Lok Sabha, New Delhi, April 2, 1954 available at http://www.indianembassy.org/policy/Disarmament/disarm2.htm, retrieved on June 15, 2013.
17. For details see Jawaharlal Nehru, "Foreword," published in Victor H. Wallace (ed.), *Paths of Peace: A Study of War, Its Causes and Prevention* (London & New York: Melbourne University Press; Cambridge University Press, 1957).
18. Jawaharlal Nehru, "The Death-Dealer," *National Herald*, April 2, 1954 published in Sarvepalli Gopal (ed.), *Jawaharlal Nehru: An Anthology* (New Delhi: Oxford University Press, 1980), pp. 395-96.
19. Nehru, n. 17.
20. Ibid.
21. Ibid.
22. Nehru, n. 16.
23. This message was conveyed by Jawaharlal Nehru to the Second World Conference against the Atomic and Hydrogen Bombs on August 4, 1956. This Conference was held in Tokyo and Nagasaki on August 6-11, 1956 under the auspices of Japan Council Against Atomic and Hydrogen Bombs. For details, see Jawaharlal Nehru, "Message of Hiroshima," A Message to the Second World Conference against Atomic and Hydrogen Bombs, New Delhi, August 4, 1956 published in H. Y. Sharada Prasad, A. K. Damodaran and Mushirul Hasan (eds.), *Selected Works of Jawaharlal Nehru*, Second Series, vol. 34, Part-I (New Delhi: Jawaharlal Nehru Memorial Fund, 2005), p. 209.
24. This type of apprehensions regarding the attitude of the United States and the Soviet Union had been shared by Jawaharlal Nehru with the Father of Indian

Nuclear Programme Homi Jehangir Bhabha. For details, see Jawaharlal Nehru, "To Homi J. Bhabha," New Delhi, August 8, 1950 published in S. Gopal (ed.), *Selected Works of Jawaharlal Nehru*, Second Series, vol. 15, Part I (New Delhi: Jawaharlal Nehru Memorial Fund, 1993), p. 493.

25. Jawaharlal Nehru, "Foreword," in Ministry of Information and Broadcasting, *Nuclear Explosions and Their Effects* (New Delhi: Publications Division, 1958), p. vi; Jawaharlal Nehru, "The Problems of Disarmament," A Speech in UN General Assembly (New York, November 10, 1961), available at http://www.indianembassy.org/policy/Disarmament/disarm5.htm, retrieved on June 14, 2013; Ministry of Information and Broadcasting (Govt. of India), *Jawaharlal Nehru's Speeches: September 1957-April 1963*, vol. 4 (New Delhi: Publications Division, 1983), p. 436; and Ministry of External Affairs (Govt. of India), *Disarmament: India's Initiatives* (New Delhi: Publications Division, 1988), p. 10.
26. Jawaharlal Nehru, "Banning the Use of Nuclear Weapons," Draft Note for Discussion at the Asian-African Conference, Bandung, April 18, 1955 published in Ravinder Kumar and H. Y. Sharada Prasad (eds.), *Selected Works of Jawaharlal Nehru*, Second Series, vol. 28 (New Delhi: Jawaharlal Nehru Memorial Fund, 2001), p. 210.
27. Jawaharlal Nehru, "The Great Adventure of Man," A Speech at Belgrade, July 2, 1955 published in Sarvepalli Gopal (ed.), *Jawaharlal Nehru: An Anthology* (New Delhi: Oxford University Press, 1980), p. 374; Jawaharlal Nehru, "The Sickness of Humanity," A Letter to Norman Cousins, March 16, 1957 published in Sarvepalli Gopal (ed.), *Jawaharlal Nehru: An Anthology* (New Delhi: Oxford University Press, 1980), pp. 427-28.
28. Jawaharlal Nehru, "A Complex and Overwhelming Problem," published in Sarvepalli Gopal (ed.), *Jawaharlal Nehru: An Anthology* (New Delhi: Oxford University Press, 1980), pp. 421-23; and Jawaharlal Nehru, "Resolution on Nuclear and Thermo-Nuclear Tests," A Statement in Lok Sabha, November 16, 1956, Lok Sabha Debates, vol. 9, Part-II, 1956, Cols. 352-361, published in H. Y. Sharada Prasad, A. K. Damodaran and Mushirul Hasan (eds.), *Selected Works of Jawaharlal Nehru*, Second Series, vol. 35 (New Delhi: Jawaharlal Nehru Memorial Fund, 2005); Nehru, n. 1, p. 429; and Nehru, n. 13.
29. Nehru, n. 16, p. 423.
30. Jawaharlal Nehru, "Non-Violence and State," A Confidential Note Written at Wardha, August 25, 1940 published in Sarvepalli Gopal (ed.), *Jawaharlal Nehru: An Anthology* (New Delhi: Oxford University Press, 1980), pp. 387-89.
31. Jawaharlal Nehru, n. 1, p. 429; Nehru, n. 13; Nehru, n. 28; and Jawaharlal Nehru, "Disarmament From Strength," A Speech at the Anti-Nuclear Arms Convention, New Delhi, June 16, 1962, available at *http*://www.indianembassy.org/policy/Disarmament/disarm6.htm, retrieved on June 15, 2013.
32. "The Need for Non-Proliferation," Minutes of Third Meeting of Commonwealth Prime Ministers' Conference, February 2, 1955 published in S. Gopal (ed.), *Selected Works of Jawaharlal Nehru*, Second Series, vol. 28 (New Delhi: Jawaharlal Nehru Memorial Fund, 2001), pp.198-99.
33. Jawaharlal Nehru, n. 1, p. 429; Nehru, n. 13; and Nehru, n. 31.

34. Nehru, n. 1, p. 429.
35. Nehru, n. 13.
36. Minutes of Third Meeting of Commonwealth Prime Ministers' Conference, n. 32.
37. Nehru, n. 16.
38. Jawaharlal Nehru, "The Root Causes of Wars," An Address to Columbia University, October 17, 1949 published in A. Appadorai (ed.), *Documents On Political Thought In Modern India*, vol. II (Bombay: Oxford University Press, 1976), p. 729.
39. Jawaharlal Nehru, "Disarmament from Strength," n. 31.
40. The UN General Assembly recognised Mongolia's NWF status through its Resolution No. 55/33S of November 2000.
41. Jawaharlal Nehru, "Atomic Energy," A Speech While Moving the Atomic Energy Bill in the Constituent Assembly, April 6, 1948, Constituent Assembly Debates, Official Report, vol. 5, 1948, pp. 3315-3334 published in S. Gopal (ed.), *Selected Works of Jawaharlal Nehru*, Second Series, vol. 5 (New Delhi: Jawaharlal Nehru Memorial Fund, 1987), p. 421.
42. Jawaharlal Nehru, "The Great Adventure of Man," A Speech at Belgrade, July 2, 1955 published in Sarvepalli Gopal (ed.), *Jawaharlal Nehru: An Anthology*, New Delhi: Oxford University Press, 1980, p. 374.
43. Jawaharlal Nehru, "Control of Nuclear Energy," A Statement in the Lok Sabha, New Delhi, May 10, 1954 available at http://www.indianembassy.org/policyDisarmament/disarm3.htm, retrieved on June 15, 2013; Jawaharlal Nehru, "International Control and Peaceful Uses of Atomic Energy," A Statement in Parliament, Parliament Debates (House of People), Official Report, vol. 5, Part II, 1954, Cols.7026-7032 published in Ravinder Kumar and H. Y. Sharada Prasad (eds.), *Selected Works of Jawaharlal Nehru*, Second Series, vol. 25 (New Delhi: Jawaharlal Nehru Memorial Fund, 1999), pp. 125-27; and Jawaharlal Nehru, "The Need for Non-Proliferation," Minutes of Third Meeting of the Commonwealth Prime Ministers' Conference, February 2, 1955 published in S. Gopal (ed.), *Selected Works of Jawaharlal Nehru*, Second Series, vol. 28 (New Delhi: Jawaharlal Nehru Memorial Fund, 2001), pp.198-99.
44. Jawaharlal Nehru, "Science and Progress," An Address to Indian Science Congress at Calcutta in 1938 published in Jagat S. Bright (ed.), *Collected Speeches of Jawaharlal Nehru*, vol. I (Lahore: The Indian Printing Works, 1945), p. 42.
45. Jawaharlal Nehru, "Atom Bomb," A Speech at Bombay, June 26, 1946 published in Jagat S. Bright (ed.), *Speeches of Jawaharlal Nehru* (Lahore: The Indian Printing Works, 1947), pp. 353-54.
46. Jawaharlal Nehru, "Atomic Energy Bill," A Speech on Atomic Energy Bill Before Constituent Assembly of India on April 6, 1948 published in Baldev Singh (ed.), *Jawaharlal Nehru on Science and Society: A Collection of His Writings and Speeches* (New Delhi: Nehru Memorial Museum and Library, 1988), p. 64.
47. Jawaharlal Nehru, "India's Policy," A Broadcast to the Nation, December 31, 1950 published in Sarvepalli Gopal (ed.), *Jawaharlal Nehru: An Anthology* (New Delhi: Oxford University Press, 1980), p. 370.

48. K. Subramanyam, "Nehru and India-China Conflict of 1962," B. R. Nanda (ed.), *India's Foreign Policy: The Nehru Years* (New Delhi: Vikas Publishing House, 1976), p. 113.
49. Nehru, n. 41, p. 427.
50. Jawaharlal Nehru, "Research on Atomic Energy," Note for Cabinet, May 22, 1948, File No.17(30)/47-PMS published in S. Gopal (ed.), *Selected Works of Jawaharlal Nehru*, Second Series, vol. 6 (New Delhi: Jawaharlal Nehru Memorial Fund, 1987), pp. 349-50.
51. Jawaharlal Nehru, "Atoms for Peace," A Speech at a Meeting of Scientists in London, October 22, 1948 published in S. Gopal (ed.), *Selected Works of Jawaharlal Nehru*, Second Series, vol. 8 (New Delhi: Jawaharlal Nehru Memorial Fund, 1989), p. 35.
52. Jawaharlal Nehru, "Atomic Research," Constituent Assembly Debates, Official Report, vol. 3, Part-I, March 23, 1949, pp. 1771-1773 published in S. Gopal (ed.), *Selected Works of Jawaharlal Nehru*, Second Series, vol. 10 (New Delhi: Jawaharlal Nehru Memorial Fund, 1990), pp. 105-6.
53. Jawaharlal Nehru, "Research in Atomic Energy," Note to S. S. Bhatnagar, March 20, 1952, File No.17(25)/56-PMS published in S. Gopal (ed.), *Selected Works of Jawaharlal Nehru*, Second Series, vol. 17 (New Delhi: Jawaharlal Nehru Memorial Fund, 1995), p. 300.
54. Ibid.
55. Jawaharlal Nehru, "The Use of Atomic Energy," Remarks at a Press Conference, Madras, October 4, 1952, published in S. Gopal (ed.), *Selected Works of Jawaharlal Nehru*, Second Series, vol. 19 (New Delhi: Jawaharlal Nehru Memorial Fund, 1996), p. 139.
56. Lok Sabha Debates, Second Series, vol. 3, no. 8, July 24, 1957, Col. 4954; and Ministry of Information and Broadcasting, *Jawaharlal Nehru's Speeches: March 1953-August 1957*, vol. 2 (New Delhi: Publications Division, 1983), p. 518.
57. Arnold Kramish, *The Peaceful Atom in Foreign Policy* (New York: Harper and Row, 1963), p. 26.
58. The United States presented the Baruch Plan prepared by Bernard Baruch before the United Nations in 1946 for the establishment of international control over the proliferation and development of nuclear technology. Jawaharlal Nehru had opposed this plan as such attempts would have prevented or made it difficult for developing countries to use nuclear technology even for industrial development.
59. G. C. Mirchandani, "India and Nuclear Weapons," T. T. Poulose (ed.), *Perspectives of India's Nuclear Policy* (New Delhi: Young Asia Publications, 1978), pp. 56-57.
60. Lok Sabha Debates, Third Series, vol. 15, March 23, 1963, Cols. 5780-5783.
61. G. C. Mirchandani, *India's Nuclear Dilemma* (New Delhi: Popular Book Services, 1968), p. 242.
62. C. Raja Mohan, "India and Nuclear Weapons," IPG4/98, available at http://library.fes.de/pdf-files/ipg/ipg-1998-4/artmohan.pdf, pp. 378-79, retrieved on June 15, 2013, pp. 379-80.
63. Ibid., p. 381.
64. Kate Sullivan, "How the World Warmed to a Nuclear India," *Inside Story*, May

3, 2012 available at inside.org.au/how-theworld-warmed-toa-nuclear-india/print/, retrieved on July 15, 2013.

65. The creation of NWFZs is considered as a regional approach to promote global nuclear non-proliferation. This approach prohibits the testing, stationing, development and use of nuclear weapons within the designated territorial framework. Countries within the designated territorial framework have the right to utilise nuclear science and technology for peaceful purposes including electricity production for domestic and industrial requirements. The establishment of NWFZs is recognised by the NPT in its article VII and also by the UN General Assembly in its Resolution No. 3472B of 1975. The UN Disarmament Commission (UNDC) in its report on April 30, 1999 has recommended a set of principles and guidelines for the establishment of a NWFZ. For details, see United Nations Office for Disarmament Affairs, "Nuclear-Weapons-Free Zones," available at www.un.org/disarmment/WMD/Nuclear?NWFZ.shtml.
66. "Obama Prague Speech on Nuclear Weapons," *Huffington Post*, June 5, 2009, available at http://www.huffingtonpost.com/2009/04/05/obama-prague-speech-on-nu_n_183219.html, retrieved on May 15, 2013; for the details of global nuclear stockpiles from 1945 to 2013, see Hans M. Kristensen and Robert S. Norris, "Global Nuclear Weapons Inventories, 1945-2013," *Bulletin of the Atomic Scientists*, vol. 69, no. 5, 2013, pp. 75-81.
67. Goldemberg, n. 7.
68. For details, see B. W. Brook and I. Lowe, *Why vs Why: Nuclear Power* (Sydney: Pantera Press, 2010).
69. Press Trust of India, "India Eyeing 63,000 MW Nuclear Power Capacity by 2032: NPCIL," *The Economic Times*, October 11, 2012.
70. Sullivan, n. 64.

13

India's Policy Towards Nepal and Bhutan: Nehru to Present

Debamitra Mitra

Nehru considered the Indian subcontinent as an exclusive sphere of influence for New Delhi. India's policy towards the Himalayan states of Nepal and Bhutan was articulated by Nehru in the form of special relationship around the issues of the ideal of democracy, treaty diplomacy, manipulation of political pragmatism and the most important determinant being the China factor. Ideal of promoting democracy got entangled with the pursuit of political pragmatism overpowered by security interests in India's perspective about the Himalayan states. Realising the strategic importance of the buffers, unlike the post-Nehruvian leaders, Nehru's earning of their trust more or less got satisfied with signing of treaties of peace and friendship with Nepal and Bhutan. Nehru-crafted India's special relationship with both the buffers raises doubts about India's big brother attitude in the post-Nehruvian era. Thus together with bilateral issues, Nehruvian and post-Nehruvian eras might be differentiated on the subtle question of attitude stimulated mostly by the Chinese overtures coupled with the pressures of globalisation.

Apart from handling India's tumultuous domestic situation after independence, Jawaharlal Nehru's major contribution lies in the field of foreign policy. His foreign policy was characterised by two major facets: first, India to be independent from the power politics of both blocs created by the Cold War and second, his faith in goodwill and honesty in matters of international affairs. Though the Chinese attack in 1962 violated the clauses of the *Panchsheel* Agreement of 1954 and had shaken his faith, it was a learning experience for him to improve Indian military strength instead of overt dependence on peaceful negotiations in matters of foreign policy. Nehru's influence was visible on the foreign policy of India. Consequently, his personal views and principles for the conduct of foreign policy became effectively co-terminous with India's. In order to ensure a congenial environment for development at home, Nehru worked abroad to ensure India's security, establishing an ideological position which accrued her goodwill among Third World countries while not antagonising either Communist or Capitalist blocs. Therefore, he articulated non-aligned policy posture to conduct India's affairs in the comity of nations. A look at Nehru's inaugural speech to the nation in 1947 provides a glimpse of the idealism his foreign policy incorporated in the subsequent decades.

> Long years ago we made a tryst with destiny and now the time comes when we shall redeem our pledge, not wholly or in full measure, but very substantially. At the stroke of the midnight hour, when the world sleeps, India will awake to life and freedom. A moment comes, which comes but rarely in history, when we step out from the old to the new, when an age ends, and when the soul of a nation, long suppressed, finds utterance. It is fitting that at this solemn moment we take the pledge of dedication to the service of India and her people and to the still larger cause of humanity.[1]

Having contempt for power politics, India tended to see its role in world politics as the harbinger of a new set of principles of peaceful coexistence and multilateralism which if applied properly would transform the world. The common perception was that Nehru's foreign policy had a unique feature of having the characteristics of both idealism and pragmatism. India's policy of non-alignment validates this perception. Non-aligned policy articulated by Nehru was the pragmatic response to the then prevailing global scenario. It was a strategy that served India's foreign policy interests while accommodating the domestic requirements of a new state struggling for nation-building. Through non-alignment India cultivated a coterie of allies on whom the country could rely to advance initiatives amenable to her interests. With diplomatic flexibility non-alignment helped India chart an independent course in international affairs, had her voice heard, and at the same time avoided the limitations of overt alignment with either superpower. Being part of India's foreign policy, neighbourhood policy was based on three assumptions. First, India being the successor state of British India had to shoulder the role and responsibilities of the Empire in a region that stretched between Iran and Indonesia, the Hindukush-Himalaya and the Indian Ocean. Second supposition postulated that India would be the leader of anti-colonial struggles and would help to create a buffer of Third World states free of fierce competition for spheres of influence between first and second world. Third, Nehru wanted to collaborate with China and thereby to keep Asia free of superpower rivalry.[2]

Nehru and Himalayan States

According to the British Raj, the regions between first (inner) and the second (outer) lines is often described as the inner ring which included Baluchistan, the North-West Frontier Province, Kashmir, Nepal, Sikkim, Bhutan, the North-East Frontier Agency, and the tribal regions of Upper Burma. The end of British rule within the subcontinent had generated the national imperative of reconsolidating India's territorial sovereignty. For that the first task was to integrate the princely states into the Indian Union. Second was to cope with the immediate consequences of the two partitions in East and West, of Bengal and of Punjab respectively, and the creation of new porous frontiers in these states. Third, and equally challenging, was the question of India's future relationship with the Himalayan kingdoms that remained critical of India's regional security scenario after independence. India had two choices to deal—first, to sustain the old framework that bound these kingdoms to the Raj and second, to simply annex them into the Indian Union and thereby to reduce any ambiguities about their status. Sardar Vallabhbhai Patel, the Home Minister in Nehru's Cabinet, believed that the kingdoms must be treated as princely states that should be brought into India's fold. Nehru, however, opted for a more complex policy that viewed these kingdoms as part of India's security perimeter and calculus of frontier defence—avoid forcible accession but bind them into stronger economic interdependence with the Republic.[3] This approach essentially meant sustaining the Raj framework of treating these kingdoms as allies and protectorates.[4] British rulers had variations in their treatment of the three kingdoms. Nepal was treated as an independent country, Sikkim as a full protectorate of India and Bhutan enjoyed a status in-between. They were strongly bound into the security framework of the Raj through the treaties signed with Nepal in 1819 and 1923, Bhutan in 1865 and 1910, and Sikkim in 1817 and 1890.

Nehru wanted to separate the three kingdoms from India and acknowledged their strategic status. He signed treaties with them during 1949-50 following almost the same template of the earlier agreements signed by the Raj. By signing the agreement with Bhutan in 1949, India retained the right to guide the kingdom's foreign policy but not to interfere in its internal affairs. Under the agreement India also had a say in Bhutan's import of arms. According to C. Raja Mohan the agreements India signed with Nepal and Sikkim in 1950 were more attuned to the challenges that China's control of Tibet posed to the security of the subcontinent. India's July 1950 Treaty with Nepal covered a wide range of aspects and included an article on mutual defence and another on regulating arms transfers. Earlier in 1947, India signed a tripartite agreement with Nepal and Britain that allowed India to recruit soldiers from Nepal, a right that was limited to Britain until then. India's December 1950 Treaty with Sikkim reaffirmed its status as a protectorate of India and gave Delhi the right to deploy troops on its territory.[5]

However, Nehru's reconstruction of the security ties with the

Himalayan kingdoms was not a replica of the Raj. He sought to accommodate many of the interests of the kingdoms in an effort to encourage them to remain part of the structure of securing India's northern frontiers. He fully recognised the sovereignty and territorial integrity of Nepal and strongly affirmed India's commitment to Bhutan's internal autonomy. He increased the annual subsidies to these kingdoms and significantly expanded their infrastructural, economic and technical assistance. Under Article 4 of the 1949 Treaty he also offered territorial concessions to Bhutan which sought the return of 32 square miles of the territory annexed by the Raj in Dewangiri district of Assam.[6] Nehru invited the representatives of Nepal and Bhutan to participate in the first Asian Relations Conference held in New Delhi in March 1947, thereby facilitating the two kingdoms for external exposure. He encouraged the establishment of ties between Nepal and China after India signed an agreement with China on Tibet in 1954. He had a balanced foreign policy with the Himalayan kingdoms where he was generous to the extent he could be, keeping in mind the importance of these kingdoms to India's defence, especially in the northern frontiers. Speaking in the Constituent Assembly on December 6, 1950, Nehru declared:

> So far as the Himalayas are concerned, they lie on the other side of Nepal, not on this side. Therefore, the principal barrier to India lies on the other side of Nepal. We are not going to tolerate any person coming over that barrier. Therefore, much as we can appreciate the independence of Nepal, we cannot risk our own security by anything not done in Nepal which permits either that barrier to be crossed or otherwise leads to the weakening of our frontiers.[7]

With the passage of time, the strategic importance of the Himalayan states for India's security in the north has increased manifold due to a few factors. First, twenty-first century Asianism has identified India along with China as two powerful actors in South and South-East Asia. Second, these two actors are competing regional powers exhibiting basic conflict of values, besides mutual suspicion and misperceptions. Third, in the corridor of states stretching from Pakistan to Myanmar, Chinese and Indian economic interests have been confronted by various security risks. This area, where mainly non-traditional violence draws strong concern from both sides, has for a long time been an arena of Sino-Indian rivalry. Fourthly, among the diplomatic objectives pursued by one over the other to gain regional supremacy, both the countries' target towards influencing the buffer states of Nepal and Bhutan is quite inevitable and also exemplary in many instances. Hence, the new Indian leaders can neither denounce Nehru nor formally reject his ideas, but are continually improvising and refashioning India's foreign policy in the basic precincts of Nehru's structure of Indian foreign policy with the Himalayan states, to suit the new requirements posed by the post-Nehruvian period.

Post-Nehruvian Phase

Implicit in the transition to globalisation, from the past emphasis on politics to new stress on economics in the making of foreign policy, has become the principal national objective for India. With the socialist straightjacket removed, and the pressures to compete with other emerging markets, Indian diplomacy now entered uncharted waters. India is now seeking foreign direct investment, and is an active player in the economically integrated world. The slow but successful economic reforms generated rapid economic growth and provided a basis to transform its relations with great powers; regional rivals like Pakistan and China, and the neighbourhood as well. Another transition from Nehruvian time is the shift from being a leader of the Third World to the recognition of the potential that India can emerge as a great power in its own right and might. *Look East Policy*, stimulated by economic diplomacy, helped India explore the cultural affinity and to forge closer economic and strategic ties with South-East, East Asian states, which can be a substitute for the Western market. The Soviet demise and China's rise demanded that India further change the anti-Western orientation of its foreign policy.

This further resulted in a change in its South Asian policy in which India embarked on a series of policy innovations that demanded greater generosity and willingness in resolving many accumulated problems with smaller neighbours. The imperatives of idealism and moralism have yet not completely disappeared, and tension between *power* and *principle* remains an enduring tenet in India's foreign policy strategy. Unlike Nehru's time, post-Nehruvian policy has limited the pursuit of national interest in order to contribute to collective interests of the international system, made almost inevitable due to globalisation. The demand on India to contribute for order and stability in its immediate and extended neighbourhood has dramatically increased. This has in turn drawn India deeper into great power rivalries in various regions and in the internal conflicts of smaller countries. In this context India's relations with Nepal and Bhutan have simultaneously shown the inheritance of Nehruvian legacy and sometimes sharp deviation from it. Interplay between power and principle has clearly reflected in India's relations with Nepal and Bhutan.

Nehruvian foreign policy had always made India sensitive to maintain an exclusive influence in her southern Himalayan neighbourhood, and Indo-Bhutan and Indo-Nepal treaties of Peace and Friendship in 1949 and 1950 respectively, were the direct offshoots of such diplomacy. At the same time, it is equally evident that China has been creating obstacles for India, for the similar objective of gaining influence on the Himalayan buffer states; since the 1950s used Nepal and Bhutan as pawns vis-à-vis India, wherever and whenever possible, especially against the backdrop of India's friendship with both Nepal and Bhutan. This has been further augmented in the present scenario of Asian supremacy, as geopolitical equations and strategic significance among the countries are shifting. Nehru's ideas of forging relationship with Nepal and Bhutan have witnessed changes in contemporary scenario notwithstanding the fact that China has remained a constant determinant of New Delhi's policy towards the Himalayan states during Nehruvian or post-Nehruvian period.

India and Bhutan

Leaders of India and Bhutan believed that the continuity and sanctity of the 1949 treaty depends ultimately on faith and trust which the two countries could inculcate in each other. R. K. Nehru, then Indian Foreign Secretary, after his visit in Bhutan in June 1955, suggested,

> We should give up the idea of pressing for closer political contacts or of asking for a political agent in Bhutan. We should concentrate more on social and economic approach. Even there, there should be no attempt at any imposition. Help should be given when asked for and not thrust upon Bhutan. The principal help that I envisage is to give opportunities to the Bhutanese for training in India in survey work, medical and health, Hindi language and general education, engineering and any other that is suggested can be considered.[8]

However he was cautious about the fact that, "If they require some persons from India to help them in any of these activities or training, we should try to send to them such persons. But the initiative should come from them."[9] Mutual trust developed between India and Bhutan was due to India's policy of not interfering in the governmental machinery run by the King of Bhutan. Nehru took decision when R. K. Nehru commented that "Bhutan was not accepting India's demand for a resident political agent there because of her concern about safeguarding her status which was higher than that of Sikkim, as the stationing of a political agent was the old British method of bringing a country under control."[10] Built on that edifice, Indo-Bhutan friendship not only qualifies as a good example of bilateral relationship in the region, at the government level, but equally at the people-to-people level closeness and interdependence.

In the late 1950s and early 1960s menacing signs of Sino-Tibet misgivings, PLA's incursion into delimited border, a vague Chinese claim and other events forced Bhutan to re-evaluate her traditional isolation policy that was detrimental to sovereignty. Developing lines of communication with India became an urgent necessity. In this respect, Jawaharlal Nehru's visit to Bhutan on horseback in September 1958 to convince Bhutan to end its isolation policy and accept India's economic assistance marked a watershed in Indo-Bhutan relations. The Chinese menace was taken into concern not only for its Tibetan policy, but when China claimed in 1910 and once again in 1948 through the Tibetan Kashag that Bhutan was their vassal state. As R. K. Nehru wrote, "we (India) cannot have special relations with Bhutan without their concurrence. They gave transit visas to the Indian party but took no special notice of the official visit to Bhutan."[11] K. M. Panikkar, Member, State Reorganisation Commission and former Ambassador to China, however stated that though the situation required careful handling there was no serious danger of the Chinese putting forward any claim to suzerainty over Bhutan.[12] Though Nehru agreed with Panikkar, he cautioned, "Our policy course should be the positive policy of friendship with these areas and contacts and help." He reiterated, "We must give no impression to the Bhutan government that we have any desire to have political and other control over it."[13]

Although Sino-Bhutan relations have been growing since the 1980s the sole purpose of Beijing has been to draw Bhutan away from its special relations with New Delhi. It has used different means to this end—refusal to discuss about Bhutan during Sino-Indian border talks, providing incentives to Bhutan for having direct relations with Beijing and linking Sino-Bhutan relations as a condition for softening Sino-Indian rapprochement. China alleged that the 1949 treaty symbolised India's expansionism and hegemonic appeals on Bhutanese nationalism. Utilising the allegation, China gave a condition to India that it would abandon recognising Bhutan as an Indian protectorate state, provided India promised to ban anti-China activities by the Tibetan refugees from Indian soil.

The more Bhutan's security is vulnerable, the more will it add to India's discomfort. Such vulnerability might increase either due to China's linking of establishing diplomatic relations directly with Bhutan or India's negligence in counterterrorism in the north-east. Even unstable domestic politics in Bhutan might go against India's interests, whether it is anti-national movement by Nepalese in Bhutan, because for New Delhi, even today, a weak Bhutan means weak buffer state between India and China. Nehruvian foreign policy assessed that and hence it was only in this connection that India had played a major role in bringing an end to Bhutan's isolation policy and drawing Bhutan into the Indian fold.

India has been supporting Bhutan in all areas of business pertaining to its holistic development since 1949. In the midst of the Indian rupee crisis in Bhutan since March 2012, it was a blessing for her to get around Rs.7 billion as grants for development projects of the 10th plan and excise refund of 2008-9 from the Government of India (GOI). Borrowings from GOI line of credit has also been enhanced to Rs.10 billion.[14] While handing over the cheques to the Finance Minister of Bhutan, Wangdi Norbu, the Indian Ambassador to Bhutan commented, "despite current fiscal and financial difficulties in India, the fund was in line with GOI's commitment for expeditious release of funds for various schemes and projects of Indo-Bhutan bilateral cooperation."[15] In the recent rupee crisis in Bhutan, the Central Bank of Bhutan has stopped replenishing commercial banks with Indian rupees needed to pay for imports from India, which has adversely hit industrialists and importers. It is a radical measure taken to curb rupee spending that had threatened to reach a crisis level. Besides this, Bhutan's ethnic problem burgeoning into an international refugee issue had also been handled adequately with Indian support almost eight years back.

With regard to security and commercial viability for India, Bhutan holds a very significant status. India fears that any direct foreign contact would pull Bhutan into big power politics that might seriously affect her social and economic stability, which could in fact destabilise the north-eastern part of India. Stability in the entire Himalayan neighbourhood became important for India's security. Thus, India unilaterally included Bhutan within India's northern security system. It was in India's national interests to prevent areas of strategic importance from falling into foreign hands. India's prudent foreign policy, during the time, made her sensitive about keeping an exclusive influence in the southern Himalayas. It was only in this connection that India had played a major role in sowing the seeds of modernity in Bhutan's traditionalism. She helped in Bhutan's socio-economic development and promoted Bhutan's international exposure through UN membership and other multilateral organisations. India's assistance during this time was indirectly tied to Bhutan's refusal of Chinese assistance.

Geopolitically, the Himalayan country's position not only acts as a cushion for Indian security in northern frontiers, there are inherent economic dimensions too, especially in import of 100 per cent hydel power from Bhutan, cross-border commerce, trade and counter-terrorism in the north-east corridor that necessitates continuous and improved relationship between the two countries. The potential and positive implications of these issues also justify the reassessment of Indo-Bhutan relations on a higher plane of realism. Though Indian support for Bhutan is quite exemplary, yet Bhutan sometimes alleges that India is taking her for granted. Against the backdrop of meeting Chinese Premier Wen Jiabao and his Bhutanese counterpart, Jigmi Y. Thinley, on the sidelines of the UN Conference on Sustainable Development, known as the Rio+20 summit in June 2012, the two heads exchanged cordial notes of establishing formal diplomatic ties between their countries. China highly appreciates Bhutan's staunch support of China's position on issues concerning Taiwan and Tibet. China is willing to complete border demarcation with Bhutan at an early date and strengthen exchanges in various fields so as to push bilateral ties to a higher level.

India was taken by surprise when Jigme Thinley appeared to be cosying up to Beijing. Indian diplomats commented that the way the previous government and Thinley went about establishing ties with China, he ignored Indian sensitivities completely.[16] Perhaps this was the reason when India had to resort to teach a lesson to Bhutan just at the eve of Bhutan's national elections on July 13, 2013, by withdrawing subsidy on cooking gas and kerosene oil being provided by New Delhi to Thimphu to Bhutan. Whatever the Indian diplomacy assessed to out-power Thinley and his party, however, there is little reason for joy in New Delhi as the People's Democratic Party trounced the ruling Druk Phuensum Tshogpa, headed by Thinley, in Bhutan's second parliamentary elections. The current trend is, if one bunch of Bhutanese politicians leans towards India, another is bound to lean towards China. Given the fragility of Sino-Indian relations, this polarisation is neither in Bhutan's interest nor in India's interest.

Due to the emerging Sino-Bhutan rapprochement, India planned to support Bhutan to conciliate to two of her urgent objectives taking Bhutan almost for granted especially on the pedestal of idealism of Indo-Bhutan relationship: first, asserting its personality on the regional scene and second, avoiding it to be dragged or entangled into shifting Himalayan politics, even if the country invents a "Chinese realpolitik" of its own. But realism has proved that already Bhutan is being drawn into Himalayan politics. Her tightrope situation of how to keep equidistant between India and China has made her more vulnerable. Added to this her transition from absolute monarchy to parliamentary democracy, from guided foreign policy to the role of full player on the world stage, and above all the change from medievalism to modernity together present enough challenges for Bhutan. Article 2 of the 1949 Friendship Treaty has been amended in 2007 where Bhutan's foreign policy is no more guided by India. After observing the Chinese overtures in Bhutan's foreign policy, it appears that India is missing the opportunities of assessing her relationship with Bhutan more on a pragmatic ground.

India and Nepal

The independence of India was followed by the establishment of the People's Republic of China (PRC) in 1949, which heralded a period of strong geopolitical change and tension around Nepal. According to New Delhi's perception, South Asia constituted an integral part of its security in which Nepal plays a critical role. Many Nepalese resented this interpretation despite Nehru's insistence that stable, independent neighbours were vital to India's security. They accused India of being insensitive to Nepal's status as an independent nation. Nepalese sources further stated that independent India did not depart from the colonial policy of the British Raj. Instead it further consolidated colonial policies especially when it came to South Asia policy and gave continuity to colonial policy in its neighbourhood. It adopted the policy of bullying and using coercive methods against its smaller and weaker neighbours, which continues even today.[17] Because of these differing attitudes, Nepal's relations with India oscillated considerably over the years, particularly in matters relating to security. In a speech before Parliament in 1950, India's Prime Minister, Jawaharlal Nehru, summed up India's security concerns vis-à-vis Nepal. Nehru stated that:

> From time immemorial, the Himalayas have provided us with magnificent frontiers ... We cannot allow that barrier to be penetrated, because it is also the principal barrier to India. Therefore, as much as we appreciate the independence of Nepal, we cannot allow anything to go wrong in Nepal or permit that barrier to be crossed or weakened, because that would be a risk to our own security.[18]

After Chinese annexation of Tibet in 1950, Nepal came to play a much larger role in India's security calculations. Fearing that China might eventually subvert or invade Nepal, India signed a Treaty of Peace and Friendship with the Rana regime on July 31, 1950. Although not a formal military alliance, the treaty required both parties to consult and devise effective countermeasures in the event of a security threat to either country. Nepal's inclusion in the Indian defence perimeter was made explicit by an exchange of secret letters—later made public—that accompanied the treaty, stating inter alia that neither government shall tolerate any threat to the security of the other by a foreign aggressor. To assuage Nepalese fears of Indian domination, the treaty also stipulated that Indian forces could be introduced into the country only at the invitation of the Nepalese government. The two sides simultaneously signed a trade and transit agreement that extended reciprocal rights with regard to bilateral trade and residential arrangements as well as trans-shipment of Nepalese goods through India.

Treaty Diplomacy

With Nepali Congress taking over power from the Rana regime, Nehru made it clear to the Prime Minister, B. P. Koirala, that though the Treaty was signed before the changeover in Nepal and seemed to be outdated, the basic points laid down in it still hold. In a letter to Prime Minister M. P. Koirala on March 23, 1954, Nehru claimed:

> In the previous talks I have had with you, as well as with the other representatives of the Nepal Government, we have discussed foreign affairs and we have agreed that there should be full coordination between the foreign policy and the defence policy of the two Governments. Indeed that was even laid down in the collateral letters exchanged at the time of the last Treaty between the two countries.[19]

As Sino-Indian tensions mounted in the late 1950s, despite close military ties with New Delhi, Nepal had never allowed garrisoning of Indian troops or joint military exercises in the country. Gradually, as Nehru got convinced that Nepal was moving away from the treaty, he himself realised that the treaty was about to lapse. To keep the value and integrity of the treaty intact and sustained, he disclosed in the Rajya Sabha on December 8, 1959 contemporaneous exchange of letters that created the groundwork behind the final version of the treaty. He revealed:

> Neither Government should tolerate any threat to the security of the other by a foreign aggressor. To deal with any such threat, the two governments shall consult with each other and devise effective countermeasures.[20]

Nepal loomed prominently in Nehru's talks with Zhou Enlai, the Chinese Premier. He asserted that India had accepted the full independence of Nepal and had not claimed some of the rights that Britain had exercised. Making a strong claim to Zhou he said, "Nepal's foreign affairs are looked after by us and we have been giving them aid and training facilities for their personnel, but we do not interfere in their internal affairs. But you will understand that traditionally Nepal and India are closely linked together and according to the treaty the foreign policy of India and Nepal is to be coordinated." According to A. G. Noorani, this claim was not warranted by the Treaty or the letters, rather it was very Curzonian and very Nehruvian.[21] Further, Nehru claimed that India had a special position in Nepal and it became necessary, therefore, for their foreign policies to be in line with each other. Hence, India did not approve of foreign intervention in Nepal in any way. He had even asked China not to post an ambassador in Kathmandu which will trigger the Western powers to do the same. The Americans, Nehru told Zhou, were "sending books for libraries and lot of money is thrown about. Nepalese are easily bribed."[22]

Subsequently, the changing geopolitical reality and Nepal's adjustment to that upset New Delhi as it saw Nepal coming close to China notwithstanding a steady increase in Nepal's economic involvement with India. Ironically China's arrival in Tibet not only reasserted the balance, but also finally cut off the remnants of trans-Himalayan trade, thus causing an about-turn of the economy of northern Nepal. These two contradictions between Indian attitude and geopolitical reality and between political and economic trends in Nepal proved to be the central factors determining the relationship between Nepal and India. According to the Nepalese viewpoint, Nepal having the geographic position of being India-locked in three sides, south, east, west, New Delhi had always tried to exploit this geostrategic and geo-economic situation of Nepal. Post-Nehru era saw the search for a new policy in India while Nepal struggled to build the economic foundations for an independent foreign policy. King Birendra did not abandon the policy of equal friendship between China and India but wanted to woo China to counter India's growing influence in the region. Nepal's overtures to China also had economic implications.

Relations between India and Nepal, though close, were yet fraught with difficulties stemming from geography, economics, and archetypal problems inherent in asymmetrical relations and common ethnic and linguistic identities that overlap the two countries' borders. It openly criticised India's 1975 annexation of Sikkim as an Indian state. Tensions reached a height in the mid-1970s, when Nepal insisted on substantial amendments in its favour in the trade and transit treaty with India. After two extensions, the two treaties expired in March 1989, resulting in a virtual Indian economic blockade for Nepal that lasted till late April 1990. Although economic issues were a major factor in the two countries' confrontation, Indian dissatisfaction with Nepal's 1988 acquisition of Chinese weapons played an important role, in spite of the fact that Nepal was declared to be a zone of peace. Indian policy linked security with economic relations and insisted on reviewing India-Nepal relations as a whole.

In December 1991 during the regime of Prime Minister V. P. Singh and the Nepalese Prime Minister G. P. Koirala, the two countries signed new, separate trade and transit treaties. Other economic agreements were designed to accord Nepal additional economic benefits. But Indo-Nepal relations underwent further reassessment when Nepal Communist Party-Maoist under the leadership of anti-India hardliner, Mohan Vaidya, demanded that all unequal treaties signed with India should be scrapped including the historic Peace and Friendship Treaty of 1950.[23] One of the most important drawbacks in India-Nepal relations has been the unrealistic priority given to the 1950 Treaty, overlooking other factors, whereas bilateral relations are not guaranteed by formal treaties alone. Many other factors and forces determine the course of bilateral relations, as Lok Raj Baral stated:

> With the formal security treaty Nepal's geopolitical situation imposes certain guidelines that can hardly go against either of the two neighbours. Nepal's policy therefore needs to be balanced despite being too close to its southern neighbours. The emerging regional and international politics have further shrunk Nepal's options forcing it to be more prudent to pursue a correct policy towards its neighbours. Geographical situation and functional interactions with southern neighbours have contributed to extensive and deep relations between Nepal and India.[24]

According to Baral the treaty of 1950 has become one of the issues for political mobilisation and politicians use this strategy when they are short of issues.[25] He further stated that the Nepalese are the principal beneficiaries in education, health and employment sectors in India, let alone the recruitment of Nepalese into the Indian army. Symbolically also, Nepal's international status has never been compromised. Nor have the policy decisions taken by Nepal on various bilateral, regional and international issues ever been strongly challenged by India.[26]

Though Nehru's foreign policy had been shaped by idealism and realism but his dealings with Nepal had been governed by realism—idealism only being used as a veil to cover the "sins" of interstate relations.[27] This continued to shape India's policy towards Nepal even after Nehru's death. King Mahendra wanted to ensure that the Indian government would not help the Nepali opposition politicians based in India, and New Delhi wanted to make sure that Nepal remained completely within its sphere of influence.[28] In 1989 India imposed economic embargo on Nepal after the two countries failed to reach an agreement on the renewal of trade and transit treaties. India closed down 19 of the 21 trade routes and 13 of the 15 transit routes used by Nepal.[29] Though bilateral issues are crucial in determining the nature of relationship, however, the essence of Indo-Nepal relations lie in attitudes rather than issues and obviously attitudes are influenced by issues and vice versa.

Except Bhutan and Maldives, it has been alleged that India has strained relationship with most of her South Asian neighbours because of these reasons: first, taking her neighbours for granted, second, not being serious about correcting trade imbalances created by its becoming a regional power and being excessively paranoid of its own security; placing undue emphasis on security at the cost of all the other facets of relationships.[30] Anti-India attitude among Nepalese leaders is infested with duplicity. They try to secure support overtly by appealing to the public's anti-India sentiments while covertly trying to keep India happy reinforcing the common perception that New Delhi's favourable attitude helps the careers of aspiring politicians of Nepal.[31] This duplicity on the part of the leadership and irrational nationalism on the part of the public, coupled with the ever suspicious approach towards New Delhi's motives, makes Nepalese attitude towards India more confusing. Relations have been strained and normalised but the attitude that formed the root cause of the problems in India-Nepal relations has remained constant for the past half century.

It is always expected that the responsibility for changing these attitudes largely lies with India because of her size and power. With this realisation, India's Prime Minister, Inder Kumar Gujral, attempted to change India's attitude through *Gujral Doctrine*, stating that India should not insist on reciprocity from small neighbours. Consequently, India improved its relations with neighbouring countries while settling some long-pending bilateral issues. It has also enabled India to settle water dispute regarding the Mahakali River with Nepal. Notwithstanding this, India did not take the rise of Maoists as a force in Nepalese politics seriously before 2000, when they directly attacked the Army posts. India declared the Nepali Maoists as terrorists even before the Nepalese Government did so. India's overall approach towards Nepal was in coordination with the US.[32]

Former Prime Minister Manmohan Singh has not appeared any different from the predecessors dealing with Nepal. The only way for Nepal is to reflect on its own shortcomings and safeguard its national interest through mature and sophisticated use of diplomacy. Because of its geographical location Nepal cannot completely remove itself from India's influence. With more wisdom in dealing with New Delhi, the degree of that influence can be reduced. Perhaps, against the backdrop of Nepal currently keeping a distance with India and tilting more towards China, Bhutan has become scary and is ready to patch up all the difficult areas with China. This makes the GOI taking more care of Bhutan so that the confidence of trust might be re-instilled rather than teach Bhutan a lesson.

Understanding the pragmatism of Indo-Bhutan relationship, during the 1950s, Nehruvian foreign policy assessed it and hence India played a major role in bringing an end to Bhutan's isolation policy. But post-Nehruvian foreign policy acted inept due to an over-enthusiastic petroleum ministry's decision for cuts in subsidies of kerosene and cooking gas in Bhutan that crippled Bhutan's economy, and India as an ally of Bhutan landed up earning distrust. Bhutan has already turned over a new leaf with its transiting from monarchical system to democracy. Inevitably, the process of debate and discussion on Bhutan's foreign and security policy has started in right earnest. Though India has a robust and comprehensive relationship with Bhutan, however, at the domestic level, issues of trade imbalance, disadvantages of overdependence on India and poor delivery mechanism and India's ineffective counterterrorism measures in the north-east are being debated in the media frequently. In the National Assembly, the representatives are pushing for settling of border dispute with China and normalising relationship with China. With China extending a rail link up to Yatung (a Chinese province whose closest Indian towns include Siliguri, Rangpur, Dinajpur and Guwahati), economic relationship with Bhutan is likely to grow at a faster pace. Together with Japan and India, China will never miss the opportunity of coming up as a major economic player in Bhutan. On the ethnic front, the issue of Bhutanese refugees of Nepalese origin remaining unresolved has the potential to strain Nepal-Bhutan relationship and complicate the internal security situation in Bhutan. There is also the likelihood of Indian north-east insurgents reusing Bhutanese territory against Indian interests. To check that, India has to be mindful of the changing political discourse especially on Bhutan as democracy takes roots there. New Delhi should be sensitive to local perceptions and encourage regular interactions at multiple levels, with an emphasis on greater people-to-people contact to dispel mutual misunderstandings and concerns.

Conclusion

To sum up, it can be articulated that India emerges as a key contributor to the prosperity of Nepal. The changing geostrategic and geo-economic reality demands that New Delhi needs to review its policy towards Kathmandu and to take steps to correct its impression as an interventionist neighbour. India's assistance should go towards building Nepal's economy and society irrespective of which party or coalition is in power in Kathmandu. Its role should be that of a trusted partner in Nepal. If India does not undertake a corrective course, Nepal will tend to fall under Chinese influence which will have far-reaching implications for India's security. However, China cannot replace India, as the latter is providing maritime route to Nepal which China cannot provide, but Beijing can certainly reduce the significance of New Delhi for Kathmandu by providing economic aid. Further, India should avoid getting drawn into Nepal-Bhutan tensions, especially on the issue of the Bhutanese refugees sheltered in Nepal. New Delhi should craft policies that would mitigate the negative effects of an unstable Nepal and the growing influence of China. India might perceive Chinese presence in Nepal to be an acute security dilemma and India needs to prepare itself for meeting such eventualities which may have low probability but high impact. Nepal's landlocked position and economic dependence does not allow Nepal to be fully independent in foreign policy decisions. India also needs to realise that Nepal will never approve to have a status like Bhutan vis-à-vis India. Nehru-crafted India's special relationship with both Nepal and Bhutan has shown signs of erosion in the post-Nehruvian period. In the current political realism this special relationship has already earned the tag of India's "insatiable" attitude. Article 2 of the India-Bhutan Treaty, where India guided Bhutan in its foreign relations, has been changed. In February 2007, the bilateral treaty of 1949 has been replaced by a new Friendship Treaty which recognises the sovereign, independent and equal status of both countries.

References

1. "A Tryst with Destiny," Great Speeches of the 20th Century. May 1, 2007. http://www.guardian.co.uk/theguardian/series/greatspeeches.
2. C. K. Lal, "From Nehru Creed to Indira Doctrine," February 2009, *Himal Southasian*, Kathmandu, Nepal, p. 1; also available on http://www.himalmag.com/.
3. Srikant Dutt, "India and the Himalayan States," *Asian Affairs*, vol. 67, no. 1, February 1980, pp. 71-81.
4. C. Raja Mohan, "India's Regional Security Cooperation: The Nehru Raj Legacy," Working Paper, no. 168, March 7, 2013, p. 6, Institute of South Asian Studies (ISAS), Singapore.
5. Ibid.
6. Debamitra Mitra, *Indo-Bhutan Relations: Political Process, Conflict and Crisis* (New Delhi: Academic Excellence, 2010), p. 26.
7. J. Lorne Kavic, *India's Quest for Security: Defence Policies, 1947-1965* (California: University of California Press, 1967), p. 56
8. Jawaharlal Nehru, "Approach to Bhutanese Problem," Note to the Foreign Secretary, MEA, July 15, 1955, Ravinder Kumar and H. Y. Sharada Prasad (eds.), *Selected Works of Jawaharlal Nehru*, Second Series II, vol. 29 (New Delhi: Jawaharlal Nehru Memorial Fund, 2001), p. 313.
9. Ibid.
10. Ibid.
11. Jawaharlal Nehru, "Policy Towards Bhutan," Note to the Foreign Secretary, July 17, 1955. Ravinder Kumar and H. Y Sharada Prasad (eds.), *Selected Works of Jawaharlal Nehru, Second Series*, vol. 29 (New Delhi: Jawaharlal Nehru Memorial Fund, 2001), p. 316.
12. Ibid.
13. Ibid.
14. *The Kuensel*, Thimphu, June 16, 2012, p. 1.
15. Passang Norbu, "India Gives Bhutan Rs. 3.61 Billion," *The Kuensel*, Thimphu, June 7, 2012, p. 2.
16. Kasturi Charu Sudan, "Ties on the Mend, Bhutan PM set to visit Delhi," *The Telegraph*, Kolkata, August 11, 2013, p. 4.
17. Nath Lamsal Yuba, "Time to Reshape Nepal's Foreign Policy," *The Weekly Mirror*, 2009, Kathmandu, p. 1.
18. Country Listing, Nepal Table of Contents, September 1991, http://www.country-data.com/cgi-bin/query/r-9187.html.
19. A. G. Noorani, "Nehru: A Democratic Curzon?" *Frontline*, vol. 17, issue 26, December 23, 2000-January 5, 2001, p. 1. See, for detail, Ravinder Kumar and

H. Y. Sharada Prasad (eds.), *Selected Works of Jawaharlal Nehru*, Second Series, vol. 27 (New Delhi: Jawaharlal Nehru Memorial Fund, 2000).

20. Avtar Singh Bhasin, *Nepal's Relations with India and China: Documents 1947-1992* (New Delhi: SIBA Exim, 1994), pp. 42-43, 67.
21. A. G. Noorani, n. 19.
22. Ibid.
23. "Anti-India Hawk Splits Maoist Party," *The Telegraph*, Kolkata, June 20, 2012, p. 3.
24. Lok Raj Baral, "Nepal-India Relations Formal Treaty and Beyond," *Think India Quarterly*, vol. 13, no. 4, October-December 2007, p. 173.
25. Ibid.
26. Ibid.
27. Baldev Raj Nayar and T. V. Paul, *India in the World Order: Searching for Major-Power Status* (Cambridge: Cambridge University Press, 2003), p. 116.
28. Rabindra Mishra, "India's Role in Nepal's Maoist Insurgency," *Asian Survey*, vol. 44, issue 5, September-October 2004, p. 632.
29. Ibid., p. 633.
30. V. Sudarshan, "Next Door Boor," *Outlook*, September 2, 2002, p. 1.
31. Rabindra Mishra, n. 28, p. 644.
32. S. D. Muni, *India's Foreign Policy: The Democracy Dimension with Special Reference to Neighbours* (New Delhi: Cambridge University Press, 2009), p. 89.

Index

Abdullah, Sheikh, 15, 65, 66, 68, 69, 71, 72, 73
Afghanistan, 67, 165, 166
Africa, 53, 148, 216, 217, 218, 225
Al Qaeda, 224
All India Congress Committee, 52
Allahabad, 28
Ambedkar, B. R, 44, 55, 108
Andhra Pradesh, 7, 16, 49, 98
Argentina, 224, 225
Article 370, 67, 73
Arunachal Pradesh, 187
Asia, 10, 19, 20, 21, 22, 24, 33, 34, 53, 75, 148, 152, 157, 161, 163, 164, 165, 166, 167, 168, 169, 170, 171, 172, 173, 174, 175, 176, 180, 188, 191, 192, 193, 194, 195, 196, 197, 201, 202, 216, 217, 218, 224, 237, 240, 247
Asian Security Structure and Challenges for India: Efficacy of the Nehruvian Approach, 163-177
    conclusion, 176-77
    emerging asian security structure, 164-170
    promoting India's interests through nehruvian approach, 170-176
Assam, 87, 97, 239
Association of South-East Asian Nations (ASEAN), 20, 22, 152, 164, 167, 168, 195, 196, 197
Austria, 217
Australia, 20, 166, 170, 193, 195
Azad, M. A. K, 29, 74, 79

Baltistan, 65, 75
Bangladesh, 188, 192, 193, 194, 195
Basu, Jyoti, 98
Bay of Bengal Muti-Sectoral Technical Economic Cooperation (BIMSTEC), 152, 161, 193
Beijing, 21, 22, 179, 183, 185, 188, 189, 190, 191, 192, 193, 195, 196, 198, 199, 200, 201, 223, 243, 245, 254
Bhabha, Homi (Dr), 5, 222
Bhutan, 11, 23, 24, 235-255
Bihar, 59, 142
Bombay, 50, 89, 218
Bose, Subhas Chandra, 27
Brazil, 19, 156, 157, 158, 198, 224, 225
Britain, 211, 216, 220, 222, 238, 249
Buddhism, 86, 120
Burma, 87, 237
Bush, George W, 160, 191, 196
Buzan, Barry, 168, 169, 196

Carr, E. H, 28, 30
Central Intelligence Agency (CIA), 183
China, 10, 11, 19, 20, 21, 22, 24, 31, 54, 75, 148, 150, 158, 160, 163, 164, 165, 166, 167, 168, 169, 170, 171, 174, 176, 179-202, 211, 221, 222, 223, 224, 225, 227, 235, 239, 240, 241, 243, 244, 245, 246, 247, 249, 250, 253, 254
Christians, 85, 87
Clinton, Bill, 22, 155, 189
Coca-Cola, 118
Community Development Programme (CDP), 16, 93, 94

Dalai Lama, 183, 184, 208
Dalits, 17, 106, 110, 113, 118, 123, 124, 126
Dev, Narendra, 29
Dey, S. K, 94, 95, 96

England, 5, 92
Enlai, Zhou, 21, 182, 249
Europe, 7, 69, 70, 81, 106, 107, 108, 111, 161, 166, 168, 170, 216, 224

Fernandes, George, 189
Food Security Act, 6, 17, 110
Foreign Policy in India's Development since Nehru Era, 145-161
France, 33, 211

Gandhi, Indira, 16, 55, 68, 69, 96, 97, 99, 117, 155, 186, 199, 222
Gandhi, Mahatma, 6, 17, 18, 27, 60, 79, 110, 133, 208
Gandhi, Rajiv, 16, 98, 155, 187, 200
Gilgit, 71, 75
Gujarat, 50, 59, 89, 95

Haksar, P. N, 170, 173, 176
Hegde, R. K, 98
Himalayas, 65, 137, 184, 239, 245, 247
Hindus, 58, 80, 82, 85, 87
Hindu Mahasabha, 80, 83
Hiroshima, 207, 209, 213, 217
Huawei, 191
Hyderabad, 94, 141

India, (*passim* throughout text)
policy towards Nepal and Bhutan: Nehru to present, 235-255
- conclusion, 254-255
- India and Bhutan, 242-248
- nehru and himalayan states, 237-240
- post-nehruvian phase, 240-241
- treaty diplomacy, 248-254

Indian National Congress, 42, 82, 186
Indonesia, 193, 195, 197, 237
Infosys, 191
Iran, 20, 159, 165, 166, 192, 225, 228, 237
Iraq, 166
Israel, 163, 165

Jallianwala Bagh, 34
Jammu and Kashmir, 14, 44, 64, 65, 66, 67, 70, 73, 75, 76
Japan, 4, 20, 22, 164, 165, 168, 169, 170, 193, 194, 195, 196, 197, 207, 253
Jinnah, Mohammad Ali, 71
Jordan, 225

Karnataka, 16, 98, 100
Kashmir, (*see also* Jammu and Kashmir), 14, 15, 44, 63-76, 86, 87, 188, 237
Kathmandu, 188, 249, 254
Katju, K. N, 52
Kher, B. G, 48
King Birendra, 249
King Mahendra, 251
Kissinger, Henry, 208
Koirala, B. P, 248

Ladakh, 65, 70, 86, 87, 185
Lal, Bansi, 97
Lehman Brothers, 160
Liberalisation, Privatisation and Globalisation (LPG), 5, 6, 92, 101, 145, 151, 152
Lok Sabha, 44, 50, 98, 99, 212, 218, 221
Lord Mountbatten, 70, 71, 76

Madhya Pradesh, 52, 59
Mahajan, Mehar Chand, 66, 69
Maharashtra, 50, 95, 100
Mahatma Gandhi National Rural Employment Guarantee Act (MGNREGA), 6, 17, 110
Malaysia, 20, 197
Maldives, 192, 252
Mandal Commission, 57
Marxism, 33, 36, 37, 92
McMahon Line, 183, 184, 199
Mehta, Balwant Rai, 16, 91, 92, 93, 98
Mekong Ganga Cooperation (MGC), 152, 161, 193
Menon, V. P, 66
Mexico, 156, 225
Mid-day Meals Programme, 17
Mohammad, Bakshi Ghulam, 67, 73
Mohan, C. Raja, 155, 238
Mongolia, 217
Moscow, 186, 199
Muslims, 65, 66, 72, 80, 82, 85, 87
Muslim League, 47, 80
Myanmar, 152, 193, 194, 197, 240

Nagaland, 51
Nagasaki, 207, 209, 217

Nanda, B. R, 9
Narayanan, M. K, 197
Nation-Building, Natural Resources and Regional Development in India: Revisiting Nehruvian Vision, 133-143
conclusion, 141-143
ideas about resources and development, 136-140
planning for the future, 140-141
National Conference, 65, 72
Nehru, Jawaharlal, (*passim* throughout text) and national unity, communalism, 79-89
communal diversity and question of national unity, 86-88
contemporary relevance, 88-89
outlook, communalism and, 80-83
religious minorities and group rights, 83-86
and India's China Policy, 179-202
border, 183-185
engagement with uneasiness, 187-202
estrangement to normalisation, 185-187
friendship to forward policy, 179-183
conception of history, 27-37
contemporary India, locating in, 1-24
contours of troubled legacy, kashmir and, 63-76
and kashmir, 68-71
chronology of events, 65-68
conclusion, 76
handling international opinion, 74-75
handling sheikh abdullah, 71-74
introduction, 64
idea of federalism and nation-building in India, 41-60
nation-building in India, 54-60
neo- liberalism and social democracy, mapping shifting trajectories of developmental state in India, 105-127
and dilemma of social democracy, 118-120
beyond "isms", prelude to social democracy, 114-118
domestic origins of social democracy, 108-113
mixed economy and deepening of democracy, 120-122
rescuing market from caste, bringing back in, 122-127
social democracy in India with difference, 106-108
outlook, nuclear technology and, 207-228
and India, nuclear technology, 218-223
and nuclear technology, 209-218
contemporary significance, 223-228
paradigm of panchayati raj and its contemporary relevance, 91-102
and panchayati raj institutions, 92-96
panchayati raj system after, 96-99
paradigm of PRIs in era of globalisation, 99-102
Nehru, Moti Lal, 28, 92
Nepal, 11, 23, 24, 235-255
New Delhi, 9, 10, 11, 21, 22, 67, 72, 73, 94, 158, 182, 188, 189, 190, 192, 195, 196, 197, 198, 199, 200, 201, 214, 221, 222, 223, 227, 228, 235, 239, 243, 244, 245, 246, 248, 249, 251, 253, 254,
New York, 154
New Zealand, 195
North Korea, 20, 163, 165, 166, 224, 225, 228

Obama, Barrack, 160, 196

Pakistan, 20, 54, 64, 65, 66, 67, 70, 71, 74, 75, 96, 148, 156, 163, 164, 165, 166, 169, 170, 181, 186, 187, 189, 191, 192, 194, 222, 224, 225, 227, 228, 240
Panchayati Raj, 15, 16, 91-100, 110
Panikkar, K. M, 180, 243

Pant, Govind Ballabh, 48
Patel, Sardar Vallabhbhai, 14, 53, 55, 64, 66, 68, 74, 181, 238
People's Liberation Army (PLA), 188, 192
People's Republic of China (PRC), 179, 180, 181, 182, 183, 189, 198, 246
Philippines, 20

Radhakrishnan, S, 30, 208
Rajagopalachari, C, 51, 208
Rajasthan, 95
Rajya Sabha, 44, 99, 248
Rao, N. T. Rama, 98
Rao, P. V. Narasimha, 187
Rashtriya Swayamsevak Sangh (RSS), 80,
Right to Education Act, 6, 17, 110
Right to Information Act, 17, 110
Roy, B. C, 52
Roy, M. N, 28
Russia, 19, 33, 67, 158, 198, 214

Sampoorna Grameen Rozgar Yojana, 17, 110
Sarkozy, Nicolas, 160
Sarva Shiksha Abhiyan, 17, 110
Second World War, 5, 42, 173, 175, 176, 207
Shastri, Lal Bahadur, 75, 96, 186, 222
Shiromani Akali Dal (SAD), 80
Sikhs, 65, 80, 85, 87
Sikkim, 11, 23, 186, 188, 189, 200, 237, 238, 242, 250
Singapore, 193
Singh, Baldev, 5, 66
Singh, Charan, 97
Singh, V. P, 250
Singh, Maharaja Hari, 65, 66, 70, 71, 72
Singh, Manmohan, 102, 108, 110, 159, 252
South Africa, 19, 157, 158, 198, 224, 225
South Asian Association for Regional Cooperation (SAARC), 167
South Korea, 20, 163, 164, 165, 197
Soviet Union, 11, 67, 75, 148, 149, 155, 164, 166, 174, 182, 186, 194, 211, 213, 214, 215, 216, 222
Sri Lanka, 192, 193, 194, 195
Tagore, Rabindranath, 27, 60
Tata Consultancy Services (TCS), 191
Tehran, 159
Thailand, 193
Tibet, 11, 21, 23, 87, 181, 182, 183, 184, 185, 187, 188, 189, 199, 201, 238, 239, 242, 245, 247, 249
Turkey, 225
United Arab Emirates (UAE), 225
United Nations (UN), 15, 66, 72, 74, 75, 149, 150, 154, 155, 158, 159, 199, 208, 213, 215, 217, 223
United States (US), 4, 11, 20, 22, 75, 124, 145, 148, 150, 151, 154, 155, 159, 160, 163, 166, 168, 169, 170, 174, 181, 183, 185, 186, 189, 190, 191, 193, 194, 195, 196, 197, 202, 209, 211, 213, 215, 216, 222, 223, 227, 252
Uttar Pradesh, 85

Vajpayee, A. B, 187, 189
Vietnam, 20, 22, 164, 165, 193, 195, 197, 225
Washington, 151, 156, 196, 200, 227
West Bengal, 16, 52, 98
World War I, 32
World War II, 107, 108, 111

Zedong, Mao, 183, 184
Zemin, Jiang, 188